PRINCIPLES OF INFORMATION PROCESSING

PRINCIPLES OF INFORMATION PROCESSING

Donald D. Spencer

To Rae

Published by
Charles E. Merrill Publishing Company
A Bell & Howell Company
Columbus, Ohio 43216

This book was set in Serifa.
Merrill Editorial
Executive Editor: Richard Abel
Developmental Editor: Annamaria Doney
Production Editor: Constantina Geldis
Text Designer: Cynthia Brunk
Cover Designer: Cathy Watterson

Illustrations by Danmark and Michaels Inc., Long Island, New York

Library of Congress Catalog Card Number: 84-62894
International Standard Book Number: 0-675-20410-0
Printed in the United States of America
1 2 3 4 5 6 7 8 9 10—89 88 87 86 85

THE CHARLES E. MERRILL INFORMATION PROCESSING SERIES

Introduction

Languages

Systems/MIS

Donald D. Spencer is an internationally known computer science consultant, educator, and writer. He received his Ph.D. degree in computer science and has worked in the computer field for over 25 years. Dr. Spencer is the author of over 100 computer science books, including *Data Processing: An Introduction* (second edition), *Data Processing: An Introduction with BASIC* (second edition), *Computers and Information Processing, An Introduction to Computers: Developing Computer Literacy, Computer Science Mathematics, Illustrated Computer Dictionary, Introduction to Information Processing* (third edition), and *Learning BASIC for Microcomputers: A Worktext,* published by Charles E. Merrill Publishing Company.

Dr. Spencer has taught computer science in college and industry and has held computer-related positions in several industrial organizations. He currently lectures to international audiences and makes presentations to teachers and students in schools and colleges on computer topics of current interest and importance. Dr. Spencer is a member of several professional and educational societies including the Association for Computing Machinery (ACM), the National Council of Teachers of Mathematics (NCTM), the Association for Educational Data Systems (AEDS), the Institute for Electrical and Electronics Engineers (IEEE), the World Future Society (WFS), and the Robotics International of the Society of Manufacturing Engineers (RI). Over one million copies of his books have been used by students, teachers, professionals, and general audience readers all over the world.

PREFACE

The concepts, techniques, and applications of information processing are continually expanding. A direct result of this phenomenal growth is an increase in student enrollments and the wide variety of classes offered in the introductory data processing course.

Principles of Information Processing is designed to be a brief overview course comprised of the most important highlights of introductory data processing. It is a compact, business-oriented essentials text that would serve well in a language-free course or in conjunction with a language text where a substantial amount of time is spent on programming. For instructors who teach BASIC, the following language manuals have been designed to complement *Principles of Information Processing:*

☐ 20436-4 Spencer: *Learning BASIC for Microcomputers: A Worktext for the IBM PC, AT, XT, and PCjr*

☐ 20435-6 Spencer: *Learning BASIC for Microcomputers: A Worktext for Apple II, IIc, and IIe*

☐ 20438-0 Spencer: *Learning BASIC for Microcomputers: A Worktext for the TRS-80 (Model 4)*

☐ 20437-2 Spencer: *Learning BASIC for Microcomputers: A Worktext* (This generic format is suitable for Commodore 64 and Macintosh—with a BASIC interpreter—and the computers listed above.)

Scope and Sequence

This book is divided into nine chapters including the basic concepts of information processing, computer system components, input/output devices, auxiliary storage devices, programming fundamentals, computer graphics, processing methods and applications, systems analysis and design, and security and ethical issues involving computers. These self-contained chapters are separated into short, manageable topics to provide flexibility in the selection of topics to be taught.

Why You Should Use This Book

Principles of Information Processing and its supplements were thoroughly researched and carefully developed to meet the present instructional needs of teachers and students.

☐ **A conversational writing style enhances student interest.** Nontechnical language has been used wherever possible and data processing jargon has been carefully explained. Special real-life applications and a carefully designed layout capture and hold students' interest.

☐ **Extensive coverage of microcomputers is integrated throughout the text.** Increasingly, students will be using microcomputers in their home, school, and work environments. Therefore, in addition to the coverage of modern computer systems from microcomputers to supercomputers, emphasis is placed on microcomputers throughout the text. A special insert, "How to Buy a Personal Computer," is also included. This insert itemizes and illustrates the step-by-step process a person should follow to buy a personal computer that suits his or her individual needs.

☐ **Four-color art, photographs, and design are used throughout the text for educational emphasis as well as visual interest.** Wherever possible, equipment and concepts are illustrated by color photographs or diagrams. The use of color is intended as an educational as well as a visual enhancement.

☐ **A topical business application appears within each chapter.** The business applications cover a wide variety of topics including integrated microcomputer software, electronic spreadsheets, popular software packages (e.g., Symphony, Framework, and WordStar), artificial intelligence, and robotics.

☐ **Computer graphics are covered in a special chapter.** Chapter 7 describes the applications of computer graphics in industry and projects the colorful future of business graphics.

In addition to these features, the textual presentation is enhanced by learning aids that help students understand the materials.

1 A brief outline appears at the beginning of each chapter.
2 Objectives are listed at the beginning of each chapter.
3 Key terms are in boldface throughout the text.
4 Key terms are defined in the Glossary at the end of the book.
5 Marginal applications of special interest topics are placed throughout the text.
6 Each chapter contains a summary and review questions. The review questions are separated into true/false and short answer categories.

Supplement Package

Several supplements have been prepared to make the *Principles of Information Processing* package more sensitive to the needs of part-time as well as full-time instructors.

An **Instructor's Resource Manual** will be provided in the form of a three-ring binder. The binder will contain lecture notes for the course and an assortment of the following supplements, customized to the individual intructor's needs.

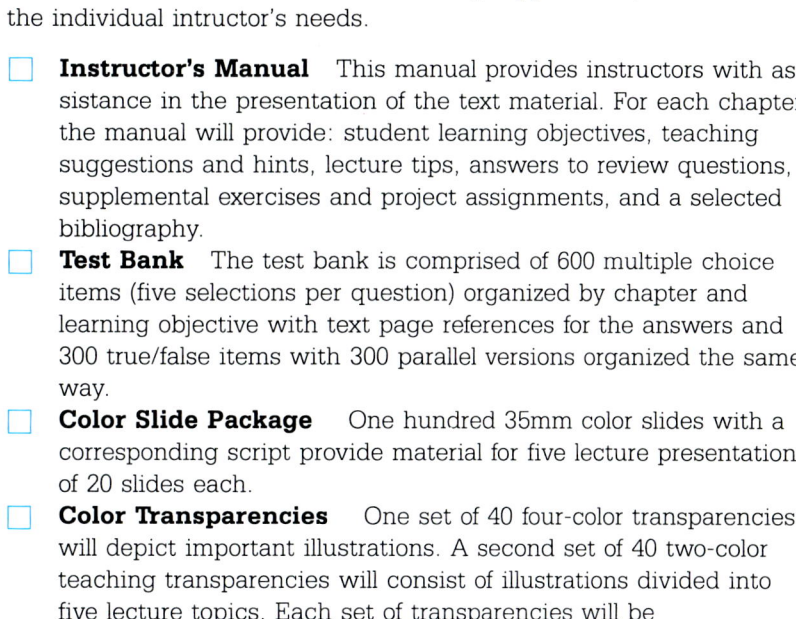

□ **Instructor's Manual**   This manual provides instructors with assistance in the presentation of the text material. For each chapter, the manual will provide: student learning objectives, teaching suggestions and hints, lecture tips, answers to review questions, supplemental exercises and project assignments, and a selected bibliography.

□ **Test Bank**   The test bank is comprised of 600 multiple choice items (five selections per question) organized by chapter and learning objective with text page references for the answers and 300 true/false items with 300 parallel versions organized the same way.

□ **Color Slide Package**   One hundred 35mm color slides with a corresponding script provide material for five lecture presentations of 20 slides each.

□ **Color Transparencies**   One set of 40 four-color transparencies will depict important illustrations. A second set of 40 two-color teaching transparencies will consist of illustrations divided into five lecture topics. Each set of transparencies will be accompanied by appropriate lecture notes.

Software   The BASIC tutorial and the Micro Payroll System are the two types of available software. The BASIC tutorial will consist of three parts: (a) a file of BASIC programs that can be called up by name and then modified according to user's instructions; (b) computer-assisted instruction in BASIC; and (c) a self-paced testing and scoring section. This tutorial will be available in the form of IBM PC, Apple II, and TRS-80 diskettes.

The Micro Payroll System is a disk/workbook package that provides hands-on use of a business data processing system. The concepts illustrated in this system include data entry and validation, word processing, spreadsheets, and computer graphics. The workbook is divided into ten lessons. Each lesson contains objectives, text, a laboratory assignment requiring use of the computer with the micro payroll system, and a set of review and evaluation questions.

Acknowledgments

Many education and publishing professionals assisted in the design, editorial, graphics, and production phases of this text and its supplement package. The efforts of hundreds of people were used in producing the final product.

I am grateful to the professionals at Charles E. Merrill Publishing Company for the many months of dedicated efforts that turned my unpolished manuscript into a colorful and informative introductory text. A special team of Merrill's key personnel coordinated the art, design, and production efforts. Richard Abel, executive editor, coordinated the supplement package. Annamaria Doney, developmental editor, guided and shaped the book from its earliest conception to the finished product. She has coordinated or been active in every facet of this project. Connie Geldis, production editor, contributed many original ideas and a superb job of editing the manuscript. Cindy Brunk, text designer, produced a design that is instructionally sound as well as visually beautiful. The efforts of these individuals made this book a reality and the end product is a testimony to their creative talents.

Additionally, I appreciate the valuable comments provided by the following instructors: Billie Bagwell, Appalachian State University; Paul Bartolomeo, Community College of Rhode Island; James W. Cox, Lane Community College; Shirley Fedorovich, Embry-Riddle Aeronautical University; Raymond O. Folse, Nicholls State University; Jay Heizer, University of Richmond; Ralph Holloway, Broome Community College; Wayne Horn, Pensacola Junior College; Bob Langley, Tennessee Technological University; John Mote, Texas A & M University; C. Terry Ordoyne, Nicholls State University; Gregory Parsons, University of Southern Maine; Ernie Phillips, Northern Virginia Community College; Barbara Price, Winthrop College; Bob Schuerman, California Polytechnic State University; and Clint Smullen, University of Tennessee.

CONTENTS

This special insert itemizes and illustrates the step-by-step process
a person should follow to buy a personal computer that suits his or
her individual needs.

1
BASIC CONCEPTS OF INFORMATION PROCESSING

OUTLINE

OBJECTIVES

1   Explain the importance of computers and information processing in today's society.

2   Understand the growth of the computer industry.

3   Identify the advantages of using computers over using manual procedures.

4   Understand the impact of the computer in business and many other areas.

5   Explain how computers have evolved.

6   Define data, information, and information processing.

7   Identify the purpose of an information system.

8   Identify the benefits of computers to the business user.

9   Briefly describe the "office of the future."

MEET THE COMPUTER

Are credit cards a part of your life? Is a quick game of Pac-Man one of the ways you unwind? If you answered yes to either one of these questions, you're already aware of the growing role computers play in everyday life.

Computers have become so essential that it's the rare individual whose life isn't affected by these versatile machines. Schools, banks, government offices, and businesses rely on computers to perform many tasks. Still, many people are unaware of how widespread the influence of computers has become (Figure 1–1).

What Computers Can Do

Computers can quote the latest price of a share of American Airlines. They can turn on your living room lights, control the thermostat on your furnace, challenge you at chess, and even make sure a fresh pot of coffee awaits you each morning. Unlike humans, they never become tired or angry.

Many people rely directly on computers to perform their jobs. Engineers use them to design bridges, cars, and airplanes. Secretaries type and store information in them, then connect them to printers that produce a copy of the information faster than any human can type. Fast-food clerks even use computers in place of cash registers.

During your lifetime, space satellites and data communication links will be vital parts of the information revolution. Information will be translated automatically into the language of the user and be made immediately available around the world. Already, computers have opened up new horizons in science, medicine, and other areas vital to human well-being. Imagine the benefits of instantly sharing information with other scientists worldwide.

Computers perform a variety of sophisticated tasks. Two of the basic things computers do are

1 Record and store information, with the ability to recall it instantly for use any time
2 Calculate tens of millions of times faster than the human brain and in seconds solve problems that would take dozens of experts years to complete

COMPUTER TECHNOLOGY AND THE WORLD MARKET

Although computers are only about 40 years old, the industry has grown so rapidly that it is now the largest in the world. Most of the early growth of computer manufacturing occurred in the United States. As a result, U.S. manufacturers dominated world markets for many years. This situation is beginning to change as other countries develop computer research and manufacturing capabilities. Japan is making great strides in this area and has produced new products ranging from microminiature

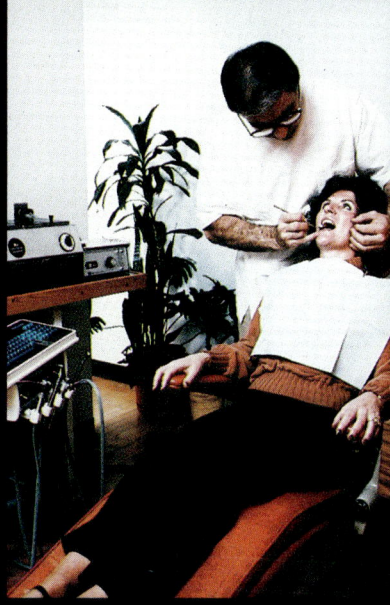

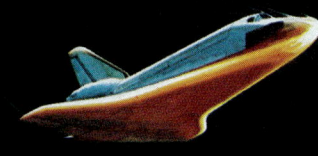

FIGURE 1–1
Computers have changed the world of the engineer, businessperson, teacher, student, doctor, and office worker. The machines are finding widespread usage in stores, offices, schools, businesses, homes, factories, government agencies, and hospitals. (Courtesy of Pertec Computer Corp., Data General Corp., Lockheed Corp., The Goodyear Tire & Rubber Co., Sperry Corp., Computer Sciences Corp., International Business Machines Corp., and NASA)

chips to supercomputers. Because of the Japanese government-sponsored development of a fifth generation of computers (machines that improve upon the silicon chip), it's expected that Japan will become a major international developer and distributor of computing equipment by the early 1990s.

The computer industry in Japan is already a very big business. Japan's 25 percent annual growth rate outstrips both Europe's 20 percent and the 15 percent annual growth rate in the United States. To keep pace, the United States will need to make a stronger commitment to research and development in the computer industry.

Worldwide, computers are a billion dollar industry. In terms of capital investments alone, this figure represents an increase from $35 million in 1955 to an expected $260 billion by 1990 (Figure 1–2). In human terms, this means that by 1990 an estimated 60 percent of all jobs will depend to some degree on computers. Twenty percent of all workers will need a working knowledge of computers to perform their jobs.

As computer use becomes widespread, prices will fall. During the next few years, millions of Americans will purchase computers ranging from small hand-held models to sophisticated desktop systems. Business use will run the gamut from portable to supercomputers. In 1985, computer cost ranged from $35 for a hand-held computer to $14 million for a supercomputer. In the future, hand-held models will be available for less than $20, and they will be as common as calculators are today.

FIGURE 1–2
Value of computing equipment in use

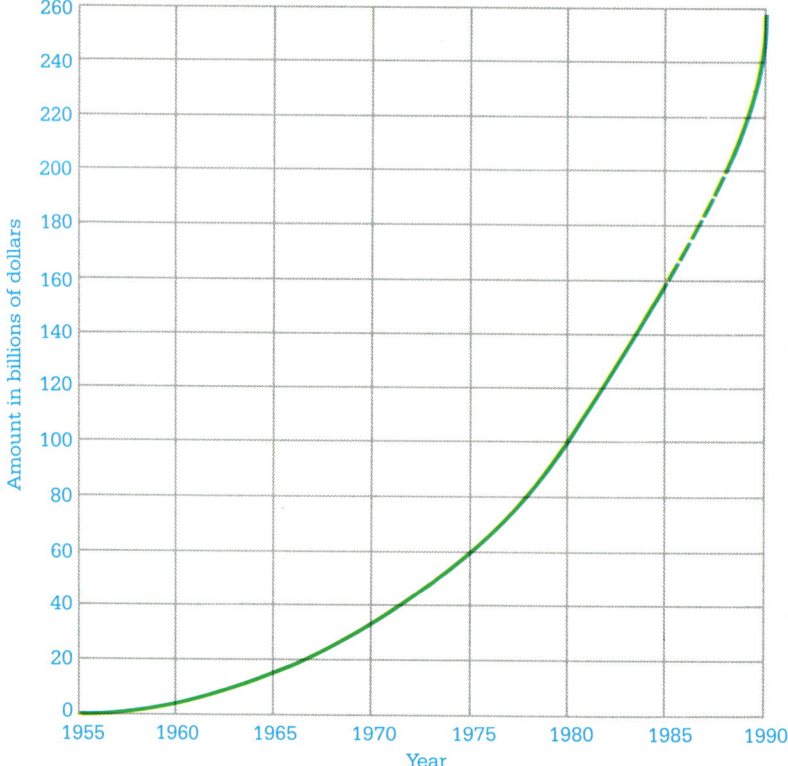

As you can see, computers have altered our life-styles and become essential to business. Throughout this text, the focus will be primarily on the impact of computers on modern business organizations.

ADVANTAGES OF THE COMPUTER

Beneath all their sophisticated trappings, computers are simply electronic problem solvers that offer the advantages of speed, accuracy, economy, and reliability.

Speed   One of the most obvious advantages of using a computer is speed. Computer speeds are measured in four ways:

1 Millisecond (thousandth of one second)
2 Microseconds (millionth of one second)
3 Nanoseconds (billionth of one second)
4 Picoseconds (trillionth of one second)

Within the half-second it takes a spilled cup of coffee to reach the floor, a medium-size computer, given the information in the computer's memory, could perform the following tasks flawlessly:

☐ Debit 3 000 checks to 400 different bank accounts
☐ Examine the electrocardiograms of 100 patients and alert physicians of possible trouble
☐ Score 250 000 answers on 5 000 tests and evaluate the effectiveness of the questions
☐ Figure the payroll for a company with 2 000 employees
☐ Perform various other chores

More powerful computers are infinitely faster. Supercomputers such as the Cray X-MP and the Control Data 205 can perform hundreds of millions of operations each second. In minutes, they can perform work that would take many smaller computers weeks to accomplish.

Accuracy   The fastest machine in the world would be of little use if it made errors that humans had to correct. Fortunately, computers are accurate machines that can process large volumes of information according to complex, repetitive procedures.

Economy   Computers not only are fast and accurate, but also economical. Businesses using computers operate more efficiently. For example, a company using a computer often reduces labor costs, increases cash flow, and cuts its investment in inventory. This company also can realize improved customer service and can provide management with fast, accurate information about customers, products, and sales.

Reliability   Like conscientious employees, computers can always be counted on to perform. Equipped with microminiature circuitry, they op-

RUN ''APPLICATION''

For every 100 people in the U.S. there are 87 telephones, 65 automobiles, and 65 television sets; but there are only about 10 electronic keyboards (typewriters, personal computers, mainframe terminals, etc.) per inhabitant. This ratio will change soon. By 1993, about 170 million keyboards will be in use. This 70 percent market penetration is greater than that of automobiles and almost as much as telephones. What it took the telephone, automobile, and television industries to achieve in 75, 70, and 30 years, respectively, will take the computer industry only 10 years.

erate without fail for long periods of time. Their built-in, self-checking features help ensure accuracy and assist in their maintenance.

AREAS OF COMPUTER APPLICATION

Computers come in all shapes, sizes, and abilities. Some are small, inexpensive, and fit on a desktop; others are huge, cost a fortune, and need entire rooms to house them. Despite these differences, computers share a common bond: they are responsible for the greatest technological revolution in world history.

The microprocessor, sometimes called a computer on a chip, is spawning a whole new world. Games, automobiles, and appliances are coming under computer control. The power of huge computers has been embedded in tiny microprocessors. In turn, the microprocessor, is being embedded in devices used by consumers. Many people believe that home computers will soon become as common as telephones. Computer applications are limited only by human imagination (Figures 1–3 to 1–11).

Why Learn About Computers?

Every educated person should become familiar with computers because of the impact that the use of computers has on our lives. Computers perform important tasks in the hospitals in which children are born, in the schools they attend, and on the jobs they will have. In short, computers touch nearly every aspect of our environment. Mastering that environment now includes absorbing at least some knowledge of the machines that have such a growing influence on your life.

EVOLUTION OF COMPUTING DEVICES

One of the earliest devices used for computation was the abacus, used around 3000 B.C. A skilled operator can use the abacus to obtain results as fast as a modern desk calculator. Although the abacus has never been widely used in the Western Hemisphere, it has been an important computational device in China, Japan, Egypt, Russia, and India for centuries.

In 1614, John Napier invented numbered calculating rods. The rods, called Napier's Bones, greatly simplified tedious multiplication problems.

By 1642, a 19-year-old Frenchman, Blaise Pascal, developed the first mechanical calculating machine (Figure 1–12). This shoe-box size calculator took over the tiresome job of adding long columns of numbers. It relied on gear-driven counter wheels to make its computations; these 300 counter wheels were used in almost every mechanical calculator for the following 300 years. Pascal's machines worked very well but could perform only addition and subtraction with ease.

About 50 years later, Pascal's calculator was improved by the German mathematician, Gottfried Leibniz. His calculator performed multiplication by repeated addition, and division by repeated subtraction. However, the calculator lacked mechanical precision in its construction and was unreliable and awkward to use.

In 1801, Joseph Marie Jacquard built a punched-card loom that has remained basically the same to this day. The Jacquard Loom, which revolutionized the weaving industry, used an endless chain of punched cards that rotated past the needles of the loom. It could weave flower designs or pictures of men and women as easily as other looms could weave plain cloth. In essence, Jacquard provided an effective means of communicating with the loom by using punched paper and cards. The language was limited to just two terms: hole and no hole. The same binary, or two-based, system is all but universal in today's machine communication.

In 1834, Charles Babbage, a mathematician at Cambridge University in England, envisioned a general purpose machine that would perform arithmetic operations in automatic sequence. This machine, called the Analytical Engine, was actually his second calculating device. His first, called the Difference Engine, was designed to compute mathematical tables, such as logarithms. Conceived by Babbage in 1812, The Difference Engine was never completed because the machine required precision parts that were unheard of at that time.

The Analytical Engine was designed to perform complex mathematical calculations and print out the results (Figure 1–13). This machine, like the Difference Engine, was never built, but its design laid the groundwork for modern computers. The Analytical Engine contained all the basic parts of a modern general-purpose digital computer: control, arithmetic/logic unit, memory, input, and output. Babbage proposed to use two types of punched cards to control its operation. Operation cards would control the arithmetic unit and specify the kind of operation to be performed; variable cards would control the transfer data to and from the memory. Babbage borrowed the punched-card principle from Jacquard's loom. Lord Byron's daughter, Ada Augusta, Countess of Lovelace, assisted Babbage in the development of the Analytical Engine and actually designed and refined some of its internal characteristics. She was a brilliant mathematician and helped to document some of Babbage's efforts. Her development of several programs for performing mathematical calculations on the Analytical Engine credits her as the world's first programmer.

Punched cards were not applied to data processing until about 20 years after Babbage's death. The first punched-card tabulating machine, called the Census Machine, was developed in 1887 by Herman Hollerith, a statistician. Because the population of the United States was growing so quickly, it had been estimated that the results of the 1890 census could not be obtained within the statutory ten years and that there would be an overlap with the next census. To prevent this possibility, Hollerith built a set of machines to reduce the processing time required for the 1890 census.

A hand-operated punch was used to punch a card for each individual in the country. The cards, similar to those Jacquard used, were the same size as the large dollar bill in use at that time. They were inserted, one at a time, in the Census Machine where the data were tabulated on

RUN "APPLICATION"

According to a report by the National Science Foundation, a shortage of qualified computer personnel is expected to develop by 1987. The study indicates that a serious worker shortage exists when industry demand exceeds the supply of new graduates in the field by at least 5 percent. When these shortages are filled by persons from other fields, the quality of the nation's computer work force diminishes. As a result, the projected shortage of qualified computer workers will range from 15 to 30 percent of the available supply, or from 115 000 to 140 000 workers, and will further affect the numbers of systems analysts, programmers, and trained support personnel.

The modern office uses word processing machines and computers for such tasks as order entry, credit checking, inventory accounting, billing, letter writing, report preparation, and the filing and retrieval of other information. (Provided by DATAPOINT® Corp. All rights reserved.)

1–3

FIGURE 1–4
Compact terminals connected to the bank's computer system provide instant access to banking information. (Courtesy of NCR Corp.)

FIGURE 1–5
These people use their home terminal to keep track of how much electricity and natural gas they use in their home. (Courtesy of Bell Laboratories)

FIGURE 1–6
Computers are rapidly changing the retailing operations of modern stores. A large department store in Mexico uses a computer to produce 300 000 credit account statements each month and, at the same time, provide internal accounting services. (Courtesy of Burroughs Corp.)

1–4

1–7

1–8

1–9

FIGURE 1–7
It takes only a few millionths of a second for a computer to tell an airline reservation clerk if a seat is available on any of their flights in any airport in the world. (Courtesy of Delta Air Lines, Inc.)

FIGURE 1–8
Young children find that small computers, such as this IBM Personal Computer, are easy to use and provide hours of enjoyment. They also can use these machines for school projects and other activities. (Courtesy of International Business Machines Corp.)

FIGURE 1–9
One computer can do the work of several lawyers by electronically sifting through thousands of cases in minutes and locating appropriate precedents for court cases. (Courtesy of Computer Sciences Corp.)

FIGURE 1–10
The auto rental agent using a computer can confirm, in a few seconds, car reservations for anywhere in the world. Reservation requests for cars at Hertz locations in Europe and Latin America are routed to the foreign section of the computerized reservation center in Oklahoma City. (Courtesy of RCA)

FIGURE 1–11
Telephone companies are increasing their use of an interactive computer graphics system to design electronic central offices. With TOPES (Telephone Office Planning and Engineering System), architects can consider alternative floor plans and establish requirements for equipment and building engineering. The system also permits rapid retrieval and processing of planning data, as well as editing of building plans at remote terminals. Besides saving engineering and drafting time, TOPES allows more efficient use of space and more accurate sizing of power plants and environmental control systems. (Courtesy of Bell Laboratories)

1–10

1–11

FIGURE 1–12
The Pascaline was the first significant calculating machine. Numbers to be added were dialed in via the row of numbered wheels at the bottom; the result appeared in the square windows at the top. The machine was also capable of subtraction.

counters, and the cards were sorted. Since the cards could be processed at a rate of 50 to 75 per minute, the 1890 census of 62 million people was completed in only two and one-half years, less than one-third the time needed to complete the 1880 census of 12 million fewer people.

Later, Hollerith organized the Tabulating Machine Company to promote the commercial use of his machines. In addition to the 1900 census, Hollerith's machines were used in insurance actuarial work, railroad car accounting, and sales analysis. Eventually he developed a more automatic card-handling machine, but he was unable to reach an agreement with the Census Bureau for its use in 1910. When his company became too large for individual control, Hollerith sold it. Hollerith's company later became one of the parents of the IBM Corporation.

At Harvard University in 1937, Howard Aiken began work on an automatic calculating machine called the Automatic Sequence Controlled Calculator (also called the ASCC or Mark I). With the help of graduate students and IBM engineers, Professor Aiken's automatic machine was completed in 1944. The machine was 51 feet long and 8 feet high, contained 760 000 parts, used 500 miles of wire, and weighed about 5 tons. It could add, subtract, multiply, divide, compute trigonometric functions, and perform other complicated calculations. Addition and subtraction were accomplished in three-tenths of one second, multiplication in less than 6 seconds, and division in less than 16 seconds.

In 1934, John V. Atanasoff, a professor of physics at Iowa State College, modified an IBM punched-card machine to perform calculations mechanically. Five years later, in conjunction with Clifford Berry, he built a prototype of a computer, called the ABC (Atanasoff-Berry Computer). The ABC, which had a memory consisting of 45 vacuum tubes, was assembled in 1942.

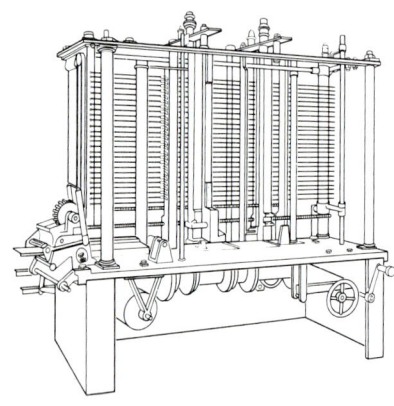

FIGURE 1–13
Even though it did not go beyond the design stage, Charles Babbage's Analytical Engine is recognized as the world's first general purpose computer.

In December, 1943, a special-purpose computer called COLOSSUS started cracking German code for the British Code and Cipher School in Bletchley Park, Buckinghamshire, England. COLOSSUS contained 1 500 thermionic valves and proved that large numbers of electronic circuits could do reliable calculations. The message to be deciphered was fed into an optical reader as a repetitive loop of punched tape in 5-bit tele-printer code, at the rate of 5 000 characters per second. Internally, CO-LOSSUS contained electronics for counting, comparison, simple binary arithmetic, and logical operations. Output was via an electric typewriter. The program, or strategy for altering trial cipher keys, was controlled from plug-boards and switches.

A limited amount of information about COLOSSUS was released in 1975. But to this day, the complete story of COLOSSUS has not been made available by the British government.

In 1946, the Electronic Numerical Integrator and Calculator (ENIAC) went into operation at the Moore School of Electrical Engineering of the University of Pennsylvania. This special computer was built to compute ballistic tables to aid army artillerymen in aiming guns (Figure 1–14).

Invented by two researchers, John W. Mauchly and John Presper Eckert, at the University of Pennsylvania, ENIAC occupied a space of 1 500 ft^2, weighed about 30 tons, contained approximately 19 000 vac-uum tubes, and required 130 kw of power. The computing elements consisted of many components with about one million hand-soldered connections. The input/output system was modified IBM card readers and punches. ENIAC could perform 5 000 additions per second, and by today's standards, this performance is relatively slow. But in 1946, the only machine that could even compete with it was the ASCC relay calcu-

FIGURE 1–14
ENIAC was built by Mauchly and Eckert at the Moore School of Electrical Engi-neering, University of Pennsylvania, in 1946. It was used by the U.S. Army to compute trajectories for new weapons and is regarded as the prototype of all later computer equipment. (U.S. Army/University of Pennsylvania News Bureau)

lator, which only performed 10 additions per second. ENIAC made all relay calculators obsolete. It could perform several additions, a multiplication, and a square root in parallel, as well as solve several independent problems at the same time. ENIAC was so successful that it marked the end of the pioneer stage of automatic computer development. After nine years of operation, ENIAC was retired from service in 1955.

Eckert and Mauchly later built the first commercial computer, UNIVAC I (Figure 1–15). In 1951, this machine was delivered to the U.S. Bureau of the Census. Not long after UNIVAC I was operational, automatic programming techniques were devised to help people use these machines. These techniques evolved into programming languages that are used extensively in solving problems on modern computers. The first UNIVAC I (serial 1) completed its last tabulation for the Census Bureau about 12 years after it went into operation.

IBM began making significant progress in the computer business about 1951. Their first computer, available in 1953, was the IBM 701. The IBM 650 was the most popular computer in the late 1950s (Figure 1–16). The first machine was installed in 1954, and more than 1 000 machines were placed in service. The IBM 650 consists of three units: a punched card input/output unit, a console unit, and a power unit. After the 701 and 650, IBM released the IBM 702 (the first large-scale computer designed for use by business), the IBM 704 (IBM's first large-scale machine for scientific users), the IBM 705, and the IBM 709.

FIGURE 1–15
UNIVAC I was the first commercial electronic computer. The Bureau of the Census became the first government agency to install this machine. The UNIVAC I was developed by J. Presper Eckert and John Mauchly (inventors of ENIAC). It contained some 5 000 vacuum tubes and had a main storage which provided for storing one thousand 12-decimal digit words. Peripheral equipment consisted of an electronic typewriter and several magnetic tape units. (Courtesy of U.S. Air Force)

FIGURE 1–16
IBM 650 computer system was a widely used general-purpose computer for business, industry, and universities. When introduced, it processed data on punched cards. Later users could add magnetic tapes and disks. The 650 had a magnetic drum memory. (Courtesy of International Business Machines Corp.)

Over the years, significant advances have occurred in computer technology. Those already mentioned represent the highlights of the early years of computer development. Generally, the advances of computer technology can be classed into four chronological categories, called computer generations.

The computers discussed earlier are classified as first-generation computers. These early computers used mainly vacuum tubes in their circuits. They were bulky, used large amounts of power, generated a great deal of heat, and were unreliable.

In 1947, Bell Laboratories invented the transistor. The transistor was only one-two hundredth of the size of the bulky vacuum tube. In addition to being smaller, it was faster and could be packaged tightly. Because it was composed of a solid substance, the transistor was far more rugged and reliable, and during operation, it generated much less heat than a vacuum tube. In 1959, more sophisticated computers were developed. These computers used transistors for arithmetic, magnetic cores for memory, and magnetic disks or tapes for storage. They could multiply two 10-digit numbers in 1/100 000 of one second. These machines were classified as second-generation computers.

The third-generation computer era is characterized by advanced miniaturization of circuitry. Electronic circuitry was etched, rather than wired, and tiny crystal structures replaced vacuum tubes and transistors. The most important advance in computer technology in the mid-1960s was the **integrated circuit**. Integrated circuits are produced as single units, containing many components fused together in a single process. They are produced on chips, thin layers of silicon or germanium so tiny that a thimble could hold 100 000 of them. Integrated circuits are very reliable and relatively inexpensive.

The early transistorized computers advanced the state of computing technology. But they had one important drawback—they weren't compatible. Users often had difficulty switching from one type of computer to another without rewriting programs. Peripheral devices designed for one computer often wouldn't work with another. What users really needed was a family of compatible computers in which peripherals and programs could be interchanged. In 1964, the IBM Corporation announced the System/360, the first family of compatible computers, ranging from small to large. The System/360, as well as other computers of this era, used integrated circuitry.

Other developments, such as MICR (magnetic ink character readers) devices, optical scanning devices, and larger, faster storage devices, helped further the third-generation computer's ability to handle data. Other important improvements in third-generation equipment included the use of communication channels to permit remote input and output, and versatile software that automated many tasks.

In the early 1970s, the IBM Corporation began delivering its System/370 computers. This family of computers, and those developed by other manufacturers in the 1970s, incorporated further refinements, including semiconductor memories and further miniaturization through **very large scale integration (VLSI)** and **large scale integration (LSI)** circuits and widespread use of virtual storage techniques. VLSI is a technological process that allows circuits containing tens of thousands of components to be densely packed on a single silicon chip.

In the late 1970s and early 1980s, microminiature circuits were used by a variety of manufacturers to produce microprocessors, microcomputers, memory chips, and other computer circuitry. By 1981, hundreds of thousands of microcomputers were used in a wide variety of areas. The early 1980s saw the introduction of hand-held computers.

The fourth-generation computer systems are characterized by VLSI and LSI circuitry, increased speeds, greater reliability, and large-capacity storage facilities. The use of visual displays has become increasingly common in today's computer systems (Figure 1–17).

THE NEXT GENERATION OF COMPUTERS

Since its birth, computer technology has consistently been aimed at high-speed operation and large capacity and has been developed mainly for processing numerical calculations. As a result, computers have had significantly limited input and output processing capabilities. As applications for computers have become widespread, from the initial scientific and technical computations to the more recent business data processing, a strong need has arisen for more extensive input/output capabilities such as speech or voice, images, and graphics, all of which are natural forms of information transmission for humans.

FIGURE 1–17
Hewlett-Packard HP9000 computer—a fourth generation computer system.
(Courtesy of Hewlett-Packard Co.)

Until now the high cost of hardware has prohibited the expansion of the number of functions built into hardware. It has also gradually increased dependence on software. The expansion of software in lieu of hardware has led to a situation called the "software crisis." This problem has had an undesirable side effect. Computer architecture has become stiff and inflexible due to continued reliance on existing software. As long as computer architecture is dependent on existing technologies, it will be unable to meet new applications.

However, a technological basis that will allow for new architectures and new functions, such as improved computer intelligence, has matured. This technological basis includes: VLSI technology, which has rapidly advanced in the past few years; the realization of larger capacity memories; increased possibility for developing high-speed elements; promotion of research into artificial intelligence and pattern recognition technology; and the technological fusion of communication and information processing. It is quite possible that in about 10 years information processing systems will appear that are based on new conceptions and architectures that are a quantum leap above the computer technology of the past 30 years.

Japan and the United States are now in a race to develop fifth generation computers. Whichever country wins will possibly become the world leader in knowledge technology. Because the Japanese government has already committed itself heavily to a concentrated research effort ($1 billion in subsidies in the first decade), the Fifth Generation project strongly challenges U.S. dominance of the international computer industry.

The Japanese Fifth Generation project focuses on "expert systems," the most practical application of artificial intelligence. Such

The term *integration* is one of the most commonly used buzz words in the microcomputer software industry. Big software development companies are getting involved in integrated software development with such enthusiasm that they are announcing products long before they are ready to market them.

In the business realm, the purpose of integration is to bring the major business computing applications together so that data can be converted into different formats without creating unnecessary confusion for users. However, integration can also mean the use of one application that can manipulate several documents in the same manner. Ultimately, it will become an intricate function of the computer and its software that will rarely be apparent to the user.

Combining very different software programs into some sort of cooperative mechanism sounds simple, but it is one of the greatest challenges facing software developers today. In addition to programs that are designed to work within dozens of hardware systems, hundreds of software vendors use different approaches to program design and structure. The proliferation of Apple II and IBM Personal Computers has created de facto hardware standards within the industry, while Digital Research's CP/M and Microsoft's MS-DOS operating systems are de facto software standards, and UNIX is becoming standard in the 32-bit microcomputer world.

The need for a common structure to support unique applications and data exchange among those applications developed naturally. As microcomputers became regarded as serious business machines, large corporations purchased them for employees who often had never even touched a typewriter keyboard. As time passed, these computer novices became users and began to feel other pressures associated with handling software. Each time they decided to use the computer to change an application, a new program with a different set of rules became the only option. Despite the apparent obstacles, however, the popularity of microcomputers in the corporate office continued to grow—and so did the need for more applications.

In 1980, a study indicated that these five applications should be offered on personal computers to support managerial tasks:

1 Remote data access (telecommunications)
2 Numerical analysis (electronic spreadsheets)
3 Sorting and searching data (data base management)
4 Memo and report writing (word processing)
5 Business graphics (screen and printed images data in the form of pie charts, bar charts, etc.)

As software developers responded to the increasing need for business-oriented programs, the integration of those applications became apparent. Today, the most frequently developed business microcomputer software include electronic spreadsheets, data/file managers, word processing graphics, and telecommunications.

DEFINING SOFTWARE INTEGRATION

There are several different levels of integrated software. Some systems are fully integrated, such as Xerox's Star system, Apple Computer's Lisa, Radio Shack's TRS–80 Model 100, Lotus Development Corporation's Symphony, and Ashton-Tate's Framework. These systems provide for integrating applications in a business environment. Other systems such as Lotus 1-2-3 and Sorcim's SuperCalc, have partially integrated programs because the interaction among applications is limited.

APPROACHES TO INTEGRATION

The most innovative technical approach to unite unique applications has been the creation of an environment in which all applications reside, cooperate, and share data. This approach is accomplished in two ways: (a) hardware/software combinations such as Apple Lisa, Apple Macintosh, and Xerox Star; or (b) software environments, such as VisiCorp's VisiOn and Microsoft's Windows. In the hardware/software combinations, the software is tied directly to the hardware, but the basic design concept is the same.

Integrated software is such a dynamic part of the microcomputer software industry that, while the mainstream players are developing the more popular technical approaches, less known developers are experimenting with newer ideas. For example, a California-based company specializing in artificial intelligence research is developing a product called a *software bus*. Theoretically, Transoft Corporation's bus is to act like a hardware or communications bus and function like data packets between structures called bus-integrated software components. These components are the actual software program modules, which are activated by the transmissions along the software bus. This approach is in the experimental stage, but it is an interesting example of the level of activity present in the area of integrated software development.

Three ways that most systems provide for interaction with users are by menus, commands, and

The Lisa 2's high resolution screen has the capacity to display multiple integrated software applications simultaneously. LisaWrite, LisaGraph, and LisaCalc have a menu bar across the top of the screen that lists the options available to start a specific task. (Courtesy of Apple Computer, Inc.)

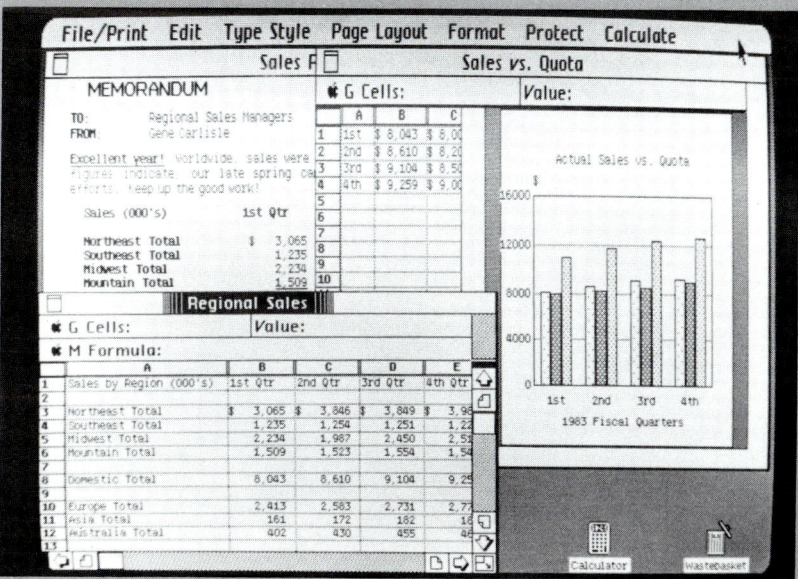

graphic icons. The use of menus to enable users to work their way through applications is perhaps the most traditional approach to interaction on microcomputers. Layers of menus make it easier to work with some programs; however, numerous menus can also become cumbersome and distracting.

Command-based applications provide more power and flexibility because users can go directly to the application of their choice and manipulate data in a direct user defined way, without encountering a menu structure. This approach is more difficult for the novice, but it is generally preferred by experienced users.

Graphic icons are small, pictorial representations of applications that appear on display screens for user selection; Apple's Lisa was the first major microcomputer breakthrough in this area. For example, if a filing function is desired, a picture of a filing cabinet may serve as its representation. Selection is generally made via a pointing device, but sometimes icons are numbered or lettered for keyboard selection. Because of its

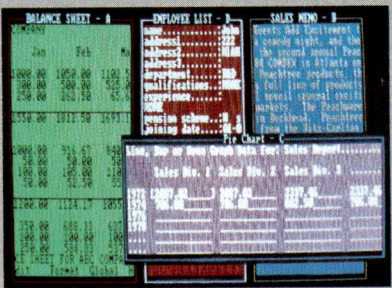

Integrated software systems allow multiple windows to be displayed on the screen at the same time. The user can move the windows and select one or just a portion of one window to fill the entire screen. (Courtesy of Peachtree Software, Inc.)

simplicity, software developers are moving toward the graphic icon approach.

When several applications are being used, the applications must reside in memory simultaneously, i.e., individual programs, such as a spreadsheet, word processor, graphics, and data management, can be loaded into the computer's RAM memory at the same time. The ability to load all applications into memory may require larger amounts of memory, but it is less time-consuming and, thus, more desirable. If it is not possible to

load all applications into memory at once, however, the disk or other storage device must be accessed whenever a particular application is needed. In this event, the system becomes disk intensive and slow. Because integrated packages are requiring increasingly larger amounts of memory, the need to move applications in and out of main memory to make room for data or other applications has become the standard rather than the exception.

One of the most important inventions in word processing is the split screen. Split screens can provide the simultaneous display and manipulation of data in different parts of the same document or within separate documents. By the same token, the development of *windows* takes the split screen a step further and allows for the manipulation of data in multiple screens from multiple documents. Because users want the power of the computer without having to understand the way it functions, the manner in which applications are displayed on a screen is becoming particularly important when integrated software is in-

Sophisticated software systems provide timely information for management. Many of these systems integrate business operations such as word processing, electronic spreadsheets, computer graphics, data base management, and telecommunications. (Courtesy of Sperry Corp.)

volved. Software developers are now trying to design software that simulates a desk in which several documents can be accessible at the same time.

GREAT EXPECTATIONS

The future of microcomputer software lies with the development of integrated applications. Experience has shown that, once people start using computers, they use them for greater numbers of applications and are less willing to learn new rules each time they change applications.

Initially, the major business use of microcomputers was for spreadsheet functions. Word processing and data management are now included. Over the next few years, more packages will include communications and sophisticated graphics, such as Apple's LisaDraw or Microsoft's Chart, and voice and touch sensitive technology for those users who find the use of an electronic mouse wearisome. The need for greater amounts of memory to facilitate these sophisticated features is crucial. For example, in 1983, the average RAM in an IBM Personal Computer was 128K; now integrated packages often require 256K, and in some cases as much as 512K. VisiOn requires 512K, and the Apple Lisa 2 has 512K of RAM. Future microcomputers will not only reflect the need for more memory, but also its decreasing cost.

RUN ``APPLICATION''

The projected decline by 1990 in the use of checks is the result of electronic funds transfer—point-of-sale deposit systems that transfer funds from buyer to seller at the time of a purchase. The United States Government already has automated nearly one-quarter of its payment transactions, and the conversion is expected to grow at a rate of 7 percent per year in the next decade.

systems solve problems roughly the way people do, by reasoning from the facts stored in a memory bank. They can make medical diagnoses, search for new oil deposits, or redesign computer microchips. Even genetic engineers seek their advice on the best way to clone a gene.

Expert systems are still in their infancy and beset by problems. The problems they are asked to solve must be well defined, and virtually all relevant information must be available to them. However, once these conditions are satisfied, their performance, in some situations, can exceed that of humans. Thus, fifth generation computers are expected to be true knowledge systems. They will be able to combine various sets of facts to produce sophisticated new solutions.

For these machines to play the central role in society that the Japanese envision, they must be much easier to use than today's machines. Fifth generation machines will have to understand spoken, written, and graphical input. Therefore, the Japanese are launching intense research and development in intelligent interfaces, including natural language processing, and speech, graphics, and image understanding. For example, speech understanding research will cover speech wave, semantic, and pragmatic analyses. Pragmatic analysis derives understanding by extracting themes in a given sentence. This extrapulation is accomplished by detecting such changes as focus shifts. Eventually the machine will be expected to understand continuous human speech with a vocabulary of 50 000 words and 95 percent accuracy from a few hundred or more speakers. The speech understanding system is also expected to be capable of running a voice-activated typewriter conducting a dialogue with users by means of synthesized speech in Japanese or English.

The Japanese also consider text analysis a part of natural language processing, although they are aware that the techniques used for large-scale text analysis are different from the techniques needed to smooth the way for an individual user to talk to a machine. Their work also involves a highly ambitious machine translation program. The goal is 90 percent accuracy (the remaining 10 percent to be processed by humans). Translations will be the product of an integrated system that takes part in each of the processes from the compilation of the text to printing the translated documents.

Picture and image processing are considered almost as important as language processing, especially as they contribute to effective analysis of aerial, satellite, and medical images.

The Japanese Fifth Generation project has captured the imagination of computer specialists around the world and is even beginning to attract popular attention. U.S. computer makers are watching the Japanese project carefully. Thus far, U.S. computer companies have shown little interest in artificial intelligence, but Japanese researchers are convinced that advances in this field will bring a revolution in computer science. Since Japan launched its Fifth Generation project in 1981, dozens of U.S. firms have started artificial intelligence departments. In 1983, the Pentagon's Defense Advanced Research Projects Agency announced that it expected to spend up to $95 million a year on new generation computers for military applications. IBM, which has traditionally taken a hands-off attitude toward such "blue sky" efforts, is said to have committed a team of 25 people to building a fifth generation machine. Perhaps the Japanese have just awakened a sleeping giant.

Japanese researchers predict that fifth generation computers will be used everywhere—in offices, factories, even homes. The machines will serve as "intelligent assistants," giving users access to a broad range of information and expertise. In the office, the machines will accept spoken requests, search through reservoirs of stored knowledge, and decide which information is most relevant to the manager's decision-making. In the home, the computers could give advice on personal money management.

WHAT IS INFORMATION PROCESSING?

Before discussing information processing, you need to understand the difference between the terms data and information. Although these terms are often used interchangeably, they refer to very different things. **Data** refers to raw material or unorganized facts. **Information** is the organized, useful knowledge derived from the processed data.

Data cannot be called information unless it has been assembled or processed in such a way as to make it useful to someone. Therefore, the major objective of any organization that uses computers is to produce usable information on which future actions can be based. Evaluating, analyzing, and processing data to produce usable information is called **information processing**.

The operational steps required to convert data to information are known as the information processing cycle. This cycle is divided into roughly four steps: (a) gathering the data; (b) processing the data; (c) producing documents and reports from the processed data; and (d) using the information. As data is processed through this cycle, information is produced which supports decisions; actions are then evaluated, thus producing more data, and the cycle repeats itself (Figure 1–18).

FIGURE 1–18
The flow of data through a business is cyclic.

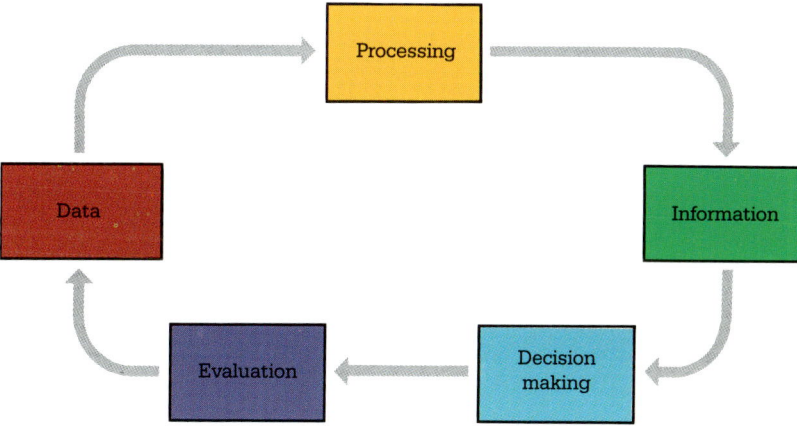

FIGURE 1–19
Data capture, or data recording, is done through the keying of data directly into a computer or onto a storage medium such as magnetic disk or tape. (Courtesy of Pertec Computer Corp.)

Gathering the data   Business forms often provide the raw data for information processing. These forms, called **source documents,** might be time cards, sales slips, purchase orders, invoices, inventory counts, credit card slips, or other items. Collecting and translating this raw data into a form acceptable to the information processing system is called **data capture** or **data recording**.

Data may also be input into a computer system via terminals connected directly to the computer system (Figure 1–19). For example, a fast-food or department store clerk might enter information on computer terminals that are linked to a computer. Whenever entries are made on such terminals, a data record describing the transaction is sent to the computer.

Processing data   Processing converts the raw data into usable information. It involves a number of steps such as classifying, sorting, comparing, calculating, summarizing, and storing (Table 1–1).

TABLE 1–1
Steps in data processing

Classify to categorize data with similar characteristics into the same group or category.
Sort to arrange data items in a desired sequence.
Compare to perform an evaluation in relation to some known measures.
Calculate to apply arithmetic functions to data.
Summarize to condense.
Store to save data in a readily available and safe place so it may be used at some future date.

FIGURE 1–20
Communication is the process of sharing information. Modern computer systems can deliver displays or documents to people who need the information. (Courtesy of Amdek Corp.)

Producing documents and reports   The output, or final result, of the processing function is frequently in the form of inventory reports, payroll checks, sales reports, business forecasts, account statements, purchase orders, business graphs, or management reports. Reports may be printed on paper or shown on a display screen.

Using the information   Unused or inaccessible information would be of little value to anyone. It's important, therefore, that the information be efficiently transmitted to those who need it. This may involve mailing a document or transmitting it via a teleprocessing system (Figure 1–20).

Regardless of the type of information processing system used, all or some of these classifying, sorting, comparing, calculating, summarizing, and storing steps must be performed for raw data to be of value. Keep in mind also that information processing does not occur in a random or haphazard fashion, but within a highly structured information processing cycle. This cycle is a sequence of operations composed of **input, processing, output, control**, and **feedback**. Different systems may perform these steps using different methods. However, the objective of information processing remains basically the same—the conversion of data to useful information.

INFORMATION SYSTEMS

The success of any business depends upon being able to communicate information. Some information processing systems can perform this task. Consider a business that has created a **data base** by storing information about all its resources in a computer. In a data base computer system, raw data are gathered from various departments, processed into information, and then sent back to appropriate departments as required. Systems act as information warehouses, accepting data from various locations, processing, storing, and releasing it on request. Figure 1–21 illustrates an information system where one central computer system serves several different departments of an organization. Information is usually stored so that users of the system can access the information and use it to prepare documents. Users at terminals can request that the computer display specific information on their terminals' screens (Figure 1–22).

BUSINESS USE OF COMPUTER SYSTEMS

The biggest use of computers in business is in information processing; over half the computers now in use were installed to control and reduce administrative paperwork and costs. Information processing is used for operations that involve routine logic and mathematics, but which require the same processing be applied to numerous similar transactions. Table 1–2 lists some business areas that use information processing methods.

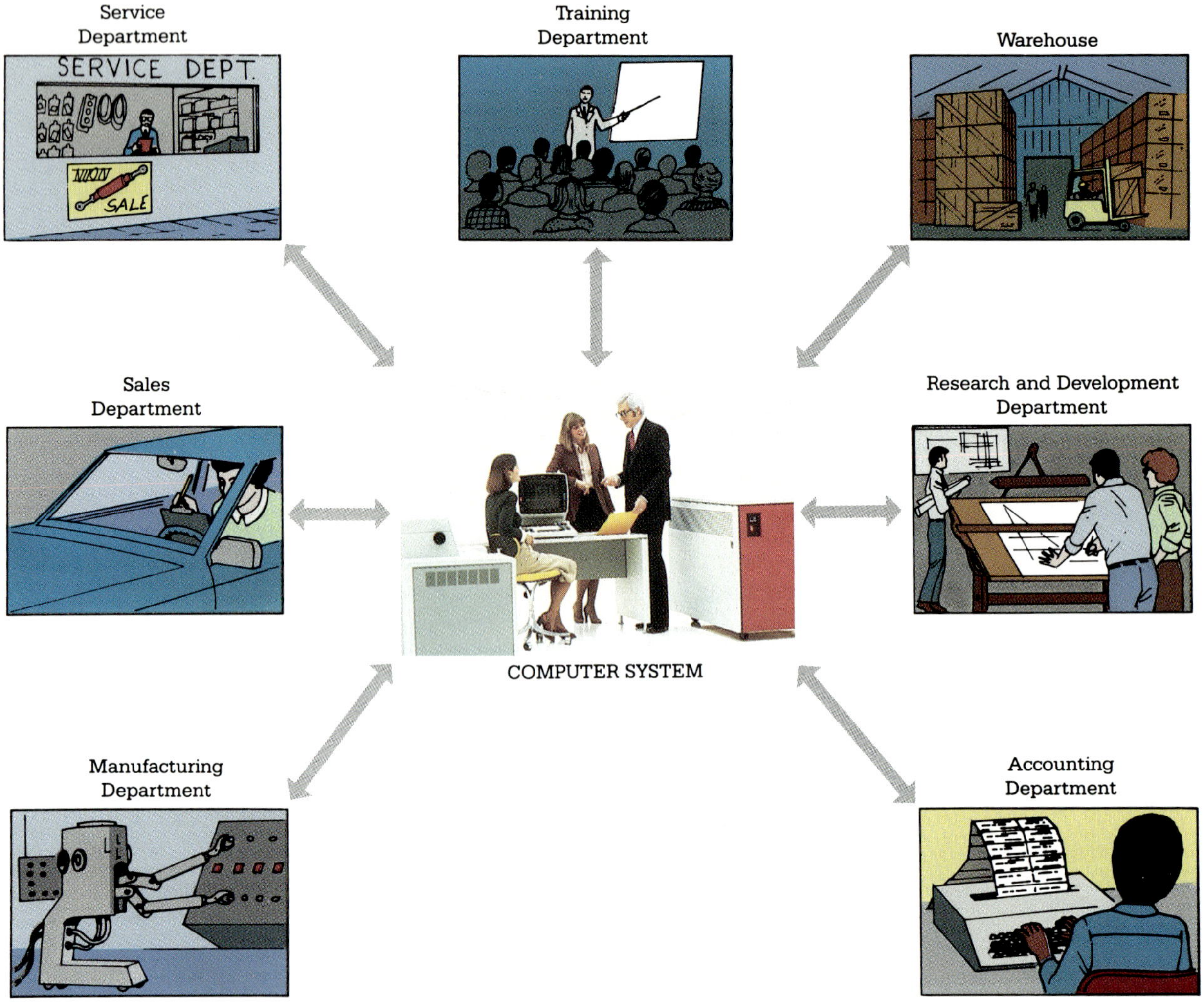
Service
Department
SERVICE DEPT.
SALE
Training
Department
Warehouse
Sales
Department
Research and Development
Department
COMPUTER SYSTEM
Manufacturing
Department
Accounting
Department

FIGURE 1–21
A computer system can facilitate communications among functional units of an organization.

FIGURE 1–22
Information is a valuable asset and important working tool within any business organization. A user has access to data stored in a data base. She can query the computer and request that it locate specific information and display it on the screen. (Courtesy of Sperry Corp.)

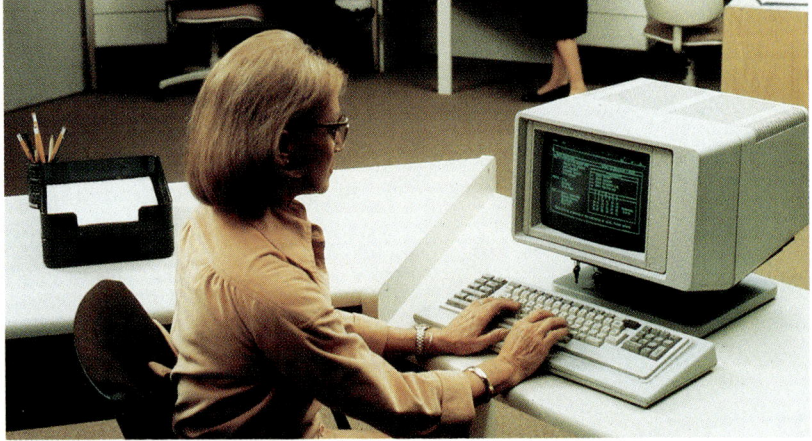

TABLE 1–2
Some business areas using information processing methods

Accounts payable	Order processing
Accounts receivable	Production scheduling
General ledger	Sales analysis
Inventory control	Warehouse control
Payroll	Labor distribution
Tax accounting	Forecasting
Utility billing	Resource scheduling
Business simulations	Credit card accounting

Payroll, accounts payable, accounts receivable, general ledger, and inventory control are the business systems encountered in most business organizations.

Payroll   A payroll system is designed to handle and provide all the information relating to the processing of an employee payroll. The functions of the payroll system include: (a) initiating all paperwork necessary to pay each employee; (b) keeping track of taxes and deductions paid; (c) maintaining records on all past earnings; and (d) providing up-to-date totals on all payroll information.

Accounts payable   Tracking money owed a firm by others is the function of accounts payable. Those owing money are usually suppliers of inventory items for resale (in the retail and distribution environments) or suppliers of raw materials used in manufacturing.

Accounts receivable   Accounts receivable deals with the flow of cash into a firm and plays a prominent role in the overall accounting scheme. Audit-trail features are especially important to accounts receivable, and money received by the firm should be recorded promptly and accurately, with appropriate updates made.

General ledger   As the heart of any accounting system, general ledger is the basis for all financial statements and makes up the sum and substance of the firm's total accounting picture.

Inventory control   An inventory control system monitors the contents and changes made in inventory—the most important asset of retailers and distributors. Consequently, a computerized inventory control system is a major ingredient in virtually all automated accounting systems.

THE OFFICE OF THE FUTURE

If you've ever wasted time looking for misplaced class notes or accidentally thrown out an important paper, tomorrow's business office will probably appeal to you. Instead of keeping paper documents stored in file cabinets or shoved in drawers, information will be stored in computer mass storage devices, on microfilm and microfiche, and in word processing systems. In many offices, this change has already begun. Workers appreciate the ease in locating documents and lack of clutter that information storage devices provide. Paper copies can be readily copied or printed when needed.

Word Processing

Office equipment has advanced more rapidly in the past decade than in all other years combined. The typewriter is perhaps the best example of this evolution. Long recognized as an essential business tool, the typewriter has been replaced, in many offices, with a faster, more efficient device called a word processor. This talented offspring of the marriage between the computer and electric typewriter is able to perform a variety of timesaving tasks. These include rearranging text, adjusting margins, and searching out and/or replacing particular words or phrases throughout documents. Many word processing systems also offer spelling checkers, which rely on a 50 000 to 100 000-word electronic dictionary to make documents letter-perfect.

Electronic Telephones and Facsimile Transmission

Another device likely to become more prevalent in the next few years is the "smart," or electronic, telephone. One smart phone now on the market is designed for use in systems with as many as nine lines. Among its functions are conference calling, call forwarding, recording, automatic dialing, multiple redialing of busy numbers, and last number redial. Other models feature built-in clocks and calculators and perform a number of interesting functions. Facsimile (FAX) transmission devices work in conjunction with the telephone to transmit exact copies of documents across the city or across the country. Scanning devices convert information into digital signals for phone transmission. Both those sending and receiving the documents must have FAX equipment. The receiving FAX reverses the process to create an exact image of the original on paper.

Other Equipment in the Office of the Future

Programmable calculators, minicomputer systems, microcomputer systems, and portable hand-held computers will be widely used in modern offices. Many employees will use computer terminals to enter information for processing or storage by a computer. They will also rely on terminals to retrieve information and send electronic messages.

Modern equipment will also make conducting business easier for travelers. Using a hand-held computer with a minicomputer and telephone interface, a business person can plug the machine into the phone and access the company's main computer system. Minutes, or even seconds, later he or she will walk away with a hard-copy printout of a client's financial statement or an up-to-the-minute quote on any number of pertinent business facts.

In the future, paper paychecks may go the way of manual typewriters. Instead of using valuable company time printing and distributing checks, employers will supply the bank with a magnetic disk or tape that will credit the employee's account and debit the employer's. Many employees will choose to conduct all their transactions with credit cards, thus eliminating paper and cash entirely from the cycle.

A century ago, most Americans were farmers. Today, more than 60 percent are engaged in work that deals with information processing. The information society is not just a fact of life in the United States. Japan, France, Canada, Germany, Sweden, Great Britain, and many other countries are involved in using computers for information processing. In the future, office workers worldwide will be dependent upon information processing equipment.

SUMMARY

- [ ] The four main advantages of computers are speed, accuracy, economy, and reliability.
- [ ] Data refers to unorganized facts or raw material.
- [ ] Information is the organized, useful knowledge derived from processed data.
- [ ] Information processing is the function of evaluating, analyzing, and processing data to produce useful information.
- [ ] The information processing cycle involves three functions: input, processing (including storage), and output.
- [ ] A data base is a collection of data stored in a computer system.
- [ ] Word processing is a process that allows you to store and manipulate text.
- [ ] Information processing activities include: accounts payable, accounts receivable, general ledger, inventory control, payroll, tax accounting, utility billing, credit card accounting, order processing, and production scheduling.

REVIEW QUESTIONS

True or False

_____ 1 The computer industry is the largest industry in the world.

_____ 2 Computers are fast and accurate; however, they are not always reliable.

_____ 3 Computers are becoming less expensive.

_____ 4 Computer applications are limited only by human imagination.

_____ 5 Sales analysis is the biggest use of computers in business.

_____ 6 Frenchman Blaise Pascal invented the first practical calculating machine in 1642.

_____ 7 Herman Hollerith developed a punched card system that was first used in the 1890 census.

_____ **8** Modern computers are faster and smaller than the early computers.

_____ **9** "Expert systems" solve problems by reasoning from the facts stored in a memory bank.

_____ **10** Japanese researchers predict that fifth generation computers will be widely used in offices, factories, and homes.

_____ **11** Information processing is the biggest use of computers in business.

_____ **12** By 1990, an estimated 60 percent of all jobs will depend to some degree on computers.

_____ **13** A word processor is a machine that is used to produce form letters, reports, manuscripts, and other paper documents.

_____ **14** One millionth of a second is called a microsecond.

_____ **15** Processing refers to the manipulation of data.

Short Answer

1 For many years, U.S. computer manufacturers have dominated world markets. Another country that is now beginning to develop and market computer equipment on a wide scale is _____.

2 A nanosecond is one _____ (thousandth, billionth) of a second.

3 The steps involved in the information processing cycle are _____, _____, _____, and _____.

4 You have decided to open your own business. Your first purchase is a computer. List five ways your new computer can be used to help in your business.

    a _____

    b _____

    c _____

    d _____

    e _____

5 The ENIAC could perform about _____ additions per second.

6 The hand-held computer was first introduced in the year _____.

7 A collection of related facts or items is a _____.

8 A technique for electronically storing, editing, and manipulating text is called _____ _____.

9 An _____ _____ is a computer system and data base that are used as a means of communicating information.

10 A _____ _____ is an original document from which basic data is extracted. Examples are invoices, sales slips, and purchase orders.

11 Fill in the blanks with the words listed below. You may need to use the same word more than once.

widespread	economy	decrease
computers	banks	world
accuracy	future	reliability
problem	impact	educated
information	farmers	speed

Stores, schools, _____, hospitals, and many other businesses rely heavily on _____ to perform many important tasks. As computer use becomes _____, prices of these machines will _____. Computers are simply electronic _____ solvers that offer the advantages of _____, _____, _____, and _____. Because of their _____ on our lives, it is essential that every _____ person become familiar with _____ and how they are used. One hundred years ago, most Americans were _____. Now, more than 60 percent are engaged in _____ work. In the _____, people all over the _____ will be dependent upon _____ processing equipment.

12 An early computer that used electronic circuits was designed by J. Presper Eckert and John W. Mauchly at the University of Pennsylvania in 1946. This machine was called the _____.

13 The first large scale electronic computer, available commercially in 1951, was the _____.

14 Time cards, sales slips, purchase orders, credit card slips, class registration cards, and invoices are all examples of _____.

OUTLINE

OBJECTIVES

1 Identify the components and functions of a computer system.

2 Explain the difference between hardware and software.

3 Identify the components and functions of a central processing unit.

4 Explain the difference between main storage and auxiliary storage.

5 Identify the different types of main storage.

6 Explain the purpose of input/output devices.

7 Explain how computers are directed to do something.

8 Explain how data are stored in computers.

2 INTRODUCTION TO THE COMPUTER

COMPONENTS OF A COMPUTER SYSTEM

Like anything that seems complicated at first, computers lose their mystery when you examine the parts that make up the whole. A **computer system** consists of a number of components, each performing a specific function (Figure 2–1). The system consists of input devices (used to send information to the computer), the central processing unit (CPU), storage devices, and output equipment that communicates computed results to humans. These physical components of the computer system are called **hardware**. Hardware includes the CPU and all input, output, and storage devices.

Hardware may be **off-line** (not controlled by or in communication with the CPU), or **on-line** (controlled by or in communication with the CPU). Data processing with punched cards, where a human operator uses a keypunch machine and transcribes data, is one example of an off-line operation. The machine attached to the computer that reads these cards is an example of an on-line device.

Complementing the hardware is a **software system**, which includes an operating system and other programs that direct or instruct the computer system to perform specific functions. One such software system is the **operating system**, a set of programs that control input and output, communicate with the computer operator, and schedule the computer's resources to allow for continuous operation with minimum manual intervention.

THE CENTRAL PROCESSING UNIT

The most complex and powerful part of a computer system is the **central processing unit (CPU)**. Like an engine in a car, the CPU is what makes the computer system go. The CPU is made up of two parts:

1 The control unit, which coordinates the operations of the entire computer system
2 The arithmetic/logic unit, which performs all calculations

The CPU has only a small amount of memory to use as high-speed storage during its calculations. The remaining memory, as well as input and output devices which enable it to communicate with humans, is external to the CPU. Depending on its purpose, the CPU can vary in size from a small chip to a room-size unit. Many older, large computer systems feature control consoles, containing switches, buttons, and sensor lights. The sensor lights show what's going on inside the CPU.

Control Unit

The **control unit** performs the most vital function in the CPU. It's the "brains behind the operation," where all program steps are interpreted and instructions are issued to carry out the programs. The control unit directs the overall functioning of the other units of the computer and regulates data flow. When the computer is operating under program control,

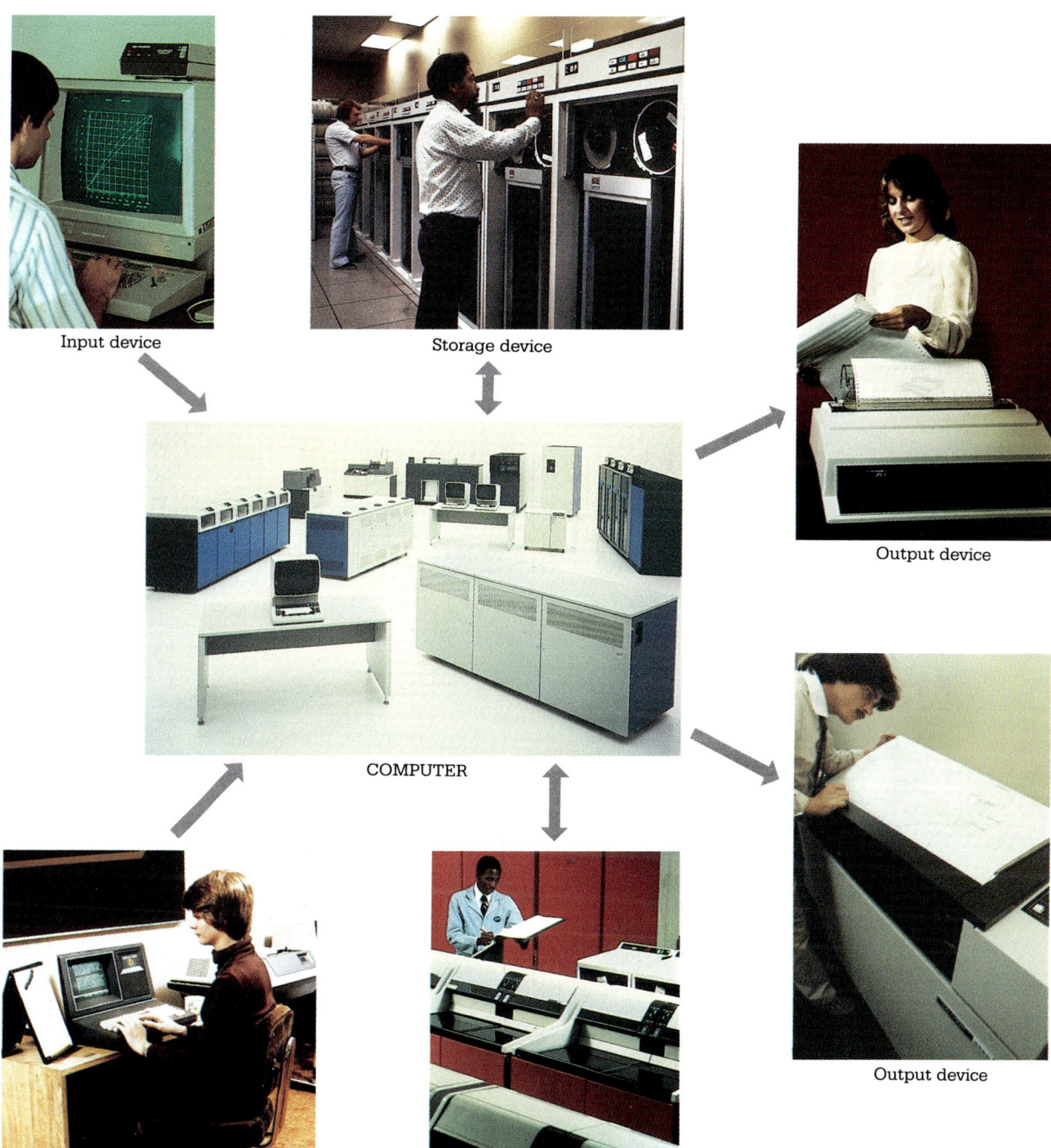

Input device

Storage device

Output device

COMPUTER

Input device

Storage device

Output device

FIGURE 2–1
A computer system consists of a number of individual components, each performing its own function. The system consists of equipment to send data to the computer (input devices), the central processing unit, storage devices, equipment to accept information from the computer (output devices), people to operate and maintain the equipment, and software. (Courtesy of Celanese Corp., Lockheed Corp., Centronics Data Computer Corp., International Business Machines Corp., Planning Research Corp., and Sanders Associates, Inc. Lower left photo provided by DATAPOINT® Corp. All rights reserved.)

the control unit brings in data, as required, from the input devices and directs the routing of results to the required output devices. This unit is similar to a central telephone switchboard; control is effected through the wires or circuit boards that connect all parts of the system to the central control board.

Another aspect of the control function of the CPU is governed by programs. A program tells the computer system how to perform the mathematical calculations necessary to solve a specific problem. It also instructs the computer how to go about storing and displaying data, as well as other functions associated with getting the problem solved.

The Arithmetic/Logic Unit

The **arithmetic/logic unit (ALU)** controls all operations of arithmetic and logic. As directed by the control unit, the ALU performs additions, subtractions, multiplications, and divisions on numerical data. The unit usually includes a small amount of storage to hold both the numbers that are to be acted upon and the partial answers generated during calculation. The ALU also can compare numeric or alphabetic information to determine whether it is the same or different. The arithmetic/logic units of most computers perform all arithmetic functions using binary numbers.

STORAGE CLASSIFICATIONS

Computer **storage**, sometimes called **memory**, is actually an electronic file in which instructions and data are placed until needed. When data come into a computer through an input unit, such as a keyboard, it is first converted to binary, then placed in storage. The data remains there until called for by the computer's control unit.

Just as you might classify the capacity of a metal file cabinet in terms of the amount of paper files it can contain, computer storage is classified as to the amount of data it can hold. Some personal computers have very small storage capacities—the equivalent of what could be printed on a couple of sheets of paper. Very large computers are able to store the equivalent of thousands, sometimes millions, of pages of data. Here are some terms related to computer storage that you should know:

- □ **Capacity** is the amount of data a storage device can hold at one time; it is measured in bytes, characters, or bits.
- □ **Bit** is a digit (1 or 0) that represents a number in a binary notation.
- □ **Byte** is a group of eight bits that represent a character, such as a letter, number, or a special symbol.
- □ **Kilobyte** (abbreviated K or KB) is 1 024 bytes.
- □ **Megabyte** is approximately one million bytes.
- □ **Access time** is the time that it takes a computer to locate and transfer data to or from storage.

The two types of computer storage are main and auxiliary storage. **Main storage** is an extension of the CPU and directly accessible to it. It accepts data from an input device during processing, exchanges data with the CPU, supplies instructions to the CPU, sends the computed data to an output device, and holds data and instructions in current use by the computer. **Auxiliary storage** is slower, less expensive, and used to supplement the main storage capacity of a computer. It may be sequential or direct. Sequential storage is nonaddressable. That is, you cannot directly refer to the contents of a particular storage location. Using sequential auxiliary storage, such as magnetic tape or cassette tape, entails going through the tape in sequence to locate the desired file. On the other hand, direct storage provides users with immediate access to files. Magnetic disks, floppy disks, Winchester disks, magnetic drums, and videodisks are all forms of direct access storage (Figure 2–2).

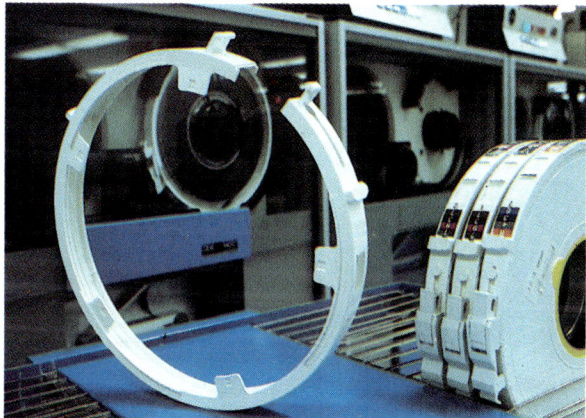

FIGURE 2–2
Floppy disks (top left), magnetic tapes (top right), magnetic disks (bottom left), and cassette tapes (bottom right) are popular forms of auxiliary storage in modern computer systems. (Courtesy of Verbatim Corp., Monsanto Co., and NASA.)

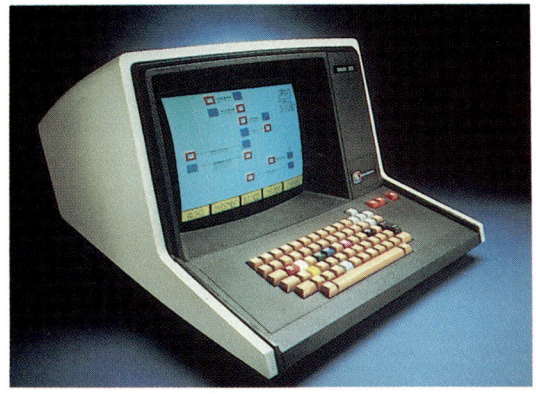

Input device

Data to be
processed

Central processing unit
(Storage and arithmetic/logic units)

Main storage

Results to be
recorded

Auxiliary storage

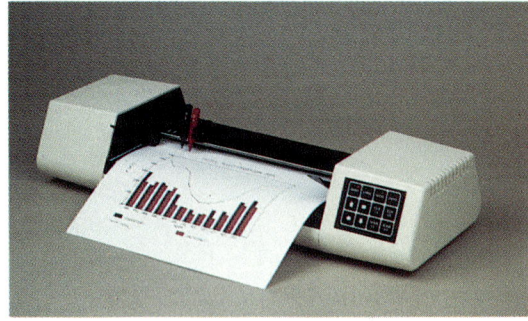

Output device

FIGURE 2–3
Schematic of main and auxiliary storage. (Courtesy of International Business Machines Corp., Intelligent Systems Corp., Bausch & Lomb Houston Instrument Division, and Boeing Co. Center photo reprinted with permission of Mostek Corp. Copyright, 1980)

Regardless of how it is stored, data must be transferred from auxiliary storage to main storage before programs can be executed. (Auxiliary storage devices are discussed in detail in Chapter 4.) The main storage, also called **primary storage** and **internal storage**, must have a capacity sufficient to retain a usable amount of data and the instructions needed for processing it. Some operations require more program statements or data than can be held in main storage at one time. That's where auxiliary storage comes in (Figure 2–3). Auxiliary storage makes up for its lack of speed with its massive capacity; it can generally store millions, even hundreds of millions, of characters.

Computer main storage consists of a large number of cells, each with a fixed capacity for storing data and a unique location called an address. Each storage cell, which is analogous to a post office box, is capable of holding a specific amount of data and, depending on the system, the unit of data may be a fixed number of binary digits (bits) or bytes (8-bits). The content of each storage cell changes constantly as data are processed and programs are executed.

Semiconductor Storage

The main storage of most modern computers consists of microminiature semiconductor circuits (Figure 2–4). Thousands, sometimes hundreds of thousands, of semiconductor storage circuits are etched on circuit chips no larger than a matchhead. Today, popular memory chips contain either 64 000 or 256 000 bits, but by the late 1980s one million-bit chips will be common. By the turn of the century, memory chips will probably contain billions of bits.

The growth of semiconductor storage and microminiature technology has resulted in the development of two basic types of **semiconductor storage: random access memory (RAM)** and **read-only memory (ROM).**

FIGURE 2–4
Miniature integrated circuits are mounted into printed circuit boards. The individual boards shown above are, in effect, complete storage systems. (Reprinted with permission of Mostek Corp. Copyright, 1980)

Electronic spreadsheets are valuable for displaying information because they can transform the personal computer screen into the rows and columns of a ledger sheet, permitting the user to work with a series of interrelated values. With them, you can record, study, and compare business data by budgeting, comparing alternatives, evaluating proposals, tracking costs, preparing bids, and measuring results. You don't have to know how to program to use spreadsheets, but because of their power, they give you a satisfying sense of control over a computer. Frequently, spreadsheets provide enough benefits to justify the cost of buying a personal computer.

VISICALC—THE FIRST SPREADSHEET

In the mid-1970s, Dan Bricklin belonged to a team of programmers who helped Digital Equipment Corporation (DEC) implement word processing concepts on DEC computer systems. This experience may have been totally uneventful had Bricklin not decided to attend Harvard Business School. At Harvard, students were often assigned the task of

preparing financial planning sheets for mock organizations. It was repetitive work that required numerous calculations before meaningful results could be obtained. Invariably, Bricklin would get to the end of a spreadsheet problem only to find that one calculation in the middle was incorrect, and he would have to refigure the entire problem. Bricklin's background in computer science, word processing, and business started him thinking about an electronic spreadsheet for use on small computers. He had a ''magic blackboard'' in mind where, when one number in the equation changed, the computer could automatically refigure the solution and change all of the numbers in the rows and columns accordingly.

Together with Bob Frankston, a friend and programmer from MIT, Bricklin founded Software Arts, Incorporated. About the same time, Dan Fylstra, another MIT graduate, had formed Personal Software Incorporated (now VisiCorp) and was selling chess games for Apple II and Radio Shack TRS-80 Model I microcomputers. The two companies formed an agreement: Software Arts provided the VisiCalc software and Personal Software sold it.

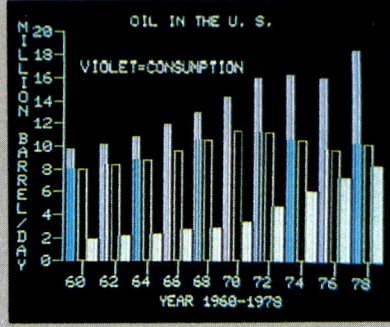

Several electronic spreadsheet vendors are incorporating graphics packages that provide automatic graphic representations of spreadsheet data. (Courtesy of Apple Computer, Inc.)

In 1978, the first test version of VisiCalc, written in BASIC, was run on Fylstra's Apple II microcomputer. The following year, the commercial version was written in machine language, and Personal Software began shipping the product to dealers. Word spread throughout the industry that VisiCalc was convenient, versatile, and inexpensive. Soon business people began buying Apple II microcomputer systems so they could run VisiCalc. Today, VisiCalc is available for dozens of different machines.

SPREADSHEET APPLICATIONS

When a user changes one value on an electronic spreadsheet, the program automatically recalculates any other affected values in seconds. This spreadsheet dramatically amplifies what can be achieved by hand. It enables complex manual ledger sheet calculations to be performed in minutes with greater accuracy. Therefore, more assumptions can also be assessed.

Although originally intended for accountants, electronic spreadsheet programs have become quite popular with managers and other white collar workers who produce budgets, sales forecasts, and action and profit plans. Many spreadsheet programs have been optimized specifically for financial modeling in disciplines

PeachCalc electronic spreadsheet is a data analysis system that allows you to use the microcomputer's memory as a large electronic spreadsheet. PeachCalc analyzes numerical and financial data, reducing traditional preparation time. (Courtesy of Peachtree Software, Inc.)

such as marketing, accounting, banking, and finance. Other common electronic spreadsheet applications are real estate analysis, cash flow projections, business plans, currency conversion, sales projections, income statements, engineering applications, budget consolidation, and tax preparation.

SECOND GENERATION SPREADSHEETS

Because of its success, VisiCalc spawned imitators. Today there are at least 70 different electronic spreadsheets for microcomputers. They account for more business microcomputer software sales that any other application. Currently more than 3 million are installed.

A new wave of second generation programs, extending the capabilities of the original, have also developed. Some leading second generation electronic spreadsheets are Multiplan, SuperCalc[3], and 1-2-3.

Multiplan, from Microsoft, has advanced features that include sorting, global search and replace, menu prompts, and an English-like language in lieu of formulas that facilitate user interaction

with the program. It permits up to six noncontiguous parts of a model to be viewed simultaneously via window splitting. Multiplan runs on virtually any microcomputer.

SuperCalc[3] from Sorcim (micros spelled backwards) is friendly, fast, and colorful. It's available on many microcomputers and is the source of several important innovations, such as the help facility and variable-width columns. It "remembers" how big your worksheet is and can automatically print wide ones; it has fast calculations and makes effective use of color to highlight protected cells and negative values.

The 1-2-3 spreadsheet from Lotus Development combines the good features from several other spreadsheets, along with the most extensive use of menus and help, to offer great power and convenience. The 1-2-3 sorts rows and can protect cells and name ranges. It can copy, move, format, and erase blocks. An unusual "what if" data table feature helps you test the sensitivity of results to changes in your assumptions. This spreadsheet also offers an enormous $255 \times 2\,048$ matrix that allows you to create sheets with elaborate levels of detail. The 1-2-3 is one of the most complete

39

A Multiplan multiwindow display is shown on the screen of this IBM Personal Computer AT. Multiplan permits up to six noncontiguous parts of a model to be shown simultaneously. (Courtesy of International Business Machines Corp.)

and popular spreadsheets available.

MAINFRAME SPREADSHEETS

Electronic spreadsheets are one of the few programs that have been adapted to run on mainframe computers and minicomputers after being developed for microcomputer use. Most microcomputer applications are scaled-down versions of previously existing mainframe and minicomputer applications. The spreadsheet is the exact opposite. Spreadsheet interaction between corporate desktop computers or terminals and centralized mainframes is becoming quite popular especially to companies that have large investments in terminals. Today, several spreadsheets are available to run on IBM mainframe computers.

FUTURE DEVELOPMENTS

In a few years, practically all business personnel will have access to a microcomputer and a spreadsheet package. This combination will be as indispensable as the pencil, eraser, and calculating machine are now. The power of its software will increase as developers produce better packages. Each new release will have more functions and commands. A new area of development is the incorporation of the electronic spreadsheet with other management-level programs. The electronic spreadsheet will eventually be replaced by a more comprehensive executive management software package, or integrated management software system, which will provide the needed tools for a complex business world.

Random access memory   RAM stores user programs and data during processing. Each storage location can be directly accessed (read or stored) in the same length of time regardless of its location in storage. Using RAM is like working on scratch paper. Unless you give the computer specific instructions to save what RAM contains, the contents are lost when the computer is turned off.

Read-only memory   ROM is used in applications where the programs or data are not to be changed. In effect, ROM is "hard-wired" into the computer when it is manufactured. For example, many manufacturers program BASIC, a popular computer language, into their machine's ROM for the convenience of users. The contents of ROM cannot be changed and are not lost when the power is turned off.

Magnetic Bubble Memory

Magnetic bubble memory gets its name from tiny, bubble-like magnetic fields embedded on the surface of garnet wafers (silicates with magnetic properties ideal for this sort of storage). Unlike semiconductor storage, which is not magnetic, bubble memories do not lose their contents when the power supply is removed. They are rugged and durable, but they are so expensive to produce that they haven't met with overwhelming commercial success.

Bubble memories can operate in harsh environments where shock, dust, or temperature might adversely affect disks or tapes. Magnetic bubbles can bridge the gap between fast but expensive semiconductor storage and relatively slow but low-cost auxiliary storage devices. Though access to data in bubble memories (measured in thousandths of one second) is slower than that of integrated circuits (measured in billionths of one second), bubble data retrieval times are comparable to those of the speediest magnetic disk.

Presently, 250 000-bit and million-bit bubble memory chips are state-of-the-art. Multimillion bit chips, created in part by reducing the size of magnetic bubbles and the distances between adjacent bubbles, are available in experimental form. These advances, combined with new methods for moving bubbles, should also reduce access time and cost.

INPUT/OUTPUT DEVICES

Regardless of its capacity or method of storage, if a computer is to be of any use to you, there must be a convenient way to enter the data to be processed and to get the results. That is the mission of **input/output equipment**, also called **I/O equipment**. **Input devices** feed data into the computer; **output devices** retrieve data from the computer's main storage. Before information can be entered, it must be converted via an input device from a form the user understands to one the computer finds intelligible. Input information is recorded on magnetic disks and tape as magnetized spots, on cards as punched holes, and on paper documents as line drawings or printed characters.

Output is data that have been processed by the computer. It may be in a form directly understandable to humans or it may be retained in machine-readable form for future use by another machine. A magnetic disk unit, used as an output device, records information in a form suitable only as input for further processing.

Some typical I/O devices are shown in Figure 2–5. Devices such as the keyboard and digitizer are used only for input, while the printer and plotter are used strictly for output. The visual display and point-of-sale terminal can be used for either input or output. (I/O devices are discussed in Chapter 3.)

THE STORED PROGRAM CONCEPT

Control is the process of directing the operation of the computer system, either manually by a human operator or automatically through program control. The instructions that guide the operation are called a **stored program**. Without these instructions, the computer is a useless machine, unable to complete work.

TELLING THE COMPUTER WHAT TO DO

Now that we've looked at computer hardware, let's see how these devices are used to solve problems.

Types of Software

Software is generally categorized as either systems software or applications software. **Systems software** consists of programs designed to facilitate the use of the computer by the user. One such software system is the operating system. **Applications software** consists of the programs written to perform specific user applications. Commercial software, purchased to insert into the computer to instruct it to play games or teach languages, is one example of applications software. A program that a company's accounting department develops to tell the computer how to keep track of employees' paychecks is another example. Primarily, applications software performs tasks that are of immediate use.

In addition to hardware and software, another important component is needed to run computer systems—human beings. Systems analysts, programmers, computer operators, and librarians are just some of the people who work with computers.

COMPUTERS AND PROBLEM SOLVING

Let's become familiar with terms relating to a computer's problem-solving capacity. A **computer program** is a set of instructions that tells the computer precisely how to perform a specific calculation or operation.

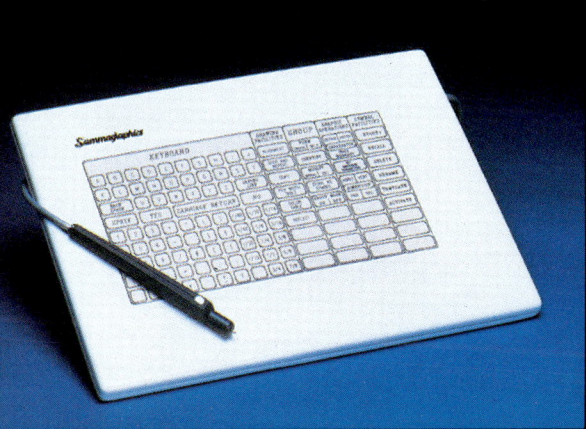
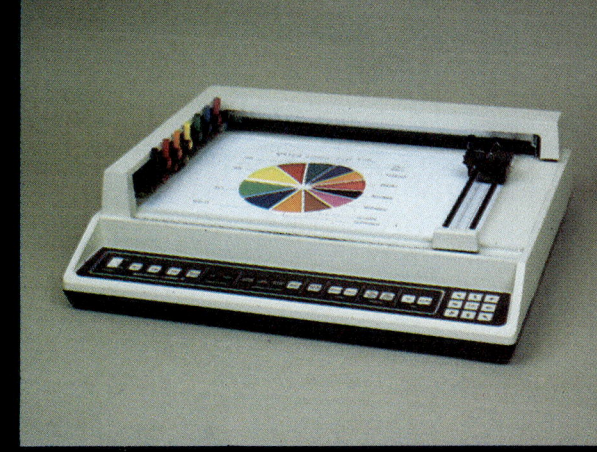

FIGURE 2–5

Input and output devices are the eyes, ears, and mouth of a computer system. Shown above are (left to right, top to bottom) visual display, printer, point-of-sale terminal, keyboard, digitizer, and plotter. (Courtesy of Control Data Corp., Dataproducts Corp., International Business Machines Corp., Bell Laboratories, Summagraphics Corp., and Bausch & Lomb, Houston Instrument Division)

43

How a Program Works

The user gives a problem to the computer via the program, which may be written in one of dozens of available programming languages. Each instruction in a program is a direction to the computer to perform a simple operation, such as adding two numbers or printing a line of results. The computer follows the sequence of instructions without deviating and is thus able to solve problems without human intervention.

Machine language   The basic language of the computer, called **machine language**, consists of a set of binary codes of 1's and 0's representing the machine's memory configurations. Machine language is obviously very difficult to use because it must be written in numbers. Depending on their architecture (the way the internal portions of the machine are put together), different machines use instructions of varying lengths of numbers. For example, a computer with 64-bit architecture only accepts instructions that are 64 bits long.

Assembly language   Symbolic codes rather than numbers are used in **assembly language**. Assembly language is on the same level as machine language, but it is simpler to use because symbols rather than numbers represent computer instructions, storage locations, and so on. Generally, each type of computer has its own assembly language.

High-level language   A language that is much easier to use than assembly or machine is **high-level language.** It enables users to write programs in terms that describe problems and solutions rather than in terms relevant to the internal operation of computers.

Before a program written in a high-level language can be executed, it must be translated into machine language inside the computer. Computers use compilers and interpreters to translate programs into machine language. Compilers and interpreters are programs themselves, whose sole purpose is to perform translations. A compiler translates each statement of a source program once into the equivalent machine language of 1's and 0's (called object code) that the computer can understand. An interpreter translates each statement of the program into machine language each time it is executed. Several microcomputers have BASIC language interpreters in ROM. One merely turns on these machines and they are ready to accept programming statements in BASIC.

DATA REPRESENTATION

All symbols convey information. The symbols themselves are not information, they represent something that is. The printed characters on this page are symbols that may convey one meaning to some persons and a different meaning to others. They may convey no meaning at all to those who don't know the significance of the symbols.

Symbols used to convey information to computer systems are called **computer codes**. As explained previously, these codes can be punched into cards, recorded as spots on magnetic disks or tapes, and so on. Computer codes provide a way for humans and machines to communicate.

Two computer codes commonly used in modern computer systems are Extended Binary Coded Decimal Interchange Code (EBCDIC) and American Standard Code for Information Interchange (ASCII) (Figure 2–6). EBCDIC, pronounced "ebseedick," represents each character with an 8-bit binary code. ASCII, pronounced "ask-ee," represents data using

Character	EBCDIC	Character	ASCII
0	1111 0000	0	011 0000
1	1111 0001	1	011 0001
2	1111 0010	2	011 0010
3	1111 0011	3	011 0011
4	1111 0100	4	011 0100
5	1111 0101	5	011 0101
6	1111 0110	6	011 0110
7	1111 0111	7	011 0111
8	1111 1000	8	011 1000
9	1111 1001	9	011 1001
A	1100 0001	A	100 0001
B	1100 0010	B	100 0010
C	1100 0011	C	100 0011
D	1100 0100	D	100 0100
E	1100 0101	E	100 0101
F	1100 0110	F	100 0110
G	1100 0111	G	100 0111
H	1100 1000	H	100 1000
I	1100 1001	I	100 1001
J	1101 0001	J	100 1010
K	1101 0010	K	100 1011
L	1101 0011	L	100 1100
M	1101 0100	M	100 1101
N	1101 0101	N	100 1110
O	1101 0110	O	100 1111
P	1101 0111	P	101 0000
Q	1101 1000	Q	101 0001
R	1101 1001	R	101 0010
S	1110 0010	S	101 0011
T	1110 0011	T	101 0100
U	1110 0100	U	101 0101
V	1110 0101	V	101 0110
W	1110 0110	W	101 0111
X	1110 0111	X	101 1000
Y	1110 1000	Y	101 1001
Z	1110 1001	Z	101 1010

FIGURE 2–6
Common internal character codes for a computer. EBCDIC (Extended Binary Coded Decimal Interchange Code) is an 8-bit code used with many computers. ASCII (American Standard Code for Information Interchange) is a 7-bit code used widely in data communications applications.

a 7-bit code. The letters making up the name SMITH are shown below in EBCDIC and ASCII code.

EBCDIC code:

11100010	11010100	11001001	11100011	11001000
S	M	I	T	H

ASCII code:

1010011	1001101	1001001	1010100	1001000
S	M	I	T	H

SUMMARY

☐ A computer system consists of a number of individual components including: input devices to send information to the computer; the central processing unit (CPU), which is the heart of the computer system; storage devices; and output equipment that communicates computed results to humans. The CPU and all input, output, and storage devices are called hardware.

☐ A software system complements the hardware and includes an operating system and other programs that direct or instruct the computer system to perform specific functions. One such software system is the operating system, a set of programs that control input and output, communicate with the operator, and schedule the computer's resources.

☐ The central processing unit (CPU) is composed of two sections: a control unit and an arithmetic/logic unit. The control unit coordinates the activities of the entire computer system, while the arithmetic/logic unit performs the calculations.

☐ Computer storage, or memory, is actually an electronic file where instructions and data are placed until needed. Incoming data input, from a keyboard or other device, is first converted to binary and then placed in storage, where it remains until called for by the computer's control unit. There are two types of computer storage: main storage, an extension of the CPU and directly accessible to it; and auxiliary storage, used to supplement main storage. Auxiliary storage may be sequential or direct. Two types of semiconductor storage, which may contain hundreds of thousands of semiconductor storage circuits etched on circuit chips no larger than matchheads, are RAM (random-access memory) and ROM (read-only memory). RAM stores user programs and data during processing, and each storage location can be directly accessed regardless of location. ROM is used in applications where the programs are not to be changed. ROM is hard-wired into the computer when it is manufactured.

☐ Magnetic bubble memory gets its name from tiny, bubble-like magnetic fields embedded on the surface of garnet wafers—silicates with magnetic properties ideal for this sort of storage.

☐ Input/output (I/O) equipment enter data into the computer and retrieve data from computer mass storage, respectively. Computer programs can be written using machine, assembly, or high-level languages. Language translators, called compilers, interpreters, and assemblers, are used to translate programs written in symbolic languages into the computer's machine language.

☐ Data are represented in storage in the form of a computer code. Two popular computer codes are called EBCDIC and ASCII.

REVIEW QUESTIONS

True or False

_____ 1 Storage external to the CPU is called auxiliary storage.

_____ 2 All activities of a computer system are coordinated and supervised by the arithmetic/logic unit.

_____ 3 The main storage of most computers is magnetic disk.

_____ 4 Computer processing is controlled by a program.

_____ 5 Calculations are performed in the storage unit.

_____ 6 Computer storage may contain instructions.

_____ 7 The digital plotter is an example of an input device.

_____ 8 Software consists of computer programs and associated paperwork.

_____ 9 An off-line device is not controlled by the central processing unit.

_____ 10 An assembler is used to translate an assembly language program into machine language.

_____ 11 Main storage may also be called auxiliary storage.

_____ 12 A megabyte is about one million bytes of storage.

_____ 13 Input/output devices are often called peripheral units.

_____ 14 On-line operation of peripheral units is possible when units are connected to and under the direct control of the computer.

_____ 15 Most peripheral units are electrical in nature, whereas the computer is mechanical.

_____ 16 Small off-line computer systems are often used to prepare data for a larger computer system.

_____ 17 A computer system is incomplete without at least one peripheral device.

_____ 18 The primary function of an output unit is to enter information into the computer.

_____ 19 Auxiliary storage is used primarily to supplement the main storage of the computer.

_____ 20 The main storage of most computers is bubble memory.

_____ 21 A computer register is similar to a cash register.

_____ 22 A register is capable of holding data temporarily.

_____ 23 A byte is the same as four bits.

_____ 24 A kilobyte is roughly one billion bytes.

_____ 25 Semiconductor memories are found only in large computer systems.

_____ 26 All activities of a computer are coordinated and supervised by the arithmetic/logic unit.

_____ 27 Symbolic codes are used in machine language.

Short Answer

1   The term _____ refers to the computer equipment while the term _____ is used to designate programs and other related items.

2   A _____ _____ consists of input/output devices, the CPU, and storage devices.

3   An _____ _____ is a unit that is in direct communication with the central processing unit.

4   The process of transferring information into and out of main computer storage is called _____ and _____ operations.

5   A _____ _____ is a set of instructions that tells the computer precisely how to perform an operation.

6   The basic language of a computer is called _____.

7   The arithmetic/logic and control units are collectively called the _____ _____ _____.

8   A register temporarily holds _____ while other parts of the CPU analyze it.

9   _____ _____ is the time that it takes a computer to locate and transfer data to and from storage.

10   Two types of semiconductor storage are _____ and _____.

11   A _____ is 1 024 bytes.

12   A _____ is roughly one million bytes.

13   A _____ is a group of eight bits that represent a character, such as a letter or number.

14   The storage unit may hold _____ and _____ simultaneously.

15   _____ is a type of storage that is used in applications where the programs and data are not to be changed.

16   The main storage of most modern computers is _____.

17   Floppy disk storage is a good example of a(n) _____ device.

18   The _____ of a storage device is expressed as the number of bytes, characters, words, or bits that it can store at any given time.

19   The _____ _____ is used to monitor a system after the computer is under program control.

20   Software is generally categorized as either _____ software or _____ software.

21   Symbols used to convey information to computers are called _____ _____.

22   _____ is an 8-bit computer code that is used to represent data inside a computer.

23   High-level programming languages are _____ (easier, harder) to use than machine languages.

24   The instructions that guide the operation of a computer are called a _____ _____.

OUTLINE

OBJECTIVES

1 Understand the purpose of
input/output.

2 Identify the different types of
input/output equipment and
understand their uses.

3 Identify the types of data preparation units.

4 Understand the purpose of
buffers.

3 INPUT/OUTPUT CONCEPTS AND DEVICES

Like humans, computers need a way to communicate. The human body receives, or inputs, information through the eyes, nose, ears, tongue, and skin. For example, when someone steps on your toes, this information is carried through the nerves to the brain where it is processed. Your brain then makes a decision on how you will respond. Your response, whether it's to say, "Ouch!," or grimace with pain, is your output—the way you communicate information.

In a computer system, input devices gather data for processing in the computer, and output devices are used to report or store the informa-

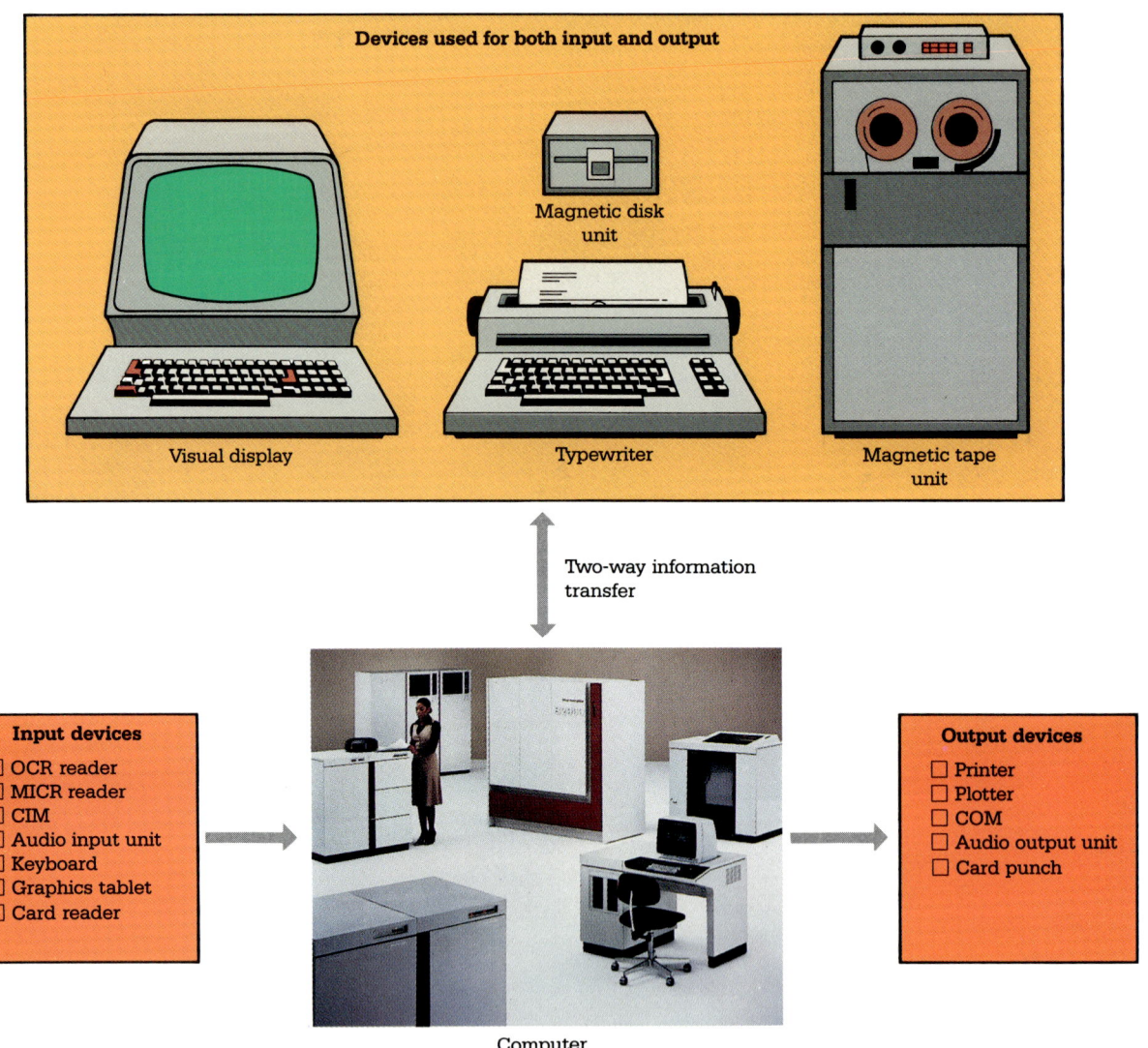

FIGURE 3–1
Input/output devices include units that can: (a) only input information to the computer; (b) only accept output from the computer; and (c) perform both the input and output functions. (Courtesy of Burroughs Corp.)

tion that has been processed. Devices that perform input, output, or both are called **peripherals**.

A computer system's input/output devices (Figure 3–1) respond to operational requests directed by a program stored in the computer. For example, an instruction to print a message causes one or more lines to be output on a device such as a visual display or printer. Just as the brain directs human communication, the instructions in the computer's program tell it what to do. These instructions select the required device, direct it to read or write, and indicate the location in computer storage where data can be stored for input or retrieved for output.

INPUT/OUTPUT DEVICES

Visual Display Devices

Visual display devices are widely used for computer input and output. Most display devices look like a cross between a typewriter and a television set. In a typical computer system, the display device is connected by wire to the computer (Figure 3–2). This might be a hard-wired connection directly to the computer, or the display might be one of many in a system network operating under the control of a communication control computer. If the display is at a remote location, its connection with the computer is usually through the telephone system. In any case, information sent from the computer to the display device is shown on the screen, and in most instances the display terminal is equipped with a keyboard for two-way communications capability (Figure 3–3).

Some visual display devices, called alphanumeric display terminals, can only show text. Others, called graphic display devices, can display graphics.

Graphic display devices not only present data in graphic form, but also manipulate and modify the data presented. Interactive graphic displays range from simple home video games shown on a television set to sophisticated computerized systems that provide complex color designs and three-dimensional displays. They can present information in

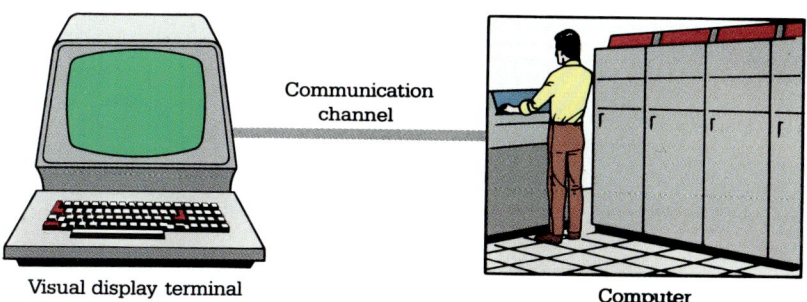

Visual display terminal

Communication channel

Computer

FIGURE 3–2
An input/output device that is connected directly to the computer is considered on-line with the computer.

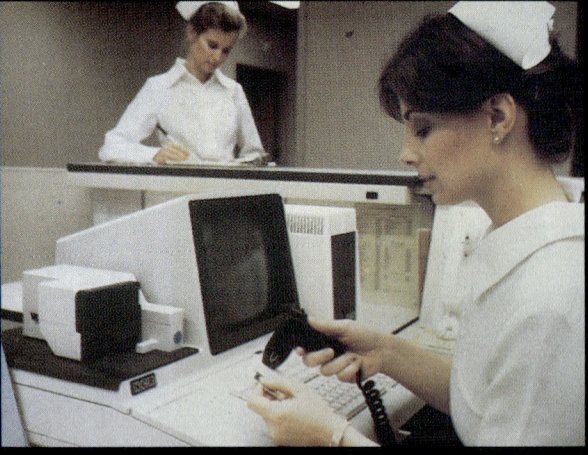

FIGURE 3–3

Most display devices include a display screen and a keyboard to give them a two-way communications capability. Display terminals are being used in hospitals (top left), homes (top right), schools (center left), businesses (center right), airlines (bottom left), and factories (bottom right). (Courtesy of NCR Corp., International Business Machines Corp., Apple Computer, Inc., Delta Air Lines, Inc., and Westinghouse Electric Corp.)

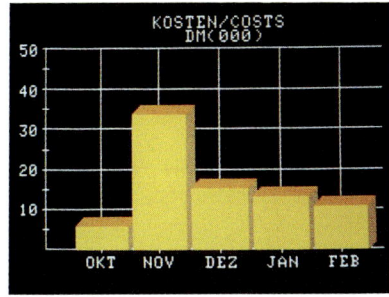

FIGURE 3–4
Graphic data provide pertinent information at a glance. (Courtesy of Polaroid Corp.)

the form of graphs or charts making it easy for an executive to note business trends (Figure 3–4).

Most graphic display systems use either refresh or storage technology. The two main types of refresh techniques are stroke writing and raster scanning. In a stroke writing display system, an electronic beam is positioned on the face of the cathode ray tube to "draw" the image, much as one would draw with pencil and paper. In a raster scanning system, the beam sequentially traces the entire face of the tube. A video signal brightens the beam of each point required for the desired display.

Displays using either the stroke writing or raster scanning technique require periodic refreshing to prevent the image from fading too quickly, causing a flickering on the screen. Raster scanning systems require more memory space because each point on the screen must reference memory. However, raster scanning tubes can provide color displays and selective image erasing features, procedures that are impractical with stroke writing systems.

The **alphanumeric display terminal**, often called a **cathode ray tube (CRT) terminal** because of its inherent display electronics, is the most popular interactive communications terminal in use today (Figure 3–5). The CRT is designed to transmit and display information from its own keyboard as well as display information from a computer. A list of control devices used with visual display devices follows.

- ☐ **Light pen**—an input device, the size and shape of a fountain pen, that allows users to point at graphic objects on the display screen and to locate positions within the displayed area; useful for preparing data at insurance companies, entering hospital patient data, identifying specific business reports in management information systems, and modifying engineers' blueprints or diagrams (Figure 3–6)
- ☐ **Joystick**—instrument that can be tilted in any direction to control the cursor on the screen
- ☐ **Paddle**—a rod that pivots on a universal ball joint allowing two simultaneous degrees of movement: left/right and forward/backward
- ☐ **Mouse**—a device for moving a cursor or other object around on the display screen; buttons used for specific actions are located on the top of a small box whose movement along a flat surface correspondingly moves the cursor on the screen (Figure 3–7)
- ☐ **Trackball**—a device consisting of a mounting set in a ball that enables an operator to control the cursor on a display

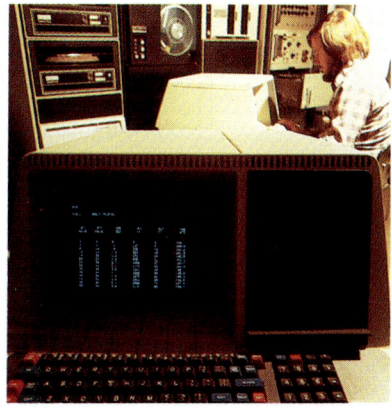

FIGURE 3–5
The alphanumeric display terminal is popular because it can display several lines of information at one time. (Courtesy of Lockheed Corp.)

Because it is fast, quiet, and costs less than a printer, the visual display terminal is the most useful microcomputer output device. The two most common types of terminals used in microcomputer systems are the video monitor and the color television receiver.

1 The video monitor (color and black and white) is made specifically for information display. Similar to a home television set, the

FIGURE 3–6
The light pen inputs position information (X + Y coordinates) into the computer. Used in conjunction with graphic display terminals, light pens are used by engineers when designing automobiles, airplanes, buildings, and bridges. (Courtesy of Lundy Electronics & Systems, Inc.)

FIGURE 3–7
The mouse (shown in the man's right hand) is used to control the cursor on the video display. (Courtesy of Radio Shack, A Division of Tandy Corp.)

FIGURE 3–8
Example of a Universal Product Code

video monitor does not include the electronics for receiving signals from a distant television station.

2 The color television receiver is simply a modified home television set.

Display devices are used with several kinds of keyboards. An alphanumeric keyboard allows the operator to compose messages or make inquiries. Keyboards that have function keys permit operators to make coded inquiries or establish operating modes. These keyboards sometimes have coded, removable overlays so that the meaning of the function keys can be changed by the operator.

With the development of portable computers, the need for more compact displays has become more evident. Several manufacturers are now producing flat panel displays (thin glass-panel displays containing gases), liquid crystal displays, or those made with the electroluminescent substances that glow when electrically stimulated. Flat panel displays offer the advantages of high daylight visibility, shock resistance, low power consumption, longer life expectancy, and compactness.

Point-of-sale Terminals

Another excellent example of an input/output device is a **point-of-sale (POS) terminal**. A POS acts both as a cash register and a data collection terminal and is widely used in supermarket and retail stores. It records all business transactions conducted at a saleperson's station and sends this information to the store's computer systems. Many terminals have special keys to calculate quantities, taxable items, trading stamp totals, and coupon refunds.

Products sold in stores using POS terminals are marked with a 10-digit **Universal Product Code (UPC)** (Figure 3–8). The code's first five digits identify the manufacturer; the second five digits identify the product. The store's salesperson runs the Universal Product Code over the optical scanner in the service counter. An optical scanning device reads the code to the computer (Figure 3–9). Upon receiving the code, the computer immediately matches it with product information, such as price, and keeps track of how many items are sold. It instantly relays this information to the cash register where it is displayed visually and printed on the customer's receipt.

POS terminals eliminate the tedious job of price-marking each item. They also eliminate checkout errors due to human error or illegible or inaccurate price marks. Finally, these terminals create a perpetually accurate inventory allowing store managers to check the inventory of any product at any time, thereby reducing the clerical costs of conducting manual inventories and providing managers with a more efficient method for reordering stock.

Automated Teller Machines

The frustration of waiting in line at a bank is a thing of the past for many people. Instead of queuing up to be served by a human teller, some peo-

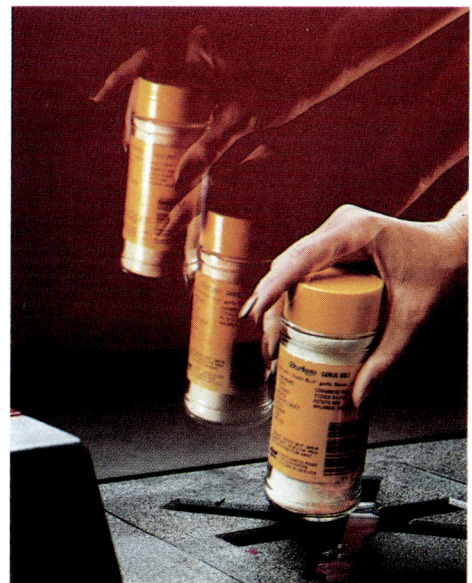

FIGURE 3–9
Computerized supermarket checkout counters are being used to increase the efficiency with which grocery items are tabulated. A Universal Product Code, printed on the grocery item, is read by an optical scanning device built into the service counter. This information is sent to the computer, which has the item's price stored in its memory. A detailed grocery list is printed for the customer and the total of the sale is calculated. (Courtesy of NCR Corp.)

FIGURE 3–10
To make their services more convenient to customers, banks and other financial institutions are beginning to install terminals in shopping malls, supermarkets, and other nonbanking locations. (Courtesy of NCR Corp.)

ple rely on an **automated teller machine** that they can use 24 hours a day (Figure 3–10). The automated teller machine is activated by the insertion of an embossed plastic card containing identifying data on a magnetic strip. The machine then leads the customer through the transaction with illuminated function keys and/or a programmable display of instructions. The automated teller machine is connected directly to the bank's computer and can transfer and accept funds and give users cash from their accounts. In the case of remote locations, a telephone connection links the automated teller machine with the bank's computer. Automated tellers enable banks to expand the physical range of their services without the cost of expensive branch buildings.

Voice Input/Output Devices

Applications of **voice input/output devices** have been limited in the past, but rapid advances in areas such as microelectronic technology have resulted in the development of microprocessor chips that synthesize human speech, thereby giving voice output capabilities to everything from children's toys to telephone communication systems. The use of voice input terminals with limited speech recognition capabilities is growing steadily in applications ranging from sales data entry to quality control.

A mouse is like a rolling function key that you slide across your desk. If you move the mouse up and to the right, the cursor on your screen moves up and to the right. It is sensitive enough to move pixel by pixel, but it can also scoot from one corner of the screen to the other in a fraction of a second. A computer mouse comes with one to three programmable buttons that enable you to edit, draw lines, or select menu choices without ever touching the keyboard.

THE FIRST MOUSE

In 1965, Douglas Englebart, a scientist at the Stanford Research Institute (SRI) in California, developed a small round-edged box on

Use of a mouse requires cleared desk space. (Courtesy of Apple Computer, Inc.)

wheels with buttons sticking up like ears and a tail-like wire connected to it. Beneath this device were two wheels mounted at right angles. The wheels were connected to devices that measured changes in movement along X and Y axes, then transferred the information to an analog-to-digital converter that told the computer where to move the on-screen cursor. The mechanism itself was not revolutionary. For decades scientists had been using "planimeters," instruments that measure the area of a figure by rolling along its perimeter on a chart. However, the SRI mouse was an ergonomical leap forward. It had three control buttons that could be pressed singly or in combinations to obtain desired effects. The mouse sat in a flat area to the right of the keyboard. To its left was a five-function binary keypad resembling a row of miniature organ keys.

Fellow researchers at SRI recall watching Englebart and fellow scientists stare fixedly into 5-inch high resolution monitors as they skittered mice back and forth with their right hands while drumming in binary rhythms with their left. They not only edited with newfound speed and ease, but also skipped through hier-

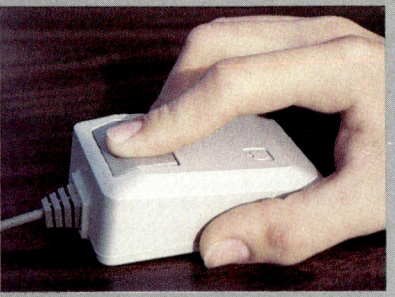

The mouse is a device for interacting with a display screen. As you roll it over a flat surface, the computer moves the cursor on the screen to correspond with the mouse's position. The button on the top of the mouse can be depressed to perform various functions.

archical menus with the flick of a wrist.

THE NEXT STAGE OF DEVELOPMENT

In 1972, Jack S. Hawley developed the first digital mouse for Xerox Corporation. Three years later, Xerox commissioned him to design a mouse that traveled on a large ball bearing rather than two orthogonal wheels. By 1981, Xerox manufactured the mouse for use in its Star computer system.

Today, computer mice are produced by several manufacturers. While they are all slightly different, most are in the shape of a box. Some have rounder corners than others, and the more recent editions are becoming smaller.

OPTICAL MICE

Most computer mice work mechanically, by counting the revolutions of a shaft attached to wheels or a ball. Some do the counting electrically, but most use optical decoders. Newer versions of computer mice are entering the marketplace. They forego moving parts and track their positions optically by moving across a precise grid and counting the lines as they pass over them. Optical mice have several advantages over mechanical ones. They have no moving parts to break or wear out, and they are quiet and relatively inexpensive to make. The range of movement can be easily varied by changing the size of the grid on which they slide. There are no wheels or ball bearings to clog with dust and no surface-gripping errors. They can also be miniaturized to fit the smallest hands. Optical mice do have drawbacks, however. The most annoying disadvantage is that they require a grid, which takes up space on a desk. Resolution is less precise than that of mechanical mice, but for most applications it is still sharper than that of the screen.

THE MAC MOUSE

The mouse used with Apple Computer's Macintosh is tiny, however, it requires at least a square foot of desk space for operation. The more room you make for it, the easier it is to control.

To use the mouse, you begin with a general on-screen menu, move the cursor over the list of selections by rolling the mouse, then click one of the mouse's buttons when the cursor points to the item you want. Successive screens offer increasingly specific choices. Users don't have to remember complex commands with their demanding syntaxes. In-

This screen illustrates the use of icons (pictorial representations of a function to be performed on the computer) to depict data and functions that can be performed on the computer. Through the use of icons, the user can easily make a choice as to which function should be performed. A mouse controls the cursor (the arrow in the center) that indicates which icon you are interested in using. (Courtesy of Apple Computer, Inc.)

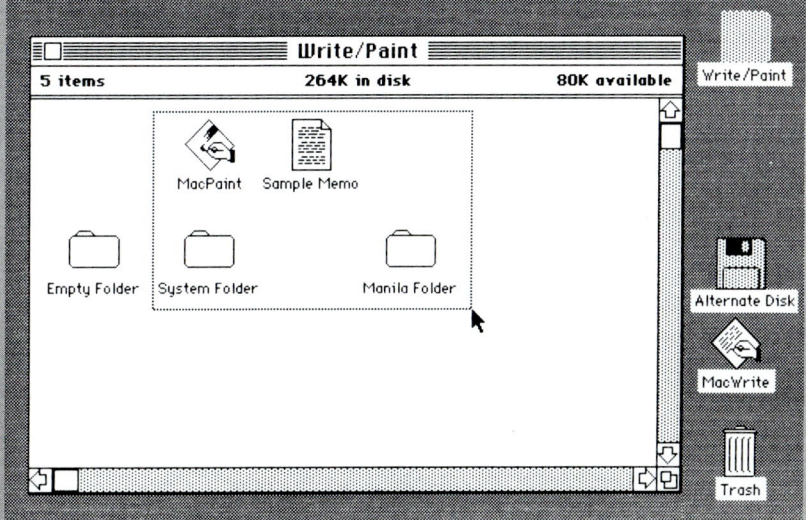

stead, they simply choose from lists of actions and let the computer handle the details. The burden is placed on the software designer to create menus that will let users do precisely what they need and want without having to learn control languages. On the other hand, the mouse restricts the user who might want to jump from one point to another without having to pause at all the intervening menus, or the experimenter who wants to try something unusual or unplanned.

At first, controlling the screen cursor with the mouse is anything but intuitive. The mouse seems cumbersome and hard to control. With a few days of practice, however, working the cursor with the mouse becomes second nature. Once you learn to lift the mouse when you run out of desk space and reposition it so that you have the room you need, you have learned the secret of using the mouse effectively.

Because the mouse has a mechanical device with a rolling ball inside it that measures relative movement, your desk area must be free of dust and particulate matter (such as cracker crumbs) for the mouse to work reliably. The Mac mouse has a single button on its top; therefore, there are no inhibitions concerning which button to press. Double-clicking the single mouse button also acts as a short-cut mechanism in obtaining other functions.

PAINTING BY MOUSE

The allure of the mouse is not limited to its efficiency in picking items in a list. Its buttons can be set to perform specific editing tasks or, for more complex jobs, can be used in conjunction with conventional function keys. By positioning one hand on the mouse and the other hand above function keys, you can make rapid text changes. The Macintosh mouse allows you to select shapes from a menu, change their sizes, shade them with patterns, and position them anywhere on the screen. It also allows freestyle sketching by turning the mouse into a sort of wheeled paintbrush. Serious designers can manipulate the mouse to enter, move, redraw, erase, or redefine lines in on-screen models. For instance, designers can select from palettes of line thicknesses and textures, colors, or standard shapes, and then create and revise complex designs in a fraction of the time it would normally take—all by rolling computer mice around on their desks.

USES IN BUSINESS

Business computer users who want to slash their editing and menu-selection time in half or turn the screen into a graphics palette can choose to use light pens, touch screens, digitizing tablets, joysticks, track balls or mice.

Computer mice are speedy and accurate. The hand movements are natural and allow the user to move the cursor without looking away from the screen. Because computer operating systems are becoming increasingly easy to use, many experts predict that computer mice will soon be standard equipment on all computers.

INPUT DEVICES

In addition to keyboards and voice recognition devices, computers receive input through graphic digitizers, magnetic ink character recognition (MICR) readers, optical character recognition (OCR) units, computer input microfilm (CIM), data entry terminals, and card readers.

Graphic Digitizers

You have learned how entering alphanumeric data into a computer system can be accomplished easily with a number of data entry devices. Suppose you wanted to enter an artist's design that is woven into a fabric, or all the dimensions of an average six-foot-tall man. You could accomplish these tasks inefficiently by writing a lengthy set of statements and then keying them into the computer via an alphanumeric keyboard. Or, you could use a graphic digitizer to accomplish either task more efficiently.

A **graphic digitizer** converts lines or graphic representations into digital or numeric data so the data can be processed by the computer. A digitizer consists of a rectangular surface, called a tablet, and a mechanism for sensing where on the surface a stylus or cursor is positioned. Digital information representing the X–Y coordinates of that position is output. The tablet is logically divided into a matrix so that the position of the stylus or cursor can be expressed with a high degree of precision.

Graphic digitizers are extremely efficient and useful tools for business. By inputting graphic data into a computer system, educational institutions, government agencies, and all types of companies can use computers to manipulate numeric models of graphic data (Figure 3–11).

FIGURE 3–11
A graphic digitizer converts lines or graphic representations into digital or numeric data that can be processed by a computer. (Courtesy of Ramtek Corp.)

Magnetic Ink Character Recognition Readers

A **magnetic ink character recognition (MICR)** reader is a special purpose input device that can read documents, such as checks, inscribed with the MICR characters. The reader works by magnetizing the magnetic ink characters on documents and sensing the signal induced by each character as it passes by a reading head. Documents can be sorted into the pockets of the MICR reader as the data are electronically captured by the computer. The American Bankers Association adopted the 14 MICR characters as the standard font for the banking industry (Figure 3–12). Nearly 100 million checks are processed each day in U.S. banks; the MICR reader processes 2 000 checks per minute. Banks would be hard-pressed to handle the processing of checks without MICR and computer technology.

Optical Character Recognition Units

In order to input data into computers with the **optical character recognition (OCR) reader**, documents are transported in a hopper past optical scanning positions. There, a powerful light and lens enable the OCR to distinguish letters, numbers, and special characters as patterns of light. These light patterns are converted into electrical pulses for use by the computer.

Presently, OCR equipment can read only certain types of printing or handwriting, though progress is being made to improve its reading abil-

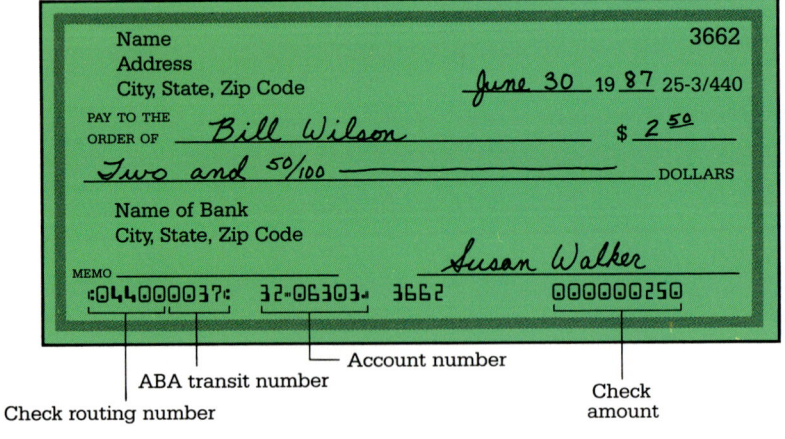

FIGURE 3–12

Magnetic ink characters are used to communicate banking information, such as identifying checking account numbers, bank numbers, and check amounts, to computer equipment. The characters are printed with magnetic ink and are read by a machine called an MICR reader.

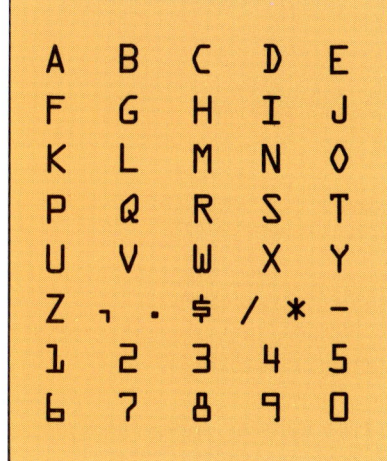

FIGURE 3–13
The characters shown here have a slightly irregular typeface. They consist of letters of the alphabet, the 10 digits, and several special characters. These characters are printed on utility bills, credit cards, and sales invoices and can be read automatically by optical character recognition equipment.

ity (Figure 3–13). OCR is used to sort mail automatically and to process business forms, credit card billing, utility bills, insurance premiums, and a variety of other forms. The Social Security Administration uses OCR readers to process the name, social security number, and quarterly earnings of more than 80 million taxpayers. Entering this information into a computer system by using a keyboard would cost taxpayers millions of dollars.

OCR equipment can also read pencil marks registered in specific positions on a form. This process is called mark-sensing and it is often used to score tests. Other OCR devices are used in supermarkets to read UPC codes and in retail department stores to read merchandise tags with hand-held wands.

Computer Input Microfilm Devices

Microfilm is a photographic image, on a reduced scale, of information that might otherwise be represented in printed form; **computer input microfilm (CIM)**, an external storage technology, involves using an input device to read the contents of microfilm directly into the computer. For example, when used with the computer, the Kodak IMT-150 microimage retrieval terminal relieves the computer of many of the control functions required by older, computer-assisted retrieval systems. The computer can load a block of data consisting of a number of addresses of microfilm images into the terminal's memory and then go on to other tasks. The terminal can be used to search out the document images without tying up valuable computer time. In effect, the microimage terminal becomes an on-line peripheral to the computer. In turn, it can direct immediate retrieval and hard-copy output from a library of millions of source documents or computer-generated images.

Data Entry Terminals

The capturing of data at their source is commonly called source data automation. Many special devices, such as the keyboard and a pen that can read Universal Product Codes, are used for this operation. The identifying data are read and kept in the storage of the device. Later the data are sent via a data communication line to a large computer system for processing. Many businesses and factories use source data collection devices to maintain employee identification, work status, and attendance, as well as work-in-progress control, material tracking, and other variable data.

Card Readers

A **card reader** is used to recognize hole patterns punched in a card and to transmit this information (in electronic form) to the computer. Card readers automatically feed, scan, and stack the punched cards. Although there are many moving parts, these readers are able to process several hundred to 2 000 cards per minute.

OUTPUT DEVICES

Printers

One of the most useful peripheral output devices is the printer, which enables operators to make paper copies of stored information. Printers come in all shapes, sizes, and price ranges. Table 3–1 lists the relative speeds of printers discussed in this section.

Impact printers   The two main classifications of printers are impact and non-impact printers. As the name implies, impact printers have a type element that produces a printed image by striking a ribbon on its way to the paper. There are two types of impact printers: solid type and matrix. Solid type impact printers use type fonts mounted on elements such as wheels or drums. The type on these machines is solid and produces sharp impressions. This printer is widely used in word processing systems where letter quality printing is required. Figure 3–14 shows a drum printer, one kind of impact printer. Drum printers contain a complete set of characters embossed around the circumference of the drum. The printing process is activated by hammers located at each print position. When the proper character is selected, the hammer strikes the paper. Drum printers provide reliable operation in the print speed range of 300 to 3 000 lines per minute.

   Daisy wheel printers use a petal-shaped wheel (thus the name "daisy") with the end of each petal containing a single character (Figure 3–15). The print wheel revolves to bring each character into print position, at which point a single solenoid (a device that converts electrical energy into mechanical energy) fires to print the character.

   A less expensive impact printer is the matrix printer, also called the dot matrix printer. This machine uses a movable print head that consists of a matrix of small tubes, each containing a fine wire or needle (Figure

Imagine a house you can talk to, where every room adjusts automatically to match your changing moods. This house would not be just a backdrop, but an active partner in your work, family life, and leisure activities. Is this some fantasy of the distant future? Not at all. The working prototype for such a house already exists. It is called Xanadu—the Computerized House of Tomorrow, and it is located a few miles outside Orlando, Florida. Xanadu showcases an astonishing array of new technologies, materials, designs, and lifestyles available today. Computers are used to control and enhance many activities, including lighting, energy control, security, appliance control, entertainment, education, environment control, information storage and retrieval, problem solving, and health monitoring. In addition to a central computer system, microcomputer systems are located throughout the house to provide stations for entertainment, education, problem solving, and kitchen help.

TABLE 3–1
Printers and their typical speeds

Type of Printer	Impact or Non-impact	Typical Speed
Typewriter	Impact	900 characters per minute
Daisy wheel	Impact	20-50 characters per second
Dot matrix	Impact	125-300 characters per second
Chain	Impact	600-2 400 lines per minute
Drum	Impact	300-3 000 lines per minute
Ink jet	Non-impact	300 characters per second
Xerographic	Non-impact	4 000 lines per minute
Electrostatic	Non-impact	5 000 lines per minute
Thermal	Non-impact	5 000 lines per minute
Laser	Non-impact	18 000-21 000 lines per minute

FIGURE 3–14
Large computer systems are capable of producing enormous amounts of processed information. Much of this information is produced in printed form. Drum printers are used to print information on continuous-form paper. High-speed line printers can print thousands of printed lines of information per minute. (Courtesy of Burroughs Corp.)

FIGURE 3–15
Daisy wheel printers offer letter quality printing at speeds of up to 55 characters per second. The font on the daisy wheel rotates to bring the desired character into position and is then struck by a hammer mechanism to form an image on the paper.

3–16). The needles are fired individually by solenoids to produce a dot matrix that varies in size and shape—the higher the density of the dots forming the matrix, the better the printing. The most common matrices are 7 × 9 dots and 9 × 9 dots (Figure 3–17). Several manufacturers now produce dot matrix printers with high density matrices that nearly equal the print quality of solid type.

Non-impact printers　　Non-impact printers produce a printed image without striking the paper. Ink jet and laser printers are examples of non-impact printers. These machines operate at high speeds without the clatter associated with impact printers, but they produce only one copy

FIGURE 3–16
A matrix printer produces 125 to 300 characters per second. (Courtesy of Dataproducts Corp.)

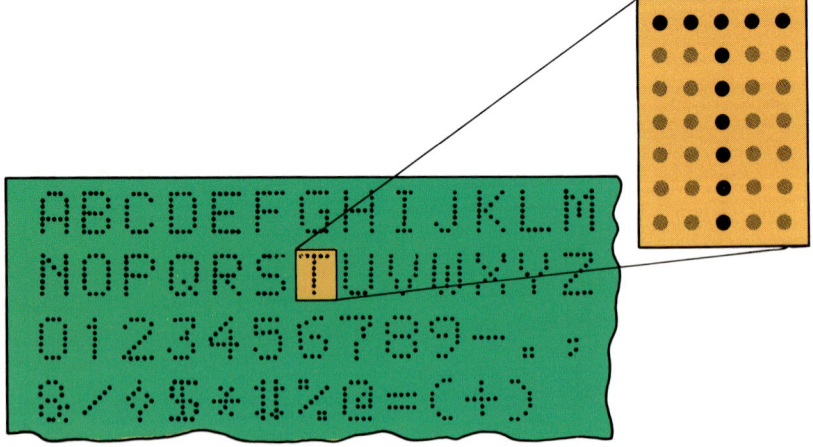

FIGURE 3–17
Dot matrix print patterns showing letters, numerals, and special characters. An enlargement of the letter T is shown.

at a time. Most use special paper that is more expensive than that used with other printers. Some non-impact printers can print graphics such as bar and pie charts.

One non-impact printer, the ink jet printer, shoots a steady stream of tiny ink droplets toward the paper (Figure 3–18). The computer controls which droplets are charged with electricity. Most droplets are magnetically attracted away from the paper, while a few hit the paper to form symbols. The resulting printed characters are about equal in quality to those produced by a cloth ribbon typewriter.

Laser printers produce a higher quality product than ink jet printers (see Figure 3–18). They are similar to photocopying machines, however, they have a laser beam that reflects off a rotating drum and paints the image, one line at a time, on an electrically charged light-sensitive sheet. The sheet loses its charge locally where it is illuminated by laser light. Once the sheet has been exposed to the laser light, it is pushed across a container filled with dry black ink. The charged particles adhere to the areas that have not been exposed to the laser light. The sheet is then run across electrically charged paper, which is compressed and baked to ensure ink adherence.

Plotters

Plotters have been around since the early days of computers. They have been used in automotive and aircraft designs, topological surveys, architectural layouts, and similar complex drafting jobs. Like other computer hardware, however, plotters have become faster, smaller, "smarter," and less expensive. Consequently, it is now both possible and practical to use these output devices to make graphic presentations of business data.

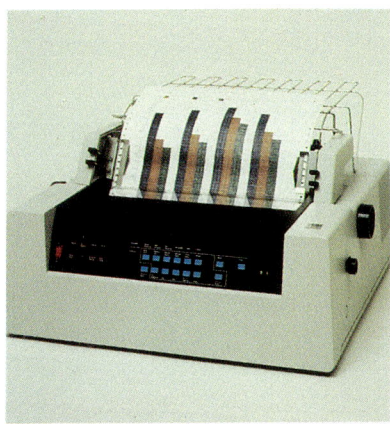

FIGURE 3–18
Ink jet and laser printers. The IBM 3287 color printer (left) is an ink jet computer that prints color. The operator at the IBM 3800 laser printer (right) is entering control information into the machine. (Courtesy of International Business Machines Corp. and Lockheed Corp.)

A **digital plotter** is a computer output device that produces drawings, charts, diagrams, and similar graphic copy (Figure 3–19). The drawings produced by the plotter may be annotated with characters, but the primary purpose of the plotter is to produce drawings. Many plotters can plot in six different colors.

Computer Output Microfilm Devices

If a CRT screen is photographed with microfilm, the microfilm is called **computer output microfilm (COM)**; this can later be viewed on a screen or transferred to hard copy. The computer produces an index to locate the proper roll and frame for a given output. A COM device displays the data stored on microfilm. COM devices are extremely useful because they free users from time-consuming searches and computers from high-volume printing tasks. They also reduce the costs of production and storage; as a result, COM lowers users' costs. Some users find the cost of storing microfilm is about one forty-fifth of the cost of storing an equivalent volume of paper. COM devices are also used wherever the Securities and Exchange Commission law requires hard copy and magnetic tape is not acceptable.

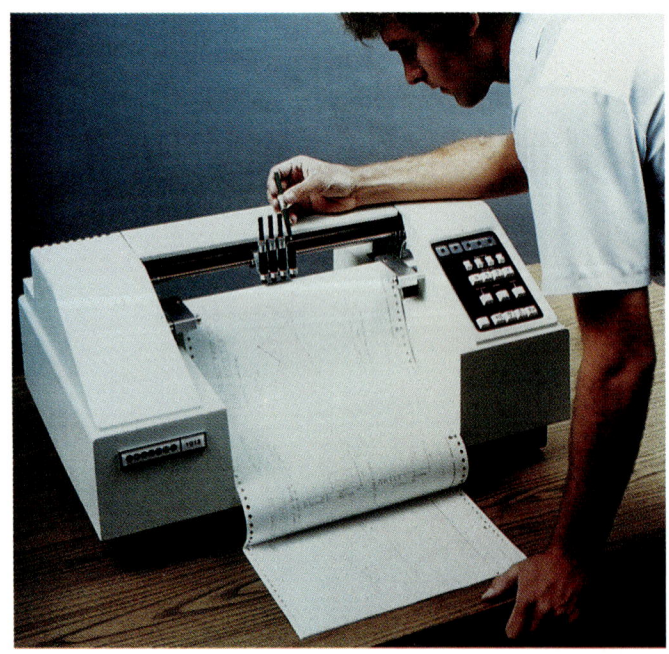
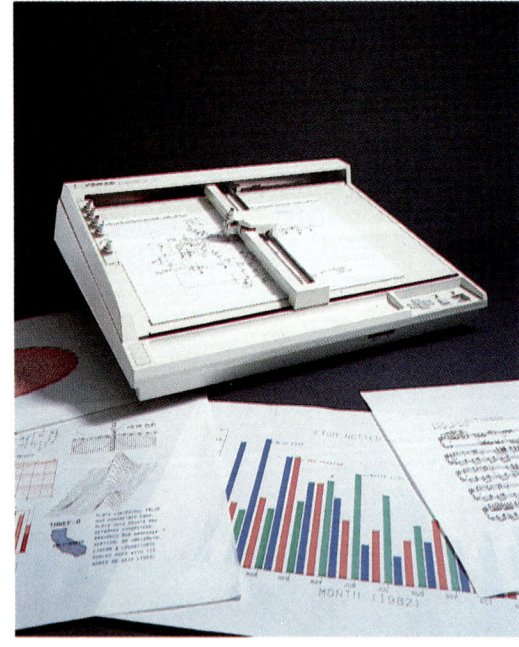

FIGURE 3–19
Digital plotters can produce drawings in several different colors. This operator is adjusting one of four color ink pens. Engineering and scientific organizations have used plotters since the early days of computers; however, it has only been in recent years that businesses have begun to use them for drawing charts, graphs, and maps. (Photos courtesy of California Computer Products, Inc. (CalComp), Anaheim, CA)

The sales staff of a Michigan car dealer watched with more than casual interest when workmen installed a large wood-grained cabinet filled with computer and video equipment. This comment, muttered by one salesperson, was inevitable: "That's going to replace us someday." Maybe so. Before long, computer systems will be doing much of a car salesperson's job. They will greet customers, compare features of competing models, figure the operating cost of an owner's car against that of a new one, tally the cost of options, and work out an estimate of monthly payments. Some systems will even write up an order and phone it to the factory.

Card Punch

Card punching is the reverse process of card reading; it converts the electrical impulses sent from the computer into holes punched in cards. A **card punch** is the device used to produce punched cards.

DATA PREPARATION UNITS

An increasingly important form of computer input using magnetic disks and tapes is the **magnetic medium device**. Magnetic media allow high density of storage and faster reading and writing; they are also reusable. These devices transcribe data via a keyboard. Once on the magnetic medium, the data are readable by the computer. Two major types of magnetic medium devices are key-to-disk and key-to-tape.

A key-to-disk system consists of one or more input keyboard stations operating under the command of a computer, usually a microcomputer or minicomputer (Figure 3–20). The computer edits the keyed data prior to storing it on a flexible disk, or diskette. Key-to-tape systems are used to record keyed data directly onto a reel of magnetic tape or a tape cassette.

BUFFERS

We have discussed the speed of computers, using terms such as microseconds and nanoseconds to describe processing capabilities. If you were to type information into a computer by using a keyboard data entry terminal, your typing speed compared to a machine capable of adding more than one million numbers a second would be minimal. It is not effi-

FIGURE 3–20
Key-to-disk system

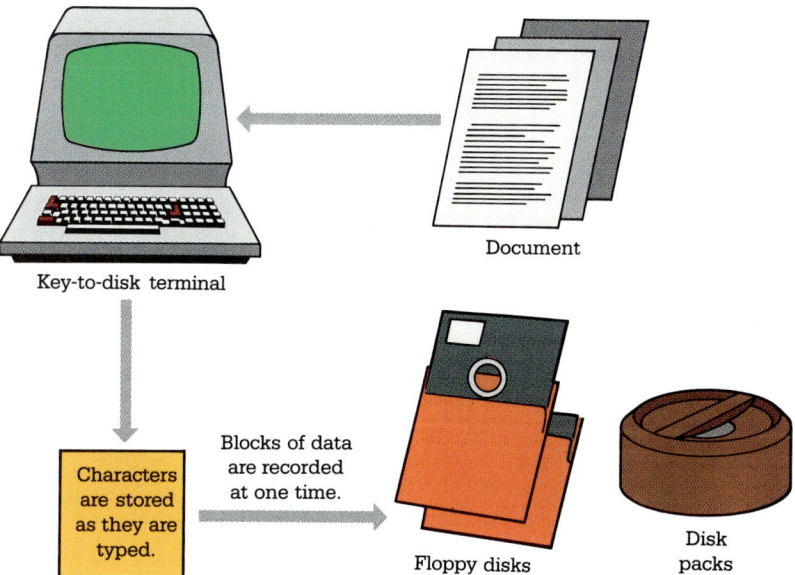

Key-to-disk terminal

Document

Characters are stored as they are typed.

Blocks of data are recorded at one time.

Floppy disks

Disk packs

cient to expect an expensive computer to wait while you type out one or two characters per second. Instead, as you type, your characters are stored in a **buffer**. A buffer is nothing more than temporary storage. It allows the speed of input or output devices to match more closely that of the computer. Character data are accumulated in blocks. A block of data (several characters) is then transferred from the buffer to the computer at a fast transfer rate. On output, a buffer is used for the reverse operation between the computer and an output device.

SUMMARY

☐ Input and output are the means by which a computer communicates with the outside world. Input devices gather or collect data for processing by the computer; output devices are used to report or store the information that has been processed. Devices that perform input, output, or both are called peripherals.

☐ Visual display devices are widely used for computer input and output. Most display devices look like a cross between a typewriter and a television set. Information sent from the computer to the display device is displayed on the screen. In most instances, the display terminal is equipped with a keyboard for two-way communications capability.

☐ Two types of visual display devices are alphanumeric display terminals (which display only text) and graphic display devices (which also display graphics).

☐ Light pens, joysticks, paddles, mice, and trackballs are control devices used with visual display devices.

☐ A point-of-sale (POS) terminal is an input/output device that acts as a cash register and a data collection terminal. It is used widely in supermarkets and retail stores.

☐ Automated teller machines are directly connected to a bank's computer. Bank customers can use the automated teller machine to transfer and deposit funds and withdraw cash.

☐ A graphic digitizer converts lines on graphic representations into digital or numeric data so the data can be processed by a computer.

☐ A magnetic ink character recognition (MICR) reader is a special purpose input device that can read paper documents inscribed with the MICR characters.

☐ An optical character recognition (OCR) reader reads letters, numbers, and special characters that are printed on paper documents. OCR is used to sort mail automatically and process business and insurance forms.

☐ Two types of printers are impact and non-impact. Impact printers have a type element that produces a printed image by striking the paper; they use type fonts mounted on elements such as wheels or drums. Non-impact printers produce a printed image without striking the paper and operate at high speeds; some can print graphics.

☐ A digital plotter is a computer output device that produces drawings, charts, diagrams, and similar graphic copy.

☐ Key-to-disk and key-to-tape systems are used to key data directly onto magnetic disks and tape, respectively.

REVIEW QUESTIONS

True or False

_____ **1** Data input devices are used to print reports.

_____ **2** The computer is used to accept data from an output unit.

_____ **3** In most computer systems, input devices are connected directly to auxiliary storage devices.

_____ **4** Printers are important hard-copy output devices, however, they cannot operate as fast as a typewriter.

_____ **5** The laser printer is one of the slowest methods of getting information out of a computer.

_____ **6** Characters inscribed with magnetic ink may be read directly into the computer by using a MICR reader.

_____ **7** Bank checks and utility bills are examples of forms that use magnetic ink characters.

_____ **8** The keyboard display terminal plays a dual role in a computer system because it performs both input and output functions.

_____ **9** The input operation is frequently inefficient and slow and may even be a bottleneck in information processing systems.

_____ **10** In a computer system, a buffer is the distance between the central processing unit and the input/output devices.

_____ **11** Buffering information is less important in data input than in data output.

_____ **12** An example of a point-of-sale terminal is a graphics tablet.

_____ **13** The capturing of data at their source is commonly called source data automation.

_____ **14** The Universal Product Code is a 12-digit code used to identify checks and utility bills.

_____ **15** Data input devices are used to print reports.

_____ **16** A color television receiver is a modified home television set.

_____ **17** An optical character recognition unit is a device used by a machine to identify characters from their shapes.

_____ **18** A daisy wheel printer uses a matrix of dots to form an image of the character being printed.

Short Answer

1 Input/output devices are sometimes called _____.

2 A _____ is a device that is attached to the computer by a cable and can control the movement of a display cursor by being rolled along a flat surface by hand.

3 A _____ _____ converts lines or graphic representations into digital data so the data can be processed by the computer.

4 The capturing of data at their source is called _____ _____ _____.

5 Printing speeds of up to _____ lines per minute are possible with laser printers.

6 A dot matrix printer is an impact printer while an ink jet printer is a _____ printer.

7 Two main types of display refresh techniques are _____ _____ and _____ _____.

8 A _____ _____ is an electrical device that resembles a pen and is used to write or sketch on the screen of a display.

9 A _____ is an output device that can be used to produce drawings or diagrams.

10 _____ systems are used to record keyed data directly onto a flexible disk.

11 OCR means _____ _____ _____.

12 A _____ is a device used to hold, temporarily, information being transmitted between main computer storage and peripheral devices.

OUTLINE

OBJECTIVES

1 Describe the two main types of auxiliary storage.

2 Understand how information is stored and accessed from magnetic tape.

3 Describe several different types of magnetic disk storage units.

4 AUXILIARY STORAGE DEVICES

MAIN STORAGE AND AUXILIARY STORAGE

The two basic types of storage are main and auxiliary. You will recall that main storage is an extension of the central processing unit and is directly accessible to it. Auxiliary storage is used to supplement the capacity of main storage.

There are two types of auxiliary storage: sequential and direct access. **Sequential access**, such as that used with magnetic tape, involves examining all recorded data in sequence. This form of storage is nonaddressable because an operator cannot directly refer to the contents of a particular storage location. Instead, sequential access storage necessitates tape searching by starting at the beginning and searching through all data records until the desired information is found.

In contrast, **direct access**, also called **random access**, devices provide immediate access to individual records and do not require reading through all data records. Direct access storage is addressable (a given item can be selected from any place in storage simply by specifying the address where it is located). The length of time it takes to locate and transfer information to or from storage is called access time.

Two terms demand further definition. A **record** is a group of logically related items read as a single unit into main storage or written from storage in the same manner. The term **file** refers to a group of logically related records. All data about an employee (name, date hired, position, etc.) would be contained in one record. The data for all employees in a company would be contained in a file.

The capacity of a storage device is expressed as the number of bytes, characters, or bits it can store at one time. The cost of storage is directly determined by the capacity and type of device. Storage capacity varies from one computer to another. The main storage capacity of a microcomputer might be as low as several thousand bytes, while the capacity of a supercomputer might be several million bytes of semiconductor storage. A kilobyte (K) is made up of 1 024 bytes. Thus, a 32K storage can hold 32 768 characters.

MAGNETIC TAPE STORAGE

Magnetic tape is a principal input/output recording medium for computer systems because it provides a rapid way of entering data and recording processed data. Here's how it works: Information is recorded on magnetic tape as magnetized spots called bits. The recording can be retained indefinitely, or the information can be erased automatically and the tape reused many times (Figure 4–1).

How Magnetic Tapes Work

Data are recorded on tracks that run the length of the tape. The spacing between rows, or channels, is generally controlled during the recording or writing operation. Character densities as high as 600 characters per cm

(1 600 characters per in) are common. Tapes that hold 2 400 characters per cm (6 250 characters per in) are being used increasingly (Figure 4–2).

Data are grouped on the magnetic tape in clusters called a logical record. Each record is physically separated from the next by a blank

FIGURE 4–1
Magnetic tapes on top of a computer are ready to be loaded.

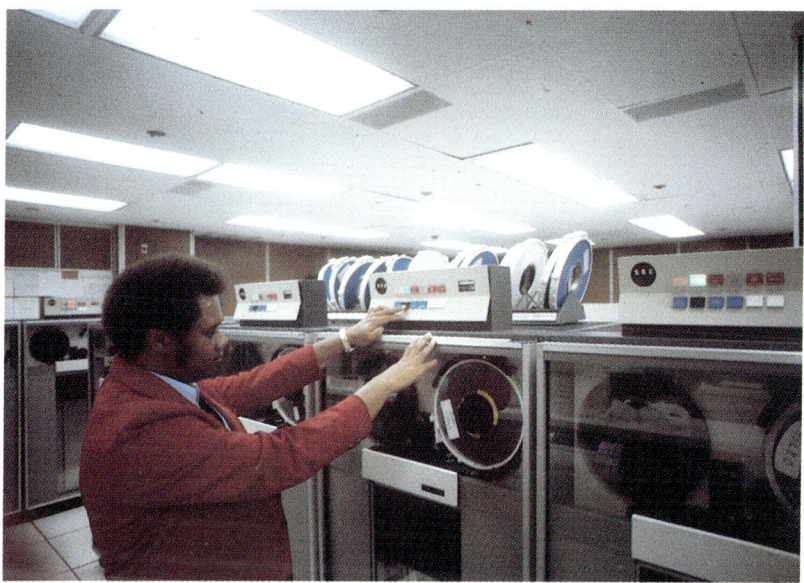

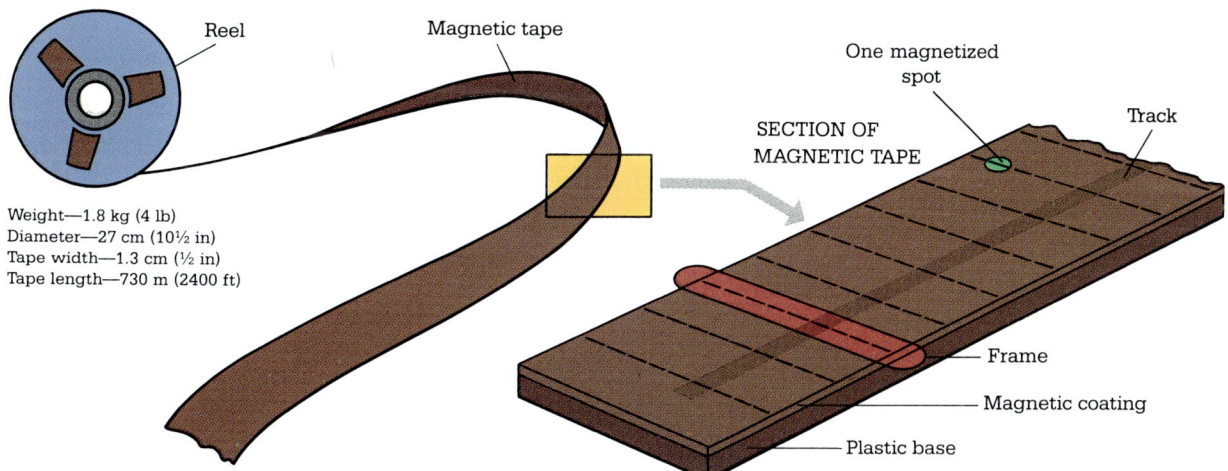

Reel

Magnetic tape

One magnetized spot

Track

SECTION OF
MAGNETIC TAPE

Weight—1.8 kg (4 lb)
Diameter—27 cm (10½ in)
Tape width—1.3 cm (½ in)
Tape length—730 m (2400 ft)

Frame

Magnetic coating

Plastic base

FIGURE 4–2
Magnetic tape is a principal input/output recording medium for use with computers. The tape is wound on individual reels or inserted in cassettes; information is stored in the form of magnetized spots. Magnetic tape is made of a nonmagnetic material, usually plastic ribbon, coated with a thin magnetic film. It is divided horizontally into nine channels, or tracks. Each vertical frame of nine positions (or bits) is a byte that represents one alphabetic or numeric character or other symbol, along with a parity bit.

space called an **interrecord gap (IRG)**. The interrecord gap serves three purposes:

1   Separates individual records
2   Allows space for the tape drive to reach its operating speed
3   Allows space for the tape drive to decelerate after a read or write operation (Figure 4–3)

For more economical use of tape storage, records that have some logical relationship may be grouped together to form a block. This block is treated as one group, or one physical record, and the records in the block are read together. The blocks of records are separated by **interblock gaps (IBG)**.

The magnetic tape drive is the mechanism that pulls the magnetic tape into position past the read/write head. The read/write head converts the magnetized bits it senses on the tape into electrical pulses and transmits them to the central processing unit. When data are being written onto the tape, the read/write head magnetizes the appropriate areas and simultaneously erases any information previously stored in that location.

Before the tape unit can perform read or write operations, it must be prepared for operation. This preparation involves loading two reels on the tape unit and threading the tape through the tape transport mechanism.

During tape read or write operations, the tape moves from one reel across a read/write head to the other reel. Writing on tape is destructive; that is, as new information is written, old information is destroyed. Reading is nondestructive; in other words, the same information can be read again and again.

A low-cost solution to the problem of large-capacity storage for small digital computer systems is the use of **cassette tape**. Cassette units are basically simple, modest-performance devices that are inexpensive and easy to operate. Figure 4–4 shows a cassette being placed in a cassette tape unit.

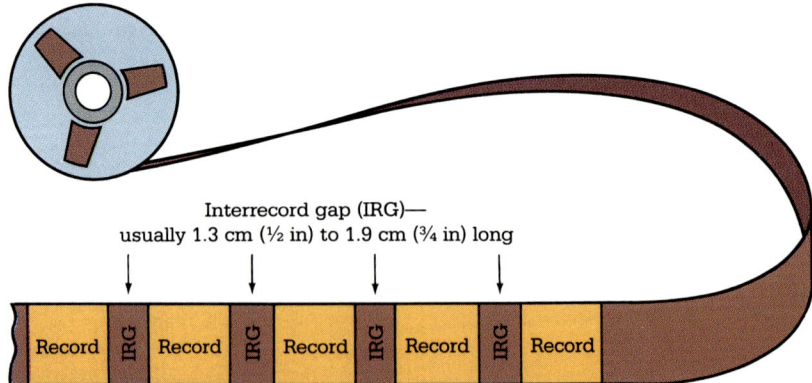

FIGURE 4–3
Data storage on magnetic tape. Each data record is separated by an interrecord gap (IRG).

FIGURE 4–4
Magnetic tape cassettes are simple, modest-performance storage devices used with microcomputers. They are relatively easy to operate and are inexpensive. Tape cassettes offer personal computer users a way to add auxiliary storage to their low-cost computer systems.

Despite the fact that it must be accessed sequentially, magnetic tape has several advantages:

- Can be erased and reused
- Provides a high-density storage facility (i.e., stores a large volume of data)
- Can be used to input and output data at high speeds
- Provides a relatively low-cost storage medium
- Provides a relatively stable storage medium over long periods of time

MAGNETIC DISK STORAGE

Magnetic disk storage is the most popular type of auxiliary storage. It provides computer systems with the ability to retrieve or read information by direct access. The physical characteristics of all **magnetic disks** are similar: thin, nonmagnetic, metal plates coated on both sides with magnetic recording material (Figure 4–5).

How Magnetic Disks Work

Disks are mounted on a vertical shaft and are slightly separated from each other to provide space for the movement of read/write assemblies. The shaft revolves, spinning the disks. Data are stored as magnetized

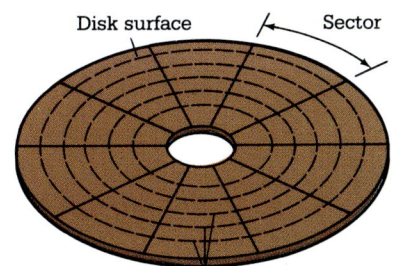

FIGURE 4–5
Schematic of a magnetic disk. A disk is a thin, nonmagnetic, metal plate coated on both sides with magnetic recording material. As the disk revolves on a disk drive, information is stored as magnetized spots on the surface of the disk. A disk contains several hundred circular tracks for storing information.

spots in concentric circles, known as tracks, on each surface of the disks; each disk contains several hundred tracks for storing data. The tracks are made accessible for reading and writing by positioning the read/write heads between the spinning disks. The read/write head mechanism is then electrically or hydraulically driven to move all heads simultaneously to any track position. After horizontal movement is completed for a specific task, the read/write heads can be directed to perform the reading and writing on the track.

Figure 4–6 illustrates a disk assembly composed of 11 disks mounted on a vertical shaft. The disk assembly provides 20 surfaces on which information can be recorded. The top and bottom surfaces are used as protective plates and are not for recording purposes. Information is read from or written on the disks by read/write heads mounted on a comb-like access mechanism that has 20 read/write heads mounted on 10 access arms. Each read/write head can either read or write information on the corresponding upper or lower disk surface. The entire access mechanism moves horizontally so information on all tracks can be either read or written.

A magnetic disk assembly can have several disks. A disk unit with 25 disks has a storage capacity of much more than 100 million characters, which can be transmitted at rates of more than 300 000 bytes per second. The magnetic disk data surface can be used repeatedly. As new information is stored on a track, the old information is erased. The record data may be read as often as desired—data remain recorded in the disks' tracks until they are written over.

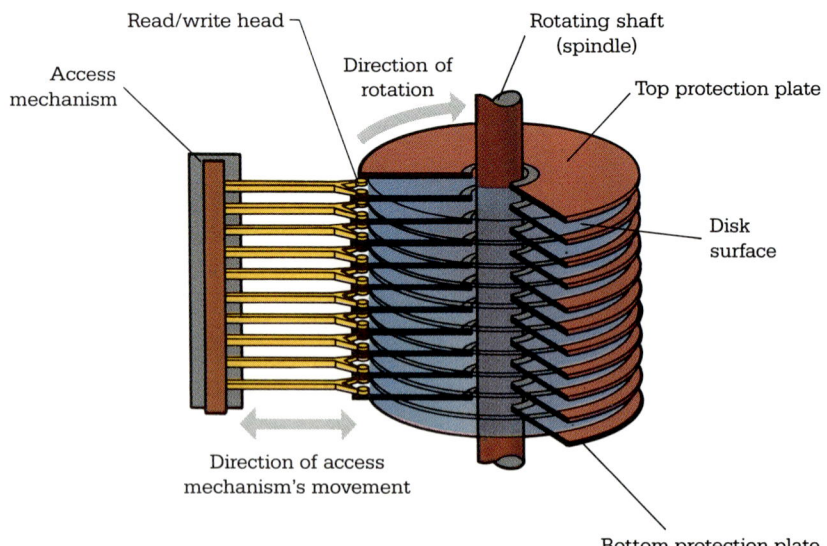

FIGURE 4–6
Schematic of a magnetic disk assembly of 11 disks. The 11 disks are mounted on a vertical shaft. The disk assembly provides 20 surfaces on which data can be recorded. Data are read from or written on the disks by a read/write head mechanism that moves horizontally so that data on all tracks can be either read or written.

The simplified disk assembly shown in Figure 4–6 illustrates the read/write head mechanism moving in a horizontal direction, enabling the disk mechanism to position itself at any specified track. The time required to locate a specific track is called the **disk access time** or **seek time**. This time is related to the lateral distance that the read/write head mechanism moves.

Another timing factor associated with disk read/write operations is **rotational delay time** or **latency**—the time required for the disk to attain the desired position at the selected read/write head. The maximum revolution time for a disk is the time required for one full revolution. The average rotational delay time is one-half the disk revolution rate. For example, if the disk revolves at 2 400 revolutions per minute (a typical speed), then the average rotational delay time would be slightly more than 11 milliseconds.

Disk Packs

Some disk units have removable and replaceable disk packs which are used as input/output units as well as storage devices (Figure 4–7). The disk pack is popular because it allows users to conveniently move the data stored in one disk unit to another so they can be processed on various computer systems. Replacement of one disk pack by another takes less than a minute, and disk packs can be taken off their drives and stored off-line. An installation with eight disk drives might well have 12 to 18 packs containing active information and switch packs to match the needs of current programs.

The removable disk pack unit usually does not provide as much disk storage capacity as the larger units made up of many permanently located disks. However, the removable unit is much cheaper and provides unlimited storage capacity because one disk pack can be replaced with another containing different information.

Computer programs that process data to and from a disk pack must inform the disk drive which disk track, surface, and sector to read or write. The drive then moves the read/write heads to that track, activates the proper head, waits for that sector to spin past the head, and reads or writes the data as directed by the program.

Data from a disk can also be retrieved without moving the read/write heads. This is accomplished by placing the records in the same track on each of the disk surfaces, which means the access time depends only on how long it takes the appropriate sector to spin around to the read/write head. Data stored in this manner are said to be stored in cylinders (Figure 4–8). The cylinder is important because one positioning of the access arm will enable all the read/write heads to reach data stored on all tracks contained in that cylinder.

Floppy Disks

Floppy disks, also called **diskettes** and **flexible disks**, are popular media for computer storage. They are widely used in microcomputer,

FIGURE 4–7
A removable disk pack. The disk pack is popular because it allows one to move the information stored on one disk unit to another so that it can be processed on other equipment. (Courtesy of Modular Computer Systems, Inc.)

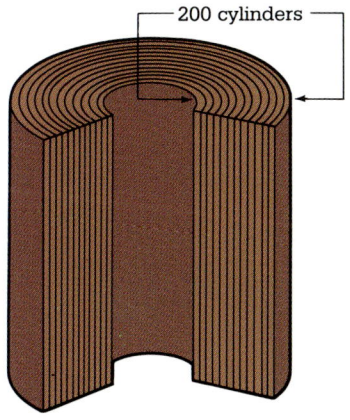

FIGURE 4–8
Cross-sectional diagram of a disk pack containing 200 cylinders of data

200 cylinders

Lotus Development Corporation's Symphony and Ashton-Tate's Framework are popular business software products that combine the five basic applications (word processing, data base management, spreadsheets, graphics, and telecommunications) into an integrated whole. A totally successful integration of these functions would result in the end of intermediary files. You would no longer have to study instructions on how to import, export, and translate files. Instead of learning several different software packages, you could use a single package with a consistent command structure to perform an analysis or create a report. The computer would be a work station and the integrated package a "toolbox" containing everything that you need.

Symphony, with its emphasis on the spreadsheet, is a number-dominated program that is designed for financial analysts who are chiefly concerned with manipulating numbers in a variety of ways. These users consider Symphony's word processing and data base management capabilities secondary to its speed, raw power, size, and ability to number-crunch.

On the other hand, Framework is a word-oriented package that is designed for managers whose principal concern is using words to bring concepts into focus. These users are impressed with Framework's outlining capability. One feature that gives Framework an overall edge is its ability to open a DOS window, enabling users to use any file that could normally be accessed through the operating system.

USING SYMPHONY

When users first enter Symphony, they are presented with a spreadsheet showing the menu at the top and work space below; other applications' work spaces follow this layout. Directly above the menu is a status line indicating the meaning of the currently highlighted menu item. In the upper right corner, the program indicates what type of application is active (e.g., sheet, doc, form); when users make a mistake, a red error message flashes there. The lower right corner contains the specific name of the worksheet. Below this, an indicator line denotes a particular lock key condition in the event that the scroll lock, caps, or numeric lock keys are engaged. A clock and calendar are in the lower left corner, as well as a message line displaying a variety of information, such as indicating when the program is printing a file or when an error has been made. These messages are usually self-explanatory, although a glossary does contain brief explanations of all possible error messages.

Once users are familiar with the basic layout of the Symphony screen, they must learn how to create and position windows. Windows are created by pressing the SERVICES key and then selecting "Window" and "Create" from the menu presented. Users are then prompted to designate the new window's area, which can be made as big or small as they desire by moving the cursor keys. After this, users can place the new window anywhere on the screen by pressing the SCROLL LOCK key and using cursor keys to position the window.

After a window is created and placed, users have a number of options. They can move the window again, delete it, hide the window, isolate it (hide all but the current window), expose or display all windows, use the pane command to split the window into two or four parts, or restrict the window's limits to certain portions of the worksheet.

Throughout their use of Sym-

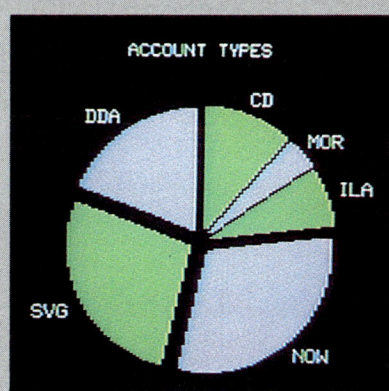

This pie chart was produced by Symphony. (Courtesy of Apple Computer, Inc.)

phony, users quickly become familiar with the program's uniform menu structure. Each application uses the SERVICES key to change windows, retrieve and store data, print, configure windows, add applications, change a file's global settings, erase the current worksheet data, and exit Symphony. Similarly, each application uses the MENU key to display the menu that is unique to that application. Despite their differences, the commands and menus themselves are fairly similar; this consistency helps to facilitate the use of the program. Once users have learned one set of menus, they know about most of the others.

Interaction with Symphony takes place through the menu which appears constantly at the top of the screen. Using the cursor arrow keys, users move the cursor or "cell pointer" along the menu until the appropriate item is highlighted. Pressing the ENTER key then initiates that command. In most instances, users can also invoke displayed menu items by pressing the first letter of the appropriate command; for example, pressing C to select "copy." Pressing the ESC key always takes users back to the previous screen; in this manner, users can change their minds about invoking a command or performing an operation. Merely making a menu selection does not automatically determine that it must be completed.

Although easy to use, Symphony's user interface presents a problem common to menu-driven programs; it is inherently slow, because users are usually forced to scroll through screen after screen in order to complete specific tasks. In addition, to properly use Symphony, users must be familiar with all of the various function keys; otherwise, users will spend too much time consulting the key chart or will not properly perform all jobs. For example, users must remember that when editing data entries in the data base module, they must first press Function Key #2 (the edit key) to activate the edit mode.

USING FRAMEWORK

Framework is an integrated package that performs as if it were more than the sum of its parts. It builds on the spreadsheet and graphic principles pioneered by VisiCalc and 1-2-3, but adds a word processor comparable to most standalone packages. Everything fits together beautifully because the same commands work throughout the package. You move text blocks the same way you move groups of spreadsheet cells, and the search-and-replace function works on a document, spreadsheet, or data base.

Framework is also distinguished by its use of the direct leverage principle, which dictates a natural, commonsense user interface incorporating pointing and doing. Choices are available on pull-down menus, and a few clearly defined keys direct the computer. This interface gives you the illusion that you are working directly on your documents and spreadsheets without the computer being present; the screen seems to be a desktop, and the documents and spreadsheets appear to be frames.

minicomputer, data entry, and word processing systems, as well as in remote terminals (Figure 4–9). The floppy disk is a compact, flexible, magnetic, oxide-coated mylar disk. It comes in three popular diameters: 20 cm (8 in), 13 cm (5¼ in), and 9 cm (3½ in).

All floppy disks are enclosed in jackets for protection, with a slot for access by the disk's reading and writing mechanism. Information is recorded in digital fashion on the disk's magnetic surface while it is rotating. The floppy disk (Figure 4–10) offers several advantages because it

1 Is easy to handle, store, and mail
2 Is readily interchangeable with other disks on the computer
3 Is reusable
4 Has a storage capacity of up to about 1.6 million bytes for double-sided, double-density disks that record data on both sides

FIGURE 4–9
A 9-cm (3½-in) micro-floppy disk and floppy disk unit. The diskette is enclosed in a jacket for protection; there is a slot for access by the floppy disk unit's reading and writing mechanism. (Courtesy of Amdek Corp. and Franklin Computer Corp.)

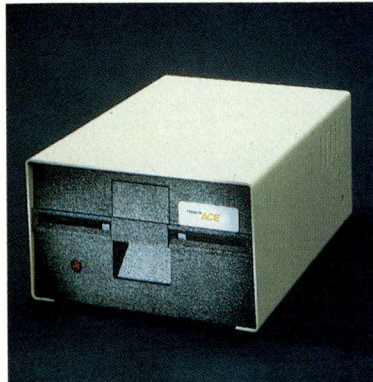

FIGURE 4–10
Operator inserting a diskette into a floppy disk unit. These units are used widely in minicomputer, microcomputer, word processing, and data entry systems. They are becoming more common because they are a relatively inexpensive means of obtaining auxiliary storage for small systems. (Courtesy of Verbatim Corp.)

Winchester Disks

The read/write head of conventional disks occasionally comes in contact with debris that may cause it to ''crash'' and lose data. Special devices have been developed to overcome this problem. One such device is the Winchester disk drive. **Winchester disks** are sealed modules that contain both a disk and a read/write head mechanism (Figure 4–11).

Because the disk module is sealed, head-to-disk alignment problems are eliminated and the risk of exposing the recording surface to airborne contaminants is reduced. Cleanliness is so vital to the operation of Winchester disks that they are assembled in rooms with vacuum-equipped walls. For these reasons, Winchester disks are extremely reliable.

Winchester disks are fast as well as dependable. The drive heads ''fly'' less than one micron above the spinning disks at speeds of over 160 kilometers per hour (100 miles an hour). This type of disk is popular because it can be used in small office computers, word processing systems, and microcomputer systems. In addition, the Winchester disk

- Provides the highest storage capacity
- Offers the lowest cost per stored byte
- Has the lowest cost of movable-head rigid magnetic disk drives
- Can supply data transfer rates ranging from 150 000 to more than one million bytes per second

Videodisks

Videodisks, also called **optical disks**, may well be the auxiliary storage system of the future. Today, videodisks are being introduced commer-

FIGURE 4–11
Winchester disk drives, such as the IBM 3340 (right), use a removable data module which contains the disks. Disk operation in these high-speed disk units exceeds 160 kilometers per hour (100 miles per hour) and any direct contact between the read/write head and the magnetized disk surface would destroy the magnetic coating. On the left is a data module containing disks, read/write heads, disk access arms, and vertical shaft. (Courtesy of Lockheed Corp.)

cially for entertainment and education in homes, schools, and industry. A videodisk can hold several hours of television pictures and sound, or the equivalent of more than 50 000 photographic slides.

The use of videodisks with computer systems is still in the early development stages. One drawback is that videodisks only have playback capability; they cannot have data written on them. We will have to wait and see what applications they may have for information processing.

MASS STORAGE DEVICES

Many businesses need direct access to extraordinarily large files of information. For example, a large insurance company may have several million policyholders whose records must be kept updated. Government agencies, computer service bureaus, and large banks also have similar needs for mass storage.

How Mass Storage Devices Work

Mass storage devices supply relatively inexpensive storage for large amounts of information. Consider how a jukebox operates. After depositing a coin, you select a song by pressing the appropriate buttons, and the machine places it on a turntable to be played. The same principle is used in several mass storage systems.

The IBM 3850 mass storage system provides up to 472 billion bytes of on-line storage (Figure 4–12) and uses up to 9 440 data cartridges. Each cartridge contains a spool of magnetic tape about 8-cm (3-in) wide

FIGURE 4–12
The IBM mass storage system—a beehive of electronic activity—contains up to 472 billion bytes (characters) of on-line information. Cartridges in each honeycomb cell contain magnetic tape. Upon receiving a signal, data being stored on tape are transferred to disks, then to the computer's main memory. The 3850 gives quick and inexpensive access to vast files of data. (Courtesy of International Business Machines Corp.)

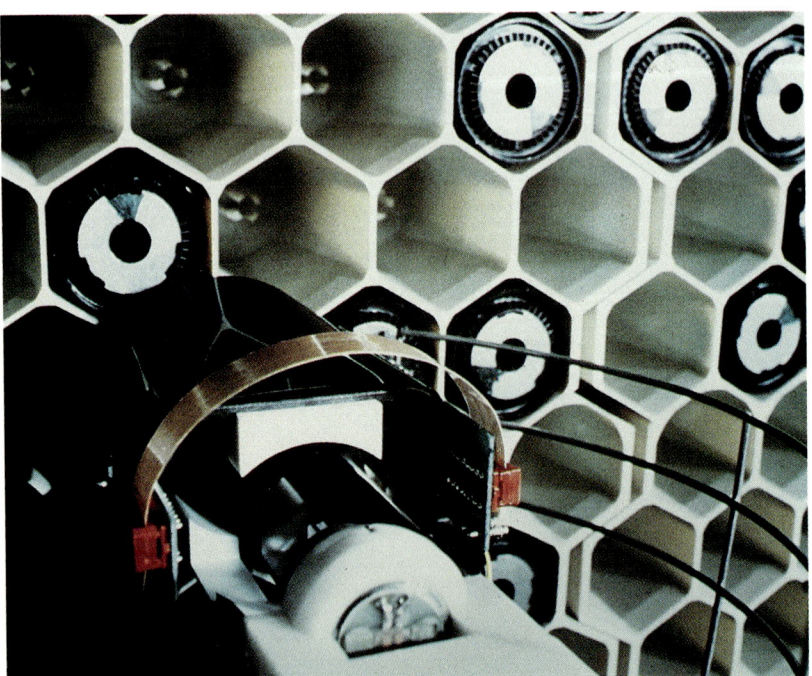

and 2 000-cm (770-in) long, which can contain 50 million bytes of information. The data cartridges are stored in a honeycomb arrangement of cells. The 3850 system uses an access arm to move the cartridges to and from the honeycomb cell bank and the read/write station. At the read/write station, the cartridge is opened and the contents of the magnetic tape strip are transferred to a disk pack on an IBM 3330 disk storage drive for immediate use. The data cartridge is then returned to its home in the cell bank.

SUMMARY

☐ The two types of auxiliary storage are: sequential and direct access. Sequential storage is nonaddressable because a user cannot directly refer to the contents of a particular storage location. Direct access storage, also called random access, provides immediate access to records and is addressable.

☐ Magnetic tape is a principal input/output and storage medium for computer systems. Data are recorded by magnetizing the iron oxide coating of the tape. Data are stored and processed sequentially.

☐ The magnetic tape drive is the mechanism that pulls the magnetic tape into position past the read/write head that converts the magnetized bits it senses on the tape into electrical pulses and transmits them to the CPU.

☐ Data are grouped on magnetic tape in clusters called records, which are physically separated from each other by a blank space called an interrecord gap. The interrecord gap also allows space for the tape drive to reach operating speed and to decelerate after a read or write operation. Some disk units have removable and replaceable disk packs used as input/output units as well as storage devices.

☐ Disk packs allow users to conveniently move data stored in one disk unit to another so they can be processed on various computer systems.

REVIEW QUESTIONS

True or False

_____ **1** Magnetic tape is an excellent example of main storage.

_____ **2** A file is a group of logically related records.

_____ **3** Main storage is indirectly accessible to the central processing unit.

_____ **4** Direct access storage is also called random access storage.

_____ **5** Magnetic disk storage is a nonaddressable form of storage.

_____ **6** In modern computer systems, it is not practical to store information on magnetic tape.

_____ **7** Access time refers to the time required to locate and transfer information to and from storage.

_____ **8** The access time for main and auxiliary storage devices is the same.

_____ **9** In addition to being used as storage devices, magnetic tape units and magnetic disk units find wide usage as input/output devices.

_____ **10** Most large computer systems employ a combination of storage devices.

_____ **11** One of the disadvantages of magnetic disk storage is the fast access to stored information.

_____ **12** When information is brought from an auxiliary storage device to the arithmetic unit, the information is lost in main storage.

_____ **13** In most magnetic disk and magnetic tape storage units, a portion of the available space is never used.

_____ **14** In a large computer system, the usual scheme is to convert source data into some fast, machine-processible medium, such as magnetic tape or magnetic disk pack.

_____ **15** It is not practical to attempt direct access processing of information recorded on magnetic tape.

_____ **16** An auxiliary storage device, such as a magnetic tape unit, is not used for storing large quantities of information.

_____ **17** All auxiliary storage devices operate on the principle of random access processing.

_____ **18** ''Destructive'' means that as new information is written, old information is destroyed.

_____ **19** Information is read from or recorded on magnetic tape devices, using magnetic read/write heads. Magnetic disks can retrieve records randomly.

_____ **20** The main storage of most computers is floppy disk storage.

_____ **21** Auxiliary storage is utilized in many computer systems because main storage is more expensive and relatively limited.

Short Answer

1 _____ storage is used primarily to supplement the _____ storage of a computer system.

2 Another name for auxiliary storage is _____ _____.

3 A _____ is a group of logically related items read as a single unit into main storage or written from storage in the same manner.

4 The length of time it takes to locate and transfer information to or from storage is called _____ _____.

5 Writing on a magnetic disk is _____, while reading is _____.

6 _____ is the time required for the disk to attain the desired position at the selected read/write head.

7 The time required to locate a specific track on a disk is called _____ _____ time.

8 There are _____ (three, four) popular sizes of floppy disks.

9 Another name for a videodisk is _____ disk.

10 A _____ _____ consists of a rigid magnetic disk in a sealed container.

11 A floppy disk is also called a _____.

12 A magnetic disk is divided into a series of concentric circles called _____.

13 The smallest floppy disk has a diameter of _____.

5 FROM MICROCOMPUTERS TO SUPERCOMPUTERS

OUTLINE

THE GROWTH OF COMPUTER
TECHNOLOGY

MICROMINIATURE CHIPS AND
MICROPROCESSORS

MICROCOMPUTERS

MINICOMPUTERS

MEDIUM- AND LARGE-SCALE
MAINFRAME SYSTEMS

SUPERCOMPUTERS

Making Computers Smarter
(Artificial Intelligence)

OBJECTIVES

1 Discuss the classifications of
computer systems and the
characteristics that define each
category.

2 Describe microprocessors and
microminiature memory chips
and their uses.

3 Distinguish between
microcomputers,
minicomputers, mainframes,
and supercomputers.

4 Discuss the need for larger and
faster supercomputers.

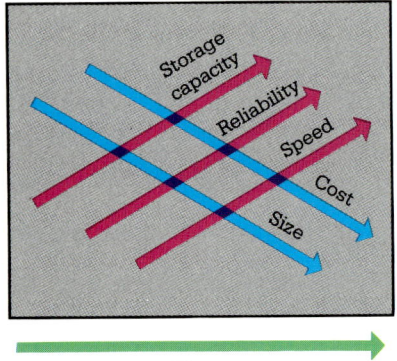

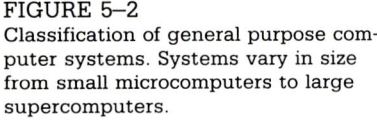

Time

FIGURE 5–1
Computer technology is a very dynamic activity. Yesterday's newest computer is tomorrow's museum piece; today's innovation will be obsolete next year. Even though changes are occurring very rapidly, the trends are going in five directions at once: Computers are becoming smaller and less expensive, as well as more reliable, faster, and capable of offering increased storage capacity.

THE GROWTH OF COMPUTER TECHNOLOGY

Recent trends in computer technology have decreased the cost of computers while increasing their speed and reliability (Figure 5–1). Trends toward smaller, more powerful, less expensive, and more reliable computers will continue through the 1980s and beyond.

The size of computer systems ranges from ultrasmall microprocessors to extra-large supercomputers. Some small computers offer computing power equivalent to large-scale systems of only a few years ago. Most systems used today are **general purpose computer systems**, but **special purpose computer systems** are designed for particular applications and to solve specific problems.

The four categories of general purpose computer systems are: microcomputer (micro); minicomputer (mini); mainframe; and supercomputer. The boundaries of these systems are continuously changing. For example, a memory size presently typical of a mini may be more typical of a micro within a few years. Also, the speed of a mainframe of a few years ago equals the speed of today's minis. Figure 5–2 illustrates the classification of general purpose computer systems.

MICROMINIATURE CHIPS AND MICROPROCESSORS

Before discussing the different types of computer systems, let's look first at **microminiature chips**. These chips are designed and built to function as memory, logic, control, arithmetic units, or some combination of these. Commonly, the arithmetic, logic, and control functions are placed on a single chip called a **microprocessor**. Memory chips and microprocessor chips are used in most of today's computers.

Microprocessors are small enough and inexpensive enough to be incorporated into other machines. Consequently, many consumer products have built-in computers that enable them to carry out complicated operations impossible for their noncomputerized counterparts to perform. Microprocessors are used in word processors, hand-held calculators,

FIGURE 5–2
Classification of general purpose computer systems. Systems vary in size from small microcomputers to large supercomputers.

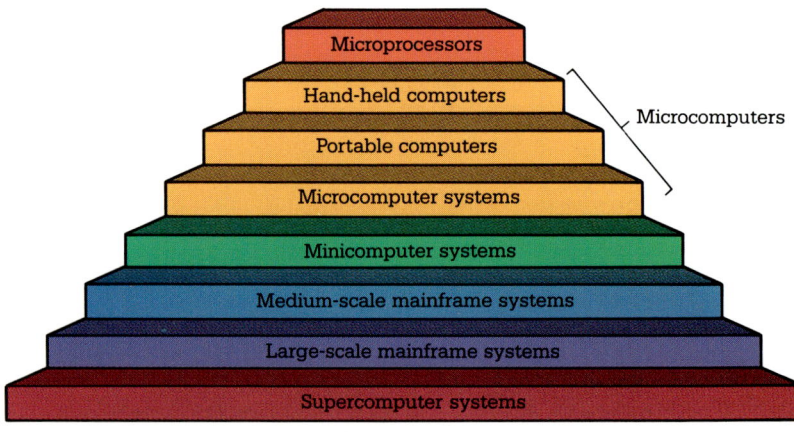

sewing machines, pinball machines, language translators, microwave ovens, cameras, cars, television sets, games, washing machines, photo-typesetting machines, gas station pumps, portable computers, slot machines, point-of-sale terminals, and many other devices (Figure 5–3).

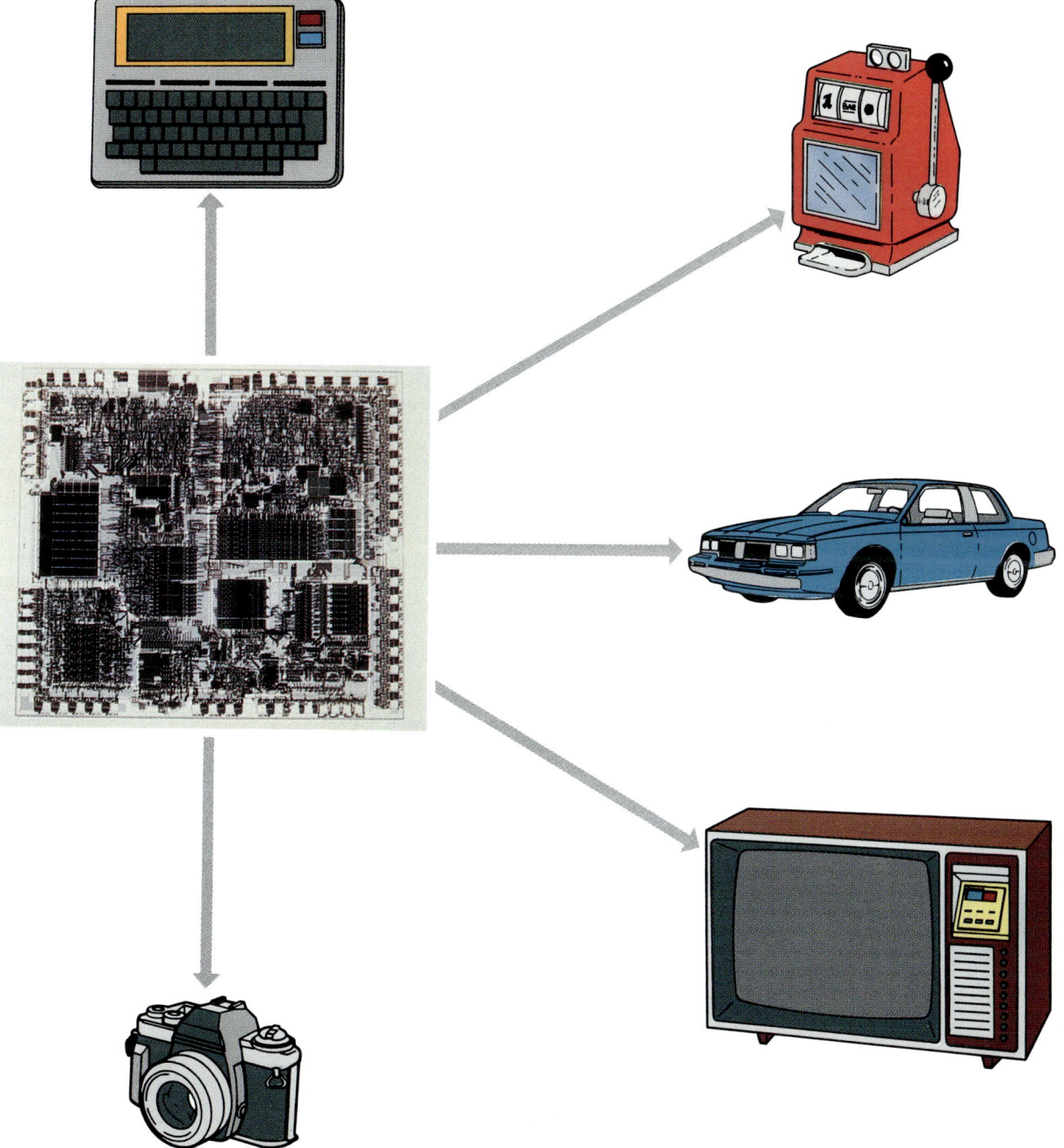

FIGURE 5–3
Microprocessors are used as the control elements in a wide variety of consumer products. (Courtesy of Intel Corp.)

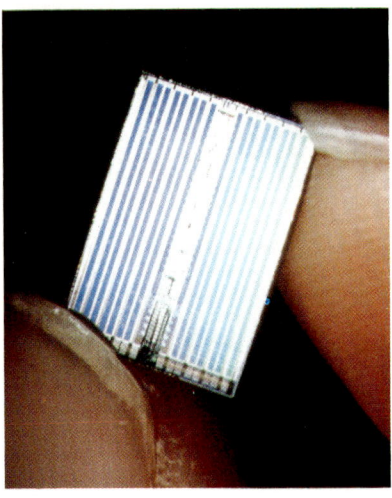

FIGURE 5–4
In early 1984, IBM announced development of a one million-bit dynamic RAM chip. The chip will probably start appearing in computers in 1985 or 1986. The 1 048 576 memory cells and their support circuitry occupy an 8 085 sq mm area of silicon. The chip dimensions are 10.5 mm × 7.7 mm. (Courtesy of International Business Machines Corp.)

Most microcomputers use either 8-, 16-, or 32-bit microprocessor chips, which serve as the central processing units of the microcomputers. In the early 1980s, most microcomputers use 8- and 16-bit microprocessors. In the mid- and late 1980s, the 16- and 32-bit microprocessors will be the main control devices for microcomputers.

A Brief Look at the Growth of Chip Technology

In the mid-1960s, several electronic devices, called **transistors**, and their connecting circuits were etched into a single piece (chip) of silicon. The result was called an **integrated circuit**. As hundreds of additional transistors were etched into the chip, the process became known as large-scale integration (LSI).

In 1981, Hewlett-Packard introduced a 0.4-cm square chip with 450 000 transistors. This event was followed by Bell Laboratories' announcement of the development of a 256K chip, which actually contains 262 144 components. In 1984, IBM Corporation and Bell Laboratories announced a one million-bit memory chip (Figure 5–4). During the late 1980s, we can expect to see several chips containing millions of elements. By the year 2000, perhaps billions of circuit elements will be contained on one small chip. The process of manufacturing chips with thousands of components is called very large-scale integration (VLSI).

How Chips Are Created

First, an engineer makes a large drawing of the circuitry to be etched on the chip. The amount of time it takes to design a chip depends on the chip's function; it can take years to complete a complex design. Drawings can be handcrafted on a drafting table or drawn on a computer (Figure 5–5). The final drawings are redone with high precision, computer-controlled plotters. The result is a precise rendering of the layers constituting the desired circuit on sheets of transparent plastic (Figure 5–6). Each of these sheets is reduced photographically to an intermediate size, and the pattern is repeated automatically enough times to fill the area of a thin silicon wafer 7.6 cm (3 in) in diameter. Great precision is required since these masks must be in nearly perfect alignment when used in the successive stages of manufacture. The mask, which resembles a photographic negative, is then used to transfer the design to a silicon wafer (Figure 5–7). The design is imprinted on the wafer by a chemical etching process using photosensitive emulsion applied to the silicon, then exposing the wafer to ultraviolet light (Figure 5–8). An acid bath is used to wash away any unexposed areas. This process can be repeated many times, creating successive layers of electrical circuitry on the chip (Figure 5–9).

Although the design layers have been etched on the wafer, the chips must also include different electrical characteristics to control the flow of electricity. Through a process call "doping," impurities are embedded in the silicon. Once the chips have been doped, they are heated for hours in large furnaces to form layers of oxide and other minerals (Figure 5–10). These layers are "etched" to form circuits.

Because the precision required exceeds that of human capability, computers are involved at every step of the manufacture of a chip. Testing begins after the chips are removed from the heat and separated from the other chips on the wafer with a laser or die-cutting saw (Figure 5–11). Usually, less than half of the chips from a wafer survive the manufacturing process and are usable. Most manufacturing stages take place in "clean rooms" containing air filters that remove the smallest particles of dust in the air so as not to contaminate the chips. Employees wear white jump suits for the same reason (Figure 5–12).

Once the chips have passed testing, they are packaged with protective casings of ceramic, plastic, or metal with gold or aluminum soldering (Figure 5–13). The packaging protects the chips and also provides electrodes for hooking up the circuits to the outside world. The lengthy manufacturing process is now complete, and the chips are available for a variety of tasks (Figure 5–14).

MICROCOMPUTERS

A **microcomputer** is an electronic machine that follows a set of instructions, called a program, to perform input, processing, storage, and output operations. Microcomputers are small, can be built with only a few chips (or even one chip for control devices like video games, cameras, and business machines), and are relatively inexpensive. They are being used in all application areas and, although they have been available for only a few years, it's clear that microcomputers will have a greater effect on society than other types of computers. Some experts even predict that their impact will be greater than that of the industrial revolution.

With prices ranging from less than $100 to several thousand dollars, microcomputers offer computer power to a wide range of individuals and businesses. Most microcomputers cost between $500 to $5 000. **Personal computers** are lower-priced microcomputer systems intended for personal rather than commercial purposes. However, many personal computers perform the same functions, such as word processing and data base filing, that business computers do.

A microcomputer system contains the same types of hardware and software of larger computer systems but is scaled down in size, speed, and price. The memory of microcomputers falls into two basic categories of semiconductor storage discussed in Chapter 2: ROM and RAM.

A typical microcomputer might have 32K to 64K of ROM and at least 128K of RAM. Peripheral devices such as keyboards, visual displays, magnetic disk units, magnetic tape units, printers, and graphical digitizers attached to microcomputers are generally quite different from those found on larger computers. The screen size of many microcomputer displays is smaller than the CRTs used on larger computers. Magnetic disks include Winchester and floppy disks; magnetic tape units are cassette tapes. The operating speed of a microcomputer is much slower than that of a mainframe computer ranging from one to four microseconds.

RUN "APPLICATION"

In January 1985, the Atari Corporation announced two new personal computers that use the powerful 16/32-bit MC68000 microprocessor. The super-fast MC68000 operates at a dazzling 8 million cycles per second, bringing advanced capabilities such as sound generation and high-speed multicolored graphics to the systems. The Atari 130ST comes standard with 128K bytes of useable RAM, while the 520ST boasts a substantial 512K bytes. Both models have 192K bytes of ROM and can be expanded to 320K bytes with a 125K byte plug-in module. Both computers use a mouse for graphic applications and a sound generator that composes and produces three-voice harmony with three separate pitch and volume settings. BASIC and LOGO programming languages are available for both machines.

FIGURE 5–5
Computers assist engineers in the design of circuits. (Courtesy of RCA)

FIGURE 5–6
A photomask, consisting of a circuit design on a sheet of transparent plastic film, can be hundreds of times larger than the finished product. (Courtesy of Intel Corp.)

FIGURE 5–7
A silicon wafer containing several chips.

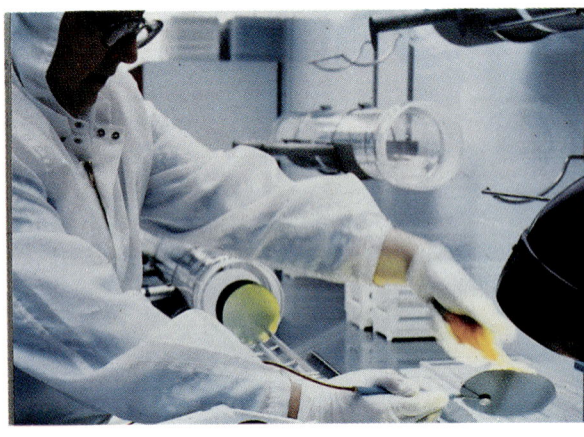

FIGURE 5–8
Wafers being prepared for etching. (Courtesy of NCR Corp.)

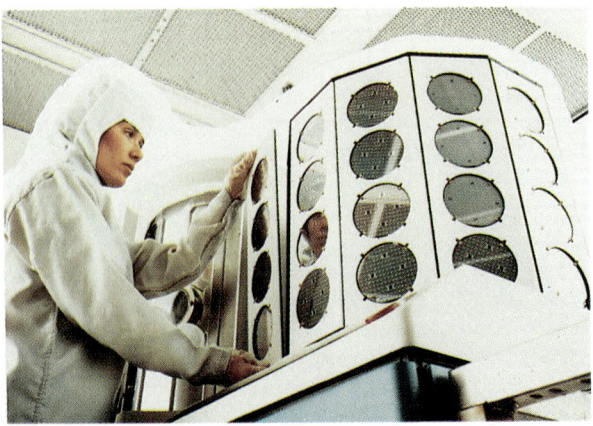

FIGURE 5–9
A technician carefully handles a wafer during a stage of chip manufacture. (Courtesy of National Semiconductor Corp.)

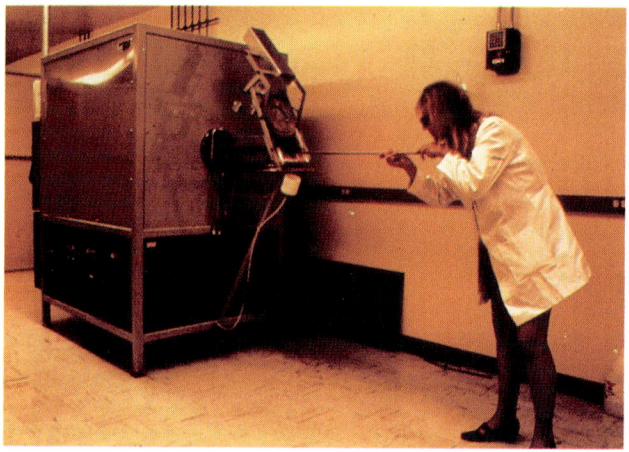

FIGURE 5–10
A tray of silicon wafers, each containing several dozen microcomputer chips, is placed into an oxygen furnace. (Courtesy of Intel Corp.)

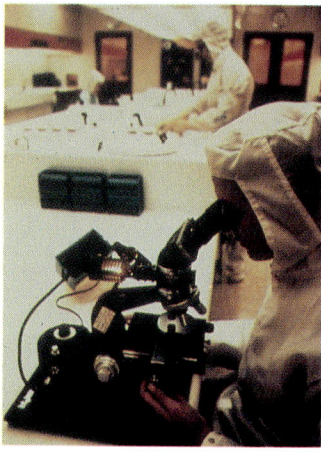

FIGURE 5–11
Chips are inspected under 400 × microscopes in the "clean room." (Courtesy of Intel Corp.)

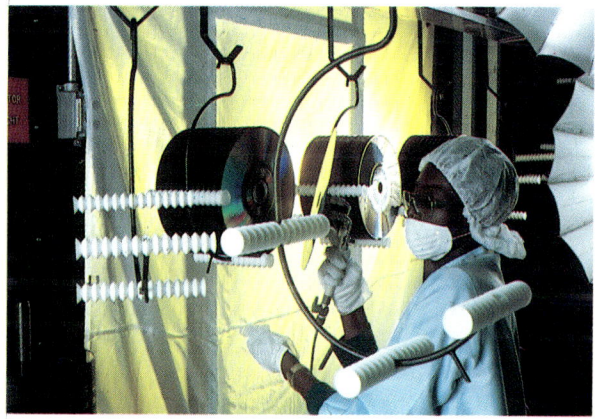

FIGURE 5–12
Most manufacturing processes take place in "clean rooms" where the air is filtered constantly and workers wear surgical-type clothing. (Courtesy of RCA)

FIGURE 5–13
The finished product—a microminiature chip. Shown here is a 32-bit very large-scale integration chip used in the NCR 9300 computer. (Courtesy of NCR Corp.)

FIGURE 5–14
Chips mounted on a circuit board. This board is used in the Hewlett-Packard HP 9000 computer and contains the CPU and memory chips. (Courtesy of Hewlett-Packard Co.)

Artificial intelligence is the behavior a computer system displays that is considered intelligent when we observe it in human beings. Artificial intelligence (AI) has the potential to affect many aspects of life, including business, health care, education, and entertainment. Although current applications are limited, growing expertise and technical capability promise significant achievements in this area.

The most common types of intelligence displayed by AI systems are the abilities of pattern recognition, learning, and problem solving. By combining these abilities, AI systems have been designed to solve various complex problems, such as investment analysis, proving theorems, and robot guidance system design. AI work has also taught computers to play chess and generate art, music, and poetry.

HISTORICAL PERSPECTIVE

AI actually predates the computer. George Boole, the founder of Boolean logic, on which AI is based, published his original works in the mid-1800s. During the 1940s ENIAC, developed at the University of Pennsylvania, was designed as a calculator using Boolean logic. John von Neumann later suggested that by using the same logic, calculators could modify their own instructions as if they were data. This modification initiated the large-scale development.

Because the stored-program computer was based on logical decision making, attempting to solve complex problems that required human intelligence was a natural next step. Early applications included theorem proving, language translation, and games such as checkers and chess. In the 25 years since these early applications were developed, however, no one has written a chess program that consistently wins against top chess players. In addition, theorem-proving programs can verify many mathematical theorems, but they have not uncovered new ones. Language translation remains an unsolved problem.

The difficulty of extending early successes to more complex applications forced AI researchers to rethink their goals and methods. They began to realize that it might be helpful to set aside the notion that AI involves a recreation of thought and to concentrate instead on specific tasks. Despite this change in emphasis, it is still useful to understand how people solve problems and to attempt to automate those problem-solving activities that the computer can perform well.

EXPERT SYSTEMS

Expert systems are computer programs that act as expert consultants to users. For example, an expert system in the field of internal medicine could help a doctor diagnose a patient's illness and prescribe treatment. Another expert system might assist a computer salesperson in interpreting a customer's needs and designing a complete computer system, including cabling and physical configuration. A third expert system might help a geologist interpret information gathered from instrumentation in the search for mineral deposits.

Expert systems consist of three components: (a) a knowledge base supplied by an expert in the field; (b) a set of facts supplied by the user; and (c) an inference engine supplied by the program. In addition, a mechanism interviews the user to determine the facts relating to the user's specific problem. The system can also describe how it is proceeding with its analysis. Potentially there is no limit to the problems that expert systems can help solve. They can be used to interpret photographic information, direct robots, assist a football coach in calling plays, pilot an airplane, and buy and sell commodities.

STATE OF THE ART

Today, AI is at a crossroads. In some instances, it has been commercially successful, however, major unsolved problems include computer creativity and learning. Research to make computers easier to use is currently underway in Japan. This effort, known as the Fifth Generation Project, is also concerned with the application of expert systems.

COMPUTERS AND CREATIVITY

Some people argue that because a computer operates with rules, it is incapable of creativity. The argument continues that although the development of rules may be creative, anything that follows from those rules is not. If whatever the computer did could be predicted by following its rules to their logical conclusion, the computer could not be considered a creative machine. Programmed with rules, however, the computer can produce results that cannot be determined in advance and have never been derived before.

The creative process, as it applies to computers, can be defined as the act of developing something that is new or an improvement. In terms of expert systems, this process can be divided into these four components:

1   The knowledge base, containing facts and rules that are useful and relevant to a set of problems
2   Option generation, using the facts and rules to create options
3   Option evaluation, testing options using information in the knowledge base
4   The environment or user, providing the final test of the option

These components must be able to communicate with each other. A control process determines the activities of each component and when those activities take place.

AI LANGUAGES

AI programs can be created using standard computer programming tools. However, these programs must be able to: (a) handle the creation and analysis of text information; and (b) develop logical inference techniques, which include the searching of large, nonnumeric data structures.

Creation and analysis of text information is handled by the list processor (LISP) programming language. LISP's popularity is based on its ability to handle strings of words. LISP contains instructions for adding and deleting words and, based on the content of the word strings, it allows program control and can perform branching.

LISP is distinguished from most languages by the programmer's ability to write subroutines that can be used later as instructions as if they were part of the original language. Users can also modify the program with string instructions during program execution, and arithmetic and algebraic calculations can be intermixed with string operations. The language is implemented as an interpreter that speeds the programmer's ability to write programs.

PROLOG is a language that is becoming widely accepted for expert systems applications. Designed specifically for expert systems, PROLOG contains direct mechanisms for implementing an inference engine as well as developing search techniques. Japan has selected PROLOG as the language for its fifth generation programs.

To be useful as a business tool, a microcomputer must be interfaced with such devices as keyboards, displays, auxiliary storage devices, and printers. When these items are incorporated with an operating system and application programs, a **microcomputer system** is set up. Several representative microcomputer systems are shown in Figures 5–15 through 5–18. Many microcomputer systems have operating systems, language translators (BASIC, Pascal, FORTRAN, LOGO), business application programs (word processing, spreadsheets, payroll, and accounts receivable), educational programs (simulations and CAI programs), and utility programs (disk copy, memory test, and sort programs).

Hand-held Computers

A **hand-held computer**, also called a **pocket-computer**, is a small microcomputer that fits in the palm of your hand (Figure 5–19). These devices resemble a hand-held calculator and are being produced by several manufacturers. They can be programmed in the BASIC language and can operate alone or, with the use of adapters, on printers, cassette recorders, display devices, and telephone modems. Memory can be expanded in many hand-held computers, which range in price from $50 to $150.

Hand-held computers have a full keyboard and a one-line alphanumeric display window. When "conversing" with the computer in BASIC, users enter statements by tapping them out on the keyboard. Future hand-held computers will probably offer more display area, lower prices, and plug-in accessories. The next step after hand-held devices is the wrist computer. In 1984, Hattori Seiko Company of Japan introduced a wristwatch that featured functions of a computer display as well as those of a standard timepiece (Figure 5–20).

Portable Computers

Portable computers that feature built-in keyboards, visual displays, floppy disk units, cassette units, and printers are also available (Figure 5–21). In 1981, the Osborne 1 was the first fully functional computer system in a portable package. Since then, many portable machines have been introduced with exotic names such as Zorba, Kaypro, Gavilan, Attache, Chameleon, Voyager, Compa, and Hyperion Plus.

Effective portable computers must pass the following tests:

1 Have microprocessor and memory components that require only a fraction of the power presently necessary
2 Feature displays that are lightweight and compact and that compare favorably to a standard-size CRT screen
3 Offer sharp and readable displays that are easy on the eyes

Fortunately, current developments will allow system designers to easily meet these requirements. Low power semiconductor technology is used to fabricate memory and microprocessor components requiring only

---

RUN "APPLICATION"

A Radio Shack TRS-80 Model 100 notebook computer aboard the U.S. Space Shuttle Challenger circled the globe once every 90 minutes as part of a Canadian government-sponsored experiment measuring the atmosphere. Marc Garneau, the first Canadian astronaut, used the Model 100 along with a sunphotometer to measure solar radiation. The first part of his measurements consisted of calibrating the sunphotometer by pointing it directly at the sun from space. This procedure could not be done directly from Earth because the effects of Earth's atmosphere would hamper the reading. By pointing the sunphotometer at the sun at sunrise and sunset, however, he was able to measure the density and distribution of the volcanic haze from El Chichon, a Mexican volcano that erupted March 26, 1982.

FIGURE 5–15
One example of a modern microcomputer is the IBM Personal Computer. Hundreds of thousands of these small machines are being used in businesses, schools, and homes. (Courtesy of International Business Machines Corp.)

FIGURE 5–17
Home entertainment and education are popular uses of the Apple IIe microcomputer. (Courtesy of Apple Computer, Inc.)

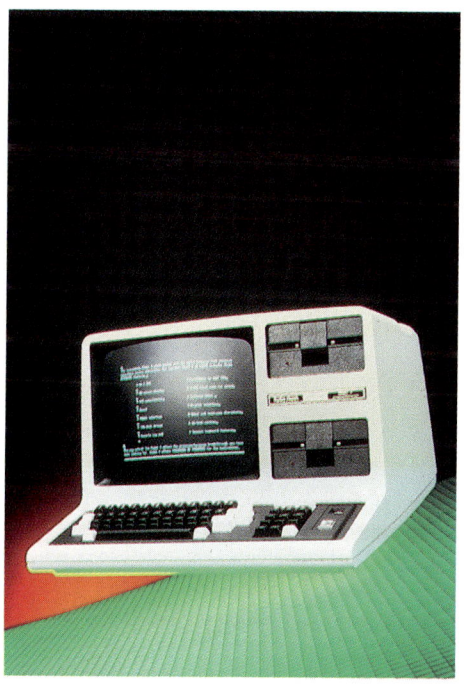

FIGURE 5–16
The Radio Shack TRS-80 Model 4 microcomputer is capable of performing many tasks in homes, small businesses, and schools. (Courtesy of Radio Shack, A Division of Tandy Corp.)

FIGURE 5–18
The IBM PCjr is the smallest and least costly computer manufactured by the IBM Corporation. (Courtesy of International Business Machines Corp.)

FIGURE 5–19
Hand-held computers are sophisticated, inexpensive microcomputers that can perform complex tasks that once required large computers. Programs written in BASIC programming language can be entered and executed on these small machines.

thousandths of watts per component, compared to the one watt per device for larger computers. In addition, flat panel displays and complementary metal oxide semiconductor technology have made the production of electronic power devices capable of extremely low power usage. Consequently, many systems requiring batteries can be designed within size limitations of smaller computers.

MINICOMPUTERS

Minicomputers have been available for two decades. The first minicomputer, 12-bit machine called the PDP-8, was introduced in 1965 by Digital Equipment Corporation (DEC). Five years later, DEC brought out the PDP-11 series, 16-bit minicomputers that were popular for many years. In 1977, DEC's VAX 11/780 made its entrance as the world's first 32-bit minicomputer. This machine is more powerful than any other brand of minicomputer and can directly address 2 million bits of primary storage. Since then, DEC has introduced the VAX-11/750 (a slightly less powerful machine), the VAX 11/782, the VAX 11/730, and the VAX 8600. Most programs designed for older DEC machines can run on the VAX family of minicomputers with little modification.

Minicomputers are general purpose computers that can be programmed to perform a variety of tasks. In the 1960s, their major use was in controlling ongoing scientific and industrial processes. Although the early machines had limited peripherals and software, they were small and sold at a relatively low price. Over the years, many users recognized the flexibility and cost benefits of using minicomputers. Gradually, manufacturers began providing lower cost peripherals and more software to meet the increasing demand.

Whether it's for school or home, work or play, a personal computer can save you time and money, increase your productivity, and process information with speed and accuracy. Because of the revolutionary changes in the industry and the marketplace, however, deciding which machine to buy can be bewildering. What tasks do I want my software to accomplish? Do I want a portable (Figure 1) or a full-size machine? Where can I go if my machine breaks down? Several issues must be addressed before you can make an intelligent choice.

WHAT COMPUTERS CANNOT DO FOR YOU

Before examining what you want a computer to do for you, it's important to understand what it *cannot* do. First, regardless of the brand you buy, a microcomputer cannot do your thinking for you. Computers can only follow specific, logical steps based on the information you enter through the keyboard or insert on software disks. For example, if you buy word processing software with the hope that it will make the human thought processes that

go into writing a report less rigorous, you're bound to be disappointed. Word processing programs can make the mechanics of writing much easier. However, they cannot miraculously equip you with the organizational and creative skills needed to produce well-written reports. You provide the inspiration; the computer relieves you of much of the drudgery involved with writing.

A corollary to this situation is that a computer can only feedback information based on the raw data you put in. For example, a financial software package used for making sales forecasts will provide results that are equivalent to the accuracy of the figures you enter. If the figures entered are

FIGURE 1
One portable computer is the Epson HX-20 notebook computer, with 16K RAM and 32K ROM. It includes a built-in word processor, microcassette drive, and other standard features. The internal power supply for this 22 cm × 30 cm (8½ in × 11½ in) portable lasts for 50 hours and can be recharged in eight hours. (Photo supplied courtesy of Epson America)

"How do you like our new home computer?"

wrong or out-of-date, the results of the computer's calculations will reflect these inaccuracies. Here again, the computer's value lies in the colossal amounts of time and frustration it saves you from doing manual, calculation tasks.

Another limitation is that the computer does only what it is told, either by the software or by a human operator. In other words, a computer is only as smart as the instructions you give it. If instructions are wrong or incomplete, you can curse and yell at "that dumb machine" as long as you like; the computer will just sit humming placidly on your desk until it receives correct directions.

Finally, no computer system is absolutely "bug-free." Since the machines are designed by humans and humans cannot think of every possible contingency and safeguard, computers may do some things that are unexplainable. With improved technology, however, most of the bugs have been worked out of systems. Considering the complexity of the parts contained inside microcomputers, these machines have amazing performance records.

WHAT COMPUTERS CAN DO FOR YOU

Unless you plan to use your computer solely for creating your own programs, software will determine what your computer can do for you. With very few exceptions, software is machine-specific; in most cases, printers and other peripheral devices are also (Figure 2). What runs on an IBM Personal Computer may not run on an Apple IIe or a Commodore 64 microcomputer. So before you even look at hardware, you must decide what tasks you want to accomplish and find the best software for the job. Then, and only then, can you make a wise selection about which computer to buy.

In practical ways, selecting a computer is like buying a car. A family of seven would be foolish to choose a sports car as its only method of transportation. The sports car might be perfect for a single

FIGURE 2
The NEC Spinwriter printer is designed for use with the IBM Personal Computer. (Courtesy of NEC Information Systems, Inc.)

person with a small garage, while a station wagon would probably be the best choice for the large family. Like cars, computers are equipped with the same basic parts, but they serve completely different needs.

The two basic types of software used with computers are

1 Systems software, which comes with the hardware and tells the computer how to operate
2 Applications software, which equips the computer to perform a specific task such as word processing accounts receivable

Most people who buy personal computers are nonprogrammers interested primarily in applications software that will equip their computers to perform specific tasks. To meet these popular applications software needs, a huge commercial market has blossomed (Figure 3). According to recent figures from FIND/SVP, a New York-based information and research firm, the microcomputer software market in this country is expected to grow from $1.85 billion in 1983 to $12 billion in 1990. The study shows IBM Corporation at the forefront of the personal computer hardware shakeout, with about

FIGURE 3
All types of software, from business to education to games, are available to users of microcomputers.

FIGURE 4
Tandy Corporation produces Radio Shack TRS-80 microcomputers. Service support is provided by 8 800 Radio Shack stores and dealers worldwide. (Courtesy of Radio Shack, A Division of Tandy Corp.)

50 percent of the market share. IBM compatible machines are expected to capture 25 percent of the market by 1990, with Commodore International Ltd., Tandy Corporation (Figure 4), Apple Computers, Incorporated, and other popular computer companies competing for the remaining 25 percent.

Because software developers respond to the demands generated by the hardware market, knowing which companies produce the best selling machines is a good predictor of the quantity—and often, the quality—of available applications software. Being informed about hardware is also a good indicator of the availability of parts, service, and peripherals such as printers and modems. As you can see, the hardware and software industries share a symbiotic relationship—they feed off one another to the mutual benefit of both.

FINDING APPLICATIONS SOFTWARE

Broadly speaking, there are two types of applications software. The first and most popular type is applications software such as data base management, business graphics, and word processing, covering a broad range of functions used by most businesses and many individuals. Some applications software, such as Lotus' Symphony software, combine various functions on one program. The second type of applications software provides specific professional or technical applications for specific types of businesses. For example, software specifically designed for use by medical doctors, dentists, architects, and engineers perform very specialized tasks.

Several categories of broad-range applications software are widely purchased for business and personal use (Figure 5). These applications software include

☐ Accounting—general ledger, payroll, accounts payable, and invoicing

☐ Communications—electronic mail interaction with central office mainframes, hookups with commercial data banks and other services offered by information utilities, and local area networks

☐ Data base management—organizing data files for central access, retrieval, and update, and compiling statistics, plot trends, and market analyses

☐ Educational programs—learning through games, tutorials, simulations, and other computer-based learning activities (Figure 6)

☐ Financial planning—performing financial tasks such as forecasting and other complicated, time-consuming predictions

☐ Graphics—displaying color graphs and charts and, combined with the proper output devices, producing color slides and other visual aids

☐ Programming—BASIC is built into most computers

The types of performance needed from various applications software packages vary with each kind

FIGURE 5
Software Publishing Corporation produces a wide variety of applications software. "PFS: Write" is an example of word processing software, and "PFS: Access" is an example of communications software. (Courtesy of Software Publishing Corp.)

FIGURE 6
Learning with Fuzzywomp, by Sierra On-Line, includes four educational games, for pre-readers featuring number sequencing, pattern matching, counting, and creative play. (Courtesy of Sierra On-Line)

of software. For example, the high color resolution and easy-to-read chart models that you need in a good graphics software package are different from the fast data handling and ease in combining files required of good data base management software. Take a realistic look at your business or personal needs when deciding upon applications software, and unless you have an unlimited income, buy only the software that you need.

For example, even though the hobbyist in you may be attracted to graphics packages that can produce color slides when used with particular computers and peripheral equipment, the cost may be prohibitive. If accounting software makes your heart beat with excitement, but your accounting needs can easily be handled with a simple, old-fashioned ledger book, then accounting software is not necessary. A little forethought will save you a lot of money.

Once you've determined your needs, there are several ways to become informed about the capabilities and ease of use of various applications packages.

☐ **Read reviews in computer publications.** *Personal Computing, Creative Computing, Byte, Computerworld,* and dozens of other computer publications provide up-to-date information on new software and hardware.

☐ **Ask your friends or colleagues for their recommendations.** If possible, arrange to drop into their homes or offices to try out the applications packages that might meet your needs.

☐ **Check your public library.** Because of copyright infringement laws, few libraries will let you take software home. However, many libraries have one or more computers and a number of software packages that you may use in the library.

☐ **Arm yourself with specific questions and visit your local computer store.** It's best to call ahead to make an appointment with a

Macintosh

Described as ''the Apple computer for the rest of us,'' the Macintosh is IBM's biggest challenger in the personal computer market. Macintosh features include

☐ MC68000 microprocessor and an advanced operating system
☐ Detachable keyboard and nine-inch, high resolution black-and-white monitor
☐ 512K RAM; 64K ROM
☐ Four-voice sound generator
☐ Modem part for communications capabilities
☐ Extensive business and recreational software selection

Cost: $3 495

sales representative. Explain that you are gathering information. Find out the store's least busy time—usually early mornings—and visit when a sales representative will have time to answer your questions and demonstrate software and compatible hardware.

☐ **At a computer store, do a trial run on software and compatible hardware that meet your specific needs.** For example, if you need a computer for financial analysis, bring your own figures to use. If it's word processing you're after, bring a report that needs to be typed and formatted. Most stores will let you sit for a couple of hours to try out products.

HOW TO SELECT HARDWARE

Computer hardware is the physical equipment that makes up the computer system. It includes the computer itself and all peripherals—the devices such as keyboard, monitor, disk drive, and printer that send information to the computer and receive information from it (Figure 7).

GUIDE TO ACCESSORIES AND PERIPHERALS

Classifications of products and services designed to expand your computer's capabilities and increase its usefulness.

Terminals
Devices for communicating with computers, typically a keyboard and CRT screen unit.

Print Buffers/Switches
Devices that hold information prior to printing, freeing the computer for other tasks. May be internal or external.

Print/Paper Feeders
Devices that translate computer output to paper copies, including letter quality and graphics.

Plotters
Devices that translate computer output to paper copies, including letter quality and graphics.

Film Image Devices
Camera systems that capture computer display images on photographic film.

Tools and Supplies
Consumables, attachments, cleaning/maintenance items used around computer work stations.

Expansion Boards
Add-in and add-on devices that increase a computer system's capabilities.

Disk Systems
Permanent data storage devices and systems that use rotating magnetic media.

FIGURE 7
A guide to accessories and peripherals (From the June 1984 issue of *Computer Accessories and Peripherals Magazine,* p. 54)

RAM and Disk Drives

The biggest question most people have about selecting a computer is determining how much memory, or storage capacity, they need. If they've done the necessary groundwork of selecting which tasks they want the computer to perform and determining which software is necessary to make this happen, the memory dilemma will have solved itself. Software packages specify the amount of RAM (random access, or read/write memory) required to run the program. If your computer will be used primarily for business purposes, experts advise that 64K RAM is the minimum advisable.

Disk drives write and read information to and from disks. Most personal computers use 5¼ in

Tape Systems
Magnetic media (data) stored on reels or in cassettes or cartridges.

Modems
Devices that connect computers to telephone lines in order to send and receive information over distances.

Power Protection
Devices that protect computers and peripherals from power surges and/or loss of power.

Security
Devices or systems that prevent unauthorized access to computer processed data, or theft of hardware.

Input Devices
Includes keyboards, voice and special electronic devices to speed or facilitate entry of data into computers.

Video Monitors
Display devices that permit operators to view computer output. Display may be green, amber, white, black.

Services
Computer-related work performed by others with special knowledge or tools.

Furniture/Accessories
Items designed to facilitate the use of computers in a particular environment.

FIGURE 7
(Continued)

IBM PCjr

Aimed at both the home and business markets, the IBM PCjr offers a standard typewriter style keyboard on all models. Some critics say the PCjr is too expensive for the home market and not capable of handling the demands of the business market. The IBM PCjr enhanced system features

- ☐ 8088 processor
- ☐ 128K RAM
- ☐ An optional 128KB memory expansion attachment to boost total user memory, in increments, to 512KB
- ☐ One 360KB built-in disk drive that can use cartridge and diskette programs
- ☐ An optional speech synthesizer with 196 built-in words and recording capabilities through a microphone input

The basic IBM PCjr system costs $700. However, attachments such as an IBM television adapter and an IBM BASIC cartridge are necessary to make the system functional. The enhanced system, excluding the memory expansion and speech attachments, costs $1 269.

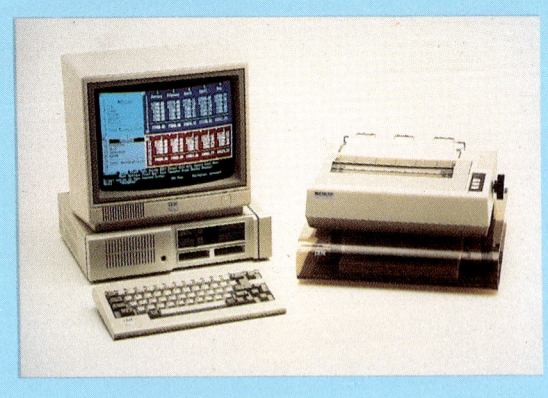

floppy mylar disks that are permanently sealed inside square plastic jackets. A cut-out slot of the disk provides access to a moving head that reads from and writes on the disk. If possible, the computer you select should be equipped with two disk drives, so that disks may be copied. Each disk should store at least 200K. Many newer machines have built-in disk drives, while other machines feature them as separate components. If speed is important, you may want to consider equipping your machine with a hard disk drive, which is about ten times faster and can store about ten times more information than floppy disk drives. Hard disk drives start at about $2 000.

Disk Operating Systems

The computer's disk operating system (DOS) makes sure the computer follows all the procedures necessary to carry out the instructions you give the machine. Most computers have their own operating systems, and applications programs are compatible only with particular operating systems. The two most widely used operating systems are CP/M for 8-bit machines and MS-DOS for 16-bit computers.

MS-DOS is the operating system for IBM Personal Computers, so a lot of MS-DOS software is being written for IBM and compatible machines. CP/M runs on several machines and has thousands of available software programs. UNIX, an operating system developed by Bell Labs for engineers, is now available for 16-bit machines (Figure 8). Presently, little software is available, and UNIX operating systems are most attractive to people who need a system that can perform complicated scientific analyses. Here again, if you decide upon software before selecting hardware, the MS-DOS versus CP/M quandary will solve itself.

Monitors and Keyboards

The quality of what you see on the screen and touch with your fingers plays a large role in the sat-

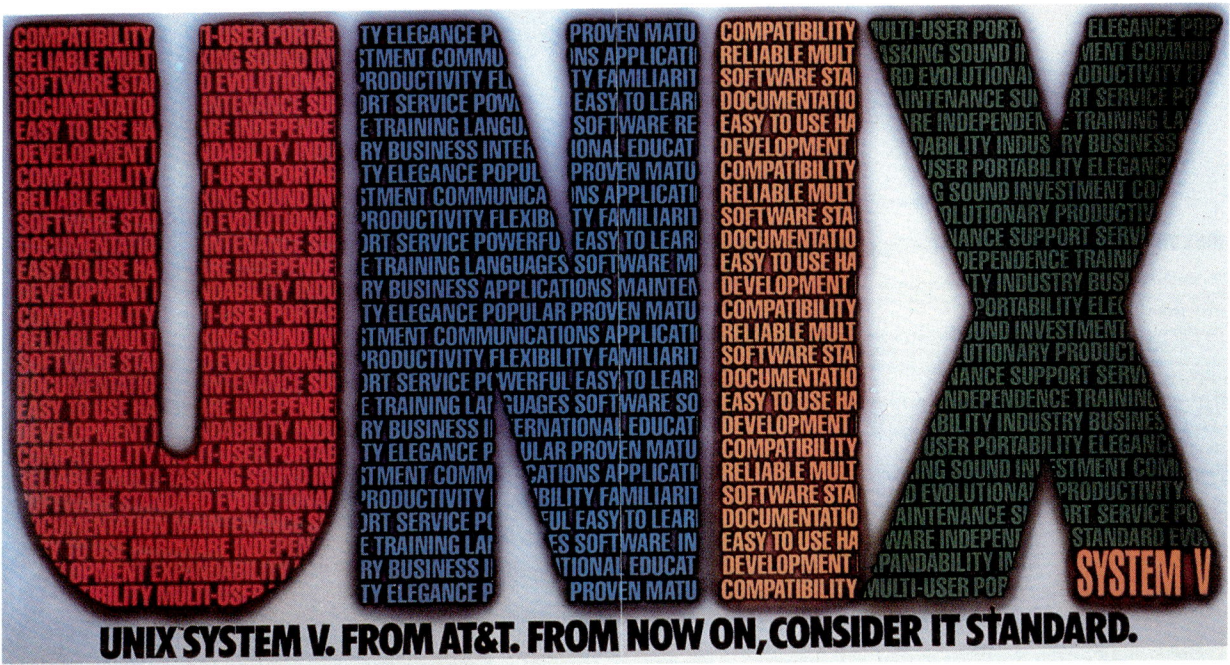

FIGURE 8
Advertising copy for the UNIX System V operating system for AT&T. (© 1984 AT&T Technologies, Inc. UNIX is a trademark of AT&T Bell Laboratories)

isfaction you will experience with your computer. The resolution, or clarity, of the image you see on the monitor is determined by the number of tiny picture elements, called pixels, it contains. The higher the density of pixels, the sharper the image displayed on the screen. Not surprisingly, monitors with sharp images are more expensive than cheaper models with fewer pixels. Some people try to save money by hooking up their computers to their televisions and using their television screens as monitors. However, the lower number of pixels in a television monitor means the resolution will not be nearly as clear as that shown on a computer monitor containing densely-packed pixels.

Unless you plan to buy graphics software or high resolution color games packages, a color monitor is not necessary. Older machines featured black and white monitors, while most newer models use green or amber on a black background. The latter are easier on the eyes and give better resolution than the old white on black screens. A nonglare screen will also help make the text easier to read. A tiltable screen is another nice, but not necessary, feature.

Screen size is also important. The length of an average, good quality screen is 24 lines—the size of about one-half a typed page. Some machines, usually word processors with vertically mounted screens, can display a full page at once. Unless word processing is the only purpose for your machine, this type of screen is not necessary.

As for keyboard selection, don't even look at the cheaper machines with the small keyboards. These flat surface, membrane covered boards make pressing keys difficult and they do not have the feel of real keyboards. In addition to moveable keys, a detachable keyboard, though not essential, is certainly worth the money in terms of comfort and convenience. A detachable keyboard allows you more mobility and less rigidity in keying in information; you can even put it on your lap. Another plus to detachable keyboards quickly becomes apparent when two people are using the machine to play a game. Instead of changing seats or sharing a chair, the keyboard can be handed or slid back and forth.

If you plan to use financial applications software, a separate numeric keypad on the right side of the keyboard will make entering numbers much easier than making the stretch to the top row of the regular keyboard (Figure 9).

Finally, how does the keyboard feel when you type? If the keys are hard to depress or the key surface is so flat that finger contact is poor, don't buy the machine. Good keyboards are designed for the comfort of touch typists.

Here is a computer hardware checklist:

1   Is the machine equipped with enough memory to handle the software you need?
2   Is the disk operating system compatible with the software you've selected?
3   Does the monitor display a clear, crisp image?
4   Is the monitor large enough, and is the displayed text easy on the eyes?
5   Does the keyboard have good height, texture, and touch control?

SELECTING PRINTERS AND OTHER PERIPHERALS

The word *peripheral* literally means "lying away from or outside the central part." That definition

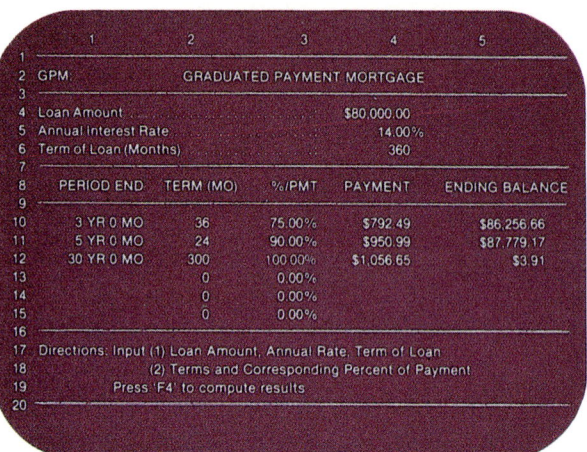

FIGURE 9
Financial Planning Mind Tools, an example of financial applications software, consists of 18 different files you can load into your regular spreadsheet program one at a time. The spreadsheet above can help you to calculate a graduated payment mortgage. (Courtesy of Howard W. Sams and Co., Inc.)

perfectly describes the relationship of this type of equipment to computers. Peripherals are not necessary to the actual computing process. However, they are important to extending the usefulness of your machine. For example, writing the great American novel on disk won't do you much good if you can't provide a paper copy for the rest of the world to read. In addition, the multitude of services such as shopping, banking, and data banks offered on-line by information utilities are unavailable to you unless you buy a modem that will connect your computer via telephone lines to that company's central mainframe.

Printers

Criteria for selecting printers include speed and print quality. Since the printer will probably be your most expensive peripheral, take great care in making your selection. Two types of printers for personal computer owners are dot matrix printers and letter quality printers (Figure 10). If speed is important and appearance is secondary, an inexpensive dot matrix printer that forms each character out of grids of dots produced by a series of tiny print hammers may be your best bet. Dot matrix printers are generally very fast, but the appearance of the finished product is not typewritten, letter quality. Dot matrix printers are good for the fast processing of lists of numbers and other computer data. Many people also use them for printing labels and other lists.

If it's a clean looking, quality appearance you're after, then the letter quality printer is what you need. Letter quality printers are slower; they produce between 12 to 60 characters per second, while dot matrix machines produce more than 250. Like dot matrix printers, most letter quality printers are impact machines. The image they produce is caused by keys striking paper. Most letter quality printers use a device called a daisy wheel that contains a letter or number at the end of each spoke. Like typewriter fonts, daisy wheels come in a

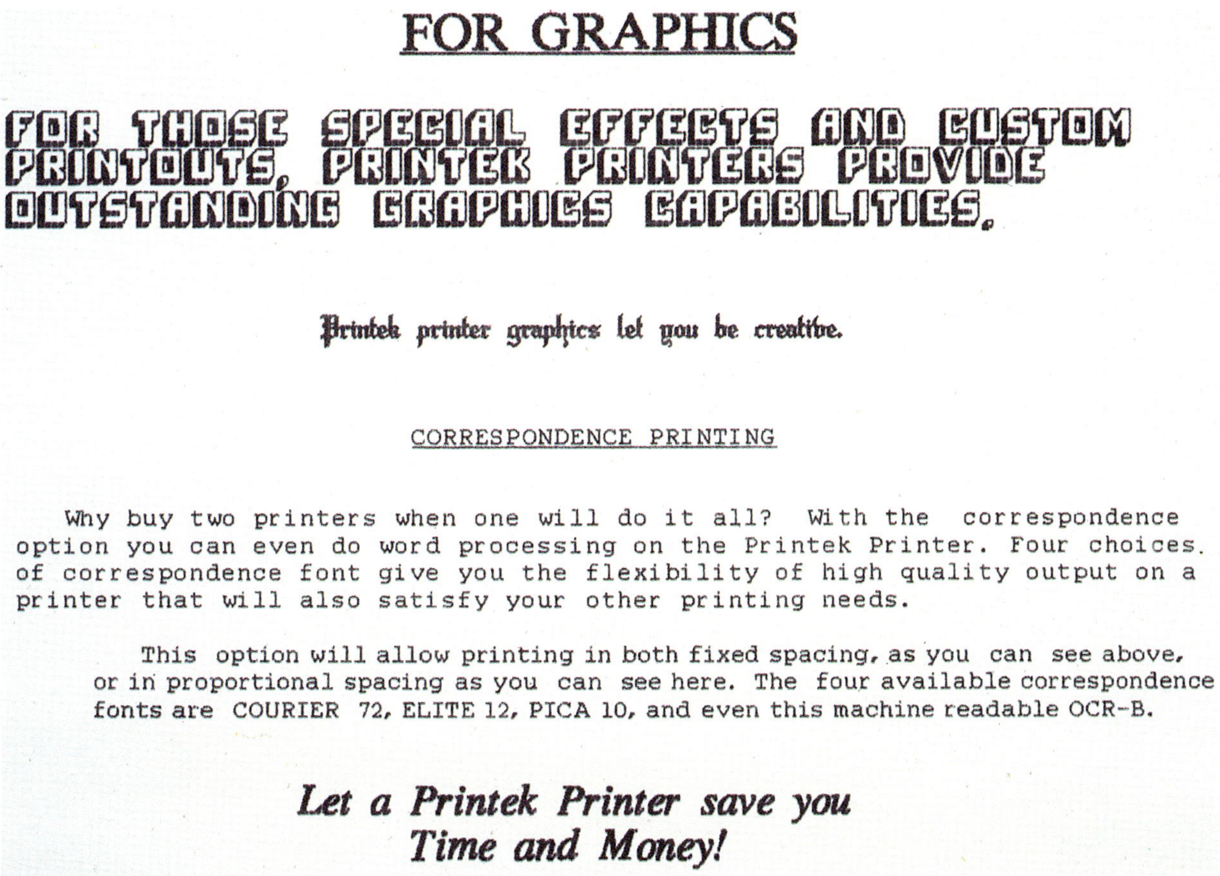

FOR GRAPHICS

FOR THOSE SPECIAL EFFECTS AND CUSTOM PRINTOUTS, PRINTEK PRINTERS PROVIDE OUTSTANDING GRAPHICS CAPABILITIES.

Printek printer graphics let you be creative.

CORRESPONDENCE PRINTING

Why buy two printers when one will do it all? With the correspondence option you can even do word processing on the Printek Printer. Four choices of correspondence font give you the flexibility of high quality output on a printer that will also satisfy your other printing needs.

This option will allow printing in both fixed spacing, as you can see above, or in proportional spacing as you can see here. The four available correspondence fonts are COURIER 72, ELITE 12, PICA 10, and even this machine readable OCR-B.

Let a Printek Printer save you
Time and Money!

FIGURE 10
Some examples of print from a dot matrix printer (Courtesy of Printek Inc.)

variety of print styles that can be easily changed. Most can also produce underlining, boldface, italics, and other special effects.

Modems

If you are interested in electronic mail capabilities, on-line conferencing, accessing commercial data bases, or just chatting on-line with other personal computer owners, you will need a modem, communications program, and telephone to make the connection (Figure 11). Communications software is every bit as important as the modem hardware you purchase. In fact, the "software first" rule applies to modem selection. As with computers, the software must be compatible with the hardware in order for the modem to work. This is particularly important when the modem is used for special purposes, such as using your home computer to access the hard disk at your office.

The speed at which modems exchange information is called the baud rate. Most newer modems are 1 200 bauds. Less expensive and much slower modems with baud rates of 300 are also available. If you plan to capture or send great chunks of text or access commercial data bases—all services which are charged based on the amount of time on the system—the faster baud rate is more practical.

SERVICE CONTRACTS

The best assortment of software won't do you any good if your computer fails to function. That's why a good service contract is essential to protect your investment. It entitles you to ask questions and demand follow-up to possible problems—even if they are your fault.

Read your warranty carefully. Make sure the service contract does not go into effect until the warranty has expired. There's no point paying for a free service. Your friends and colleagues can also advise you about various stores' reputations.

Other questions you need to investigate include:

- [ ] Does the dealer do on-site repairs, or is work on equipment done only at the shop?
- [ ] Will the dealer pick up and deliver equipment to be serviced, or is that your responsibility?
- [ ] If the dealer does pick up and deliver, is there a charge?
- [ ] Will the dealer supply "loaner" equipment while yours is being repaired?
- [ ] If you decide to "trade up" later to a more expensive machine, will the dealer give you a trade-in allowance?
- [ ] Does the contract include regular check-ups and cleaning, or is there a charge for this?

FIGURE 11
CompuServe, the largest videotex service available, offers personal computer users hundreds of data bases and services. (Courtesy of CompuServe)

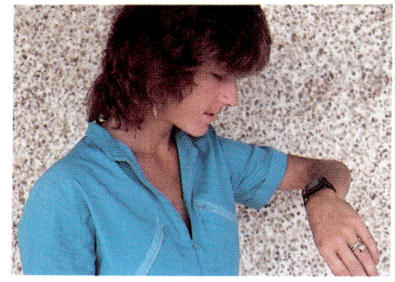

Minicomputer systems are usually larger and more powerful than microcomputer systems, and smaller and less powerful than mainframes. However, this is not always the case. There are microcomputer systems more powerful than the smallest minicomputer and large minicomputer systems that are more powerful than mainframes.

MEDIUM- AND LARGE-SCALE MAINFRAME SYSTEMS

It becomes more difficult to develop categories distinguishing between super-minicomputers, medium-scale systems, large-scale systems, and supercomputer systems as you move up to medium- and large-scale computer systems. Distinguishing among them is often more a matter of degree than a matter of clearly delineated categories.

The price of medium-scale computer systems normally starts at about $150 000 and goes up to more than $1.5 million. Large-scale computer systems overlap this range, starting at about $1 million and increasing beyond $5 million. Medium- and large-scale computer systems are used by universities, large businesses, airlines, hospitals, government agencies, and manufacturing companies.

FIGURE 5–20
The Seiko 2000 is a wristwatch-sized computer that offers 6K of ROM, 2K of RAM, and a 10-character by four-line display. It can store 200 lines (10 characters each) of data, display four lines at a time, and scroll through all 200, using the watch as a personal phone directory or electronic note pad. A separate keyboard is used to enter data. The computer can be programmed in BASIC.

FIGURE 5–21
Portable computers are as useful as desktop microcomputer systems, however, they can fit easily inside a briefcase and can be used almost anywhere. Computers, like the one shown here, are also called notebook computers and lap computers. (Courtesy of Radio Shack, A Division of Tandy Corp.)

Moving up in size also increases everything else, number of peripherals, word size, internal and auxiliary storage devices, and operating speeds. The speed of mainframe computers is often measured in millions of instructions per second (MIPS) or thousands of operations per second (KOPS). The MIPS measures processor speed based on the average instruction cycle times. The KOPS calculation is based on a "typical" group of programs being executed. The KOPS rating for an IBM System 34 is 110; an IBM 4331 is 213; and an IBM 3033 is 5900. The KOPS rating for the CDC Cyber 205 and the Cray 1 supercomputer is 800 000. As you can see, there is a large speed difference between mainframe computers and supercomputers.

The major manufacturers of mainframes are Burroughs Corporation, Control Data Corporation, Honeywell, IBM Corporation, NCR Company, and Sperry Corporation. In contrast to microcomputers and minicomputers, about half of the mainframes in use are rented from the manufacturer or from leasing companies. Several representative mainframe systems are shown in Figure 5–22.

SUPERCOMPUTERS

A **supercomputer** is a very large-scale mainframe computer system that acts as a big number-crunching machine. It can process great quantities of data extremely quickly and can do, in several hours, the work that normally takes weeks on conventional large mainframe computers. To qualify as a supercomputer, a machine must perform more than 20 million (20 megaflops) computations per second.

The fastest supercomputers—selling from $6 million to $17 million each—operate at about 800 million operations per second, compared with only thousands of operations per second for most microcomputer systems. Although the cost of a supercomputer is great, it can often be more cost-effective than using several smaller mainframes. For example, a supercomputer that costs $10 million is more efficient than five mainframe systems costing $2 million each.

Two major vendors dominate the supercomputer business: Control Data Corporation and Cray Research, Incorporated; they make the Cyber 205 and the Cray X-MP and Cray 2, respectively. The Cray X-MP is five to eight times faster than the Cray 1, which was for many years the fastest computer in the world (Figure 5–23). The Cray X-MP features two central processing units (CPUs), each more powerful than the Cray 1's single CPU. Four million 64-bit words of central memory are shared by the XMP's processors.

The Cray 2 is a triumph of miniaturization. Its central processing unit is only 66-cm (26-in) high and 97-cm (38-in) long. No wire in the Cray 2 is longer than 41-cm (16-in). The Cray 2 operates in a glass aquarium, immersed in liquid fluorocarbon like a brain bathed by cerebrospinal fluid. With its temperature balance carefully maintained, the Cray 2 can function at speeds of more than one billion operations per second. The first Cray 2 was installed in California at the Lawrence Livermore National Laboratory (Figure 5–24).

FIGURE 5–22
Some mainframe computer systems—IBM 3084 (top left), Burroughs B7900 (top right), Amdahl 5860 (center left), Control Data Cyber 170 Model 855 (center right), NCR 8400 (bottom left), and IBM 4341 (bottom right). (Courtesy of International Business Machines Corp., Burroughs Corp., Amdahl Corp., Control Data Corp., and NCR Corp.)

FIGURE 5–23
The Cray X-MP supercomputer system is one of the largest, fastest, and most expensive computers in existence. A Cray 1 supercomputer system is shown in the background. (Courtesy of Cray Research, Inc.)

FIGURE 5–24
The Cray 2 supercomputer can process results at speeds of more than one billion operations per second. Cray's new technology involves the immersion of the computer in a clear, inert fluorocarbon liquid that provides cooling for the system. Because of this cooling method's efficiency, components can be packaged in greater density. For purposes of display, the module shown above was immersed in the coolant in a small aquarium. (Courtesy of Cray Research, Inc.)

Control Data's Cyber 205 can perform up to 800 million operations per second (Figure 5–25). Circuitry in the 205 is large-scale integration (LSI) logic, and the central processing unit uses 29 different LSI chips. The purchase price of a Cyber 205 system ranges from $8 million to $17 million.

The Japanese government has several research projects underway to produce supercomputers that are much faster than those of Control Data or Cray Research. By 1989, a group of Japanese companies expects to complete a $300 million project, largely funded by the government, to develop a supercomputer that is one thousand times faster than the Cray 1.

To date, several Japanese companies have produced supercomputers with processing speeds varying from 500 million operations per second to 1 300 million operations per second. The NEC SX-2, Hitachi S-810-20, and Fujitsu VP-400 are the first supercomputers to be developed by Japanese companies.

Supercomputers will continue to be used for scientific number-crunching, but will find a broadened appeal in corporations requiring complex simulations. Businesses dealing with oil, natural gas, water, and seismic and weather explorations can profit by computer simulations. So can automobile, aircraft, and nuclear reactor designers.

FIGURE 5–25
The Control Data Cyber 205 supercomputer system can operate up to 800 million operations per second. (Courtesy of Control Data Corp.)

SUMMARY

☐ Microminiature chips are built to function as memory, logic, control, or arithmetic units, or some combination of these. When the arithmetic, logic, and control units are placed on a single chip, a microprocessor, which can be used in word processors, hand-held calculators, microwave ovens, language translators, washing machines, portable computers, and in many other objects, is created.

☐ With the ability to etch hundreds of transistors onto a single silicon chip, large-scale integration (LSI) began. Very large-scale integration (VLSI) is the process of manufacturing chips with thousands of components.

☐ Making chips is a painstaking process. First, a large engineering drawing of the circuitry to be etched on the chip is developed; then a precise rendering is made on sheets of transparent plastic. Next, each plastic sheet is reduced photographically to intermediate size and the pattern is repeated automatically enough times to fill the area of a thin, 3-inch diameter silicon wafer. The design is then transferred and imprinted onto a tiny silicon wafer via a chemical etching process that can be repeated many times to create successive layers of electrical circuitry on the chip. The chips are "doped" to include different electrical characteristics to control the flow of electricity and heated for hours in furnaces to form layers of oxide and other minerals on the chips. These layers are "etched" to form circuits. After they are tested, chips are packaged using protective casings and the manufacturing process is complete.

☐ There are two types of computer systems: general purpose systems and special purpose systems. Special purpose systems are designed for a particular application, while general purpose systems can perform a variety of applications. Types of general purpose computers include: microcomputers (small, inexpensive machines used in businesses, schools, and homes); larger minicomputers; and mainframe computer systems used in universities, large businesses, manufacturing firms, and government agencies.

☐ Supercomputers are big number-crunching machines that can process great quantities of data extremely quickly. A supercomputer system costs between $6 million and $17 million.

REVIEW QUESTIONS

True or False

_____ **1** Modern computers using LSI and VLSI circuits are smaller, faster, and more reliable than earlier computers using vacuum tube or transistor circuitry.

_____ **2** Microcomputer systems that cost less than $100 are available.

_____ **3** Large-scale integration is a mathematics technique for solving large complex integration problems.

_____ **4** Supercomputers are powerful machines that cost millions of dollars.

_____ **5** A minicomputer is larger than a mainframe computer.

_____ **6** LSI means large-scale integration.

_____ **7** Supercomputers are the largest, fastest, and most expensive computers available.

_____ **8** Today, low-cost microcomputers are being used rather widely in homes by personal computer users.

_____ **9** Supercomputers range in price from $5 000 to $5 million.

_____ **10** One of the reasons that information processing has become important in our economy is that it is always more economical to do everything by machines.

Short Answer

1 A _____ _____ computer would be used to control the operations of a steel mill.

2 The four categories of general purpose computer systems are _____, _____, _____, and _____.

3 Recent trends in computer technology have _____ cost while _____ the _____ and _____ of computers.

4 During the past few years, computer equipment has become _____, _____, and _____ expensive to operate.

5 Examine Figure 5–21 in the text. The computer shown in this photograph _____ (can, cannot) solve problems without a program.

6 _____ are widely used as control devices in consumer products, such as cameras, video game machines, sewing machines, automobiles, and word processing machines.

7 A _____ is a storage chip that is programmed at the time of its manufacture and cannot be reprogrammed by the computer user.

8 The process of manufacturing chips with thousands of components is called _____ _____ _____ _____.

9 The man shown in Figure 5–21 is using a notebook computer. This machine is also called a _____ computer.

10 A computer small enough to fit in your hand is called a _____ computer.

11 The two basic types of memory found in microcomputers are _____ and _____.

12 _____ _____ are low-priced microcomputer systems intended for personal rather than commercial purposes.

13   _____ systems are usually larger and more powerful than microcomputer systems, and smaller and less powerful than mainframe computers.

14   The speed of mainframe computers is often measured in MIPS. The acronym MIPS means _____ _____ _____ _____ _____.

15   In 1984, several Japanese companies introduced supercomputers with processing speeds varying from 500 to 1 300 million operations per second. The NEC SX-2, Hitachi S-810-20, and Fijitsu VP-400 are the first supercomputers to be developed by Japanese companies. The two largest manufacturers of supercomputers in the United States are _____ and _____. These two companies have produced the _____, _____, and _____ supercomputers.

16   Rank the following computer types by relative size from the smallest to the largest.
         _____   **a**   Medium-scale computer system
         _____   **b**   Microprocessor
         _____   **c**   Microcomputer system
         _____   **d**   Supercomputer system
         _____   **e**   Large-scale computer system

17   In order for a machine to qualify as a supercomputer, it must perform more than _____ million calculations per second.

18   In 1984, IBM Corporation and Bell Laboratories introduced a memory chip that contained _____ bits.

6 AN INTRODUCTION TO COMPUTER PROGRAMMING

OUTLINE

OBJECTIVES

1 Understand how a program is developed from the time it is first conceived until the finished product is working on the computer system.

2 Explain the individual stages of program development.

3 Describe the purpose and use of algorithms, flowcharts, pseudocodes, decision tables, and HIPO charts.

4 Identify the two types of software.

5 Explain the differences among machine, assembly, high-level and natural programming languages.

COMPUTER PROGRAMMING STEPS

Whether or not you are consciously aware of it, you go through steps to solve daily problems. Using a computer to solve problems involves a more formal series of steps than those you might use to decide where to go for dinner.

The process of producing a set of instructions that makes a computer perform some specific activity is called programming. The activity can be as diverse as producing a company payroll or solving a complex mathematical problem. The set of instructions that controls the computer is called a program. Preparing and checking out a computer program are time-consuming, important operations. Since the computer cannot make unplanned decisions, each step of the problem has to be accounted for in the program.

An overview of the steps taken to solve a problem follows:

☐ A computer user studies the problem and prepares a plan of action.

☐ The **programmer** decides which steps the computer must take to obtain the desired results and specifies the form of input and output.

☐ The plan of action is then coded into a set of steps in a programming language.

☐ These instructions are prepared for input by keying them directly into the computer's memory via a keyboard or by keying them onto magnetic disk or magnetic tape.

☐ Once in the computer's memory, the program is translated into machine language (the only language the computer understands) by a translating program called an interpreter, compiler, or assembler.

☐ Now the program is ready to be executed by the computer. The steps of the program are carried out on the data used with the program and the output is generated. (The stages of program development are illustrated more fully in Figure 6–1.)

Step One: Defining the Problem

Before any other steps can be taken, you must first be able to define the problem. This means you have to study the problem to the point that you understand it completely. An incomplete understanding of the problem guarantees that the solution will be inadequate or incorrect. The importance of properly defining a problem cannot be over-emphasized, since developing a method for solving the wrong problem would obviously be unsatisfactory. Finding answers to the following questions will help to define the problem.

☐ Is the problem worth solving?
☐ Is a computer solution practical?
☐ Do we know how to use a computer to solve the problem?
☐ Is the available computer equipped to solve the problem?

1	**DEFINING THE PROBLEM** The problem is studied and defined; a method of solution is developed.	
2	**PROGRAM DESIGN** The problem's solution is represented as an algorithm.	
3	**CODING THE PROGRAM** Each step of the problem's solution is converted into computer instructions in the form of a language such as BASIC.	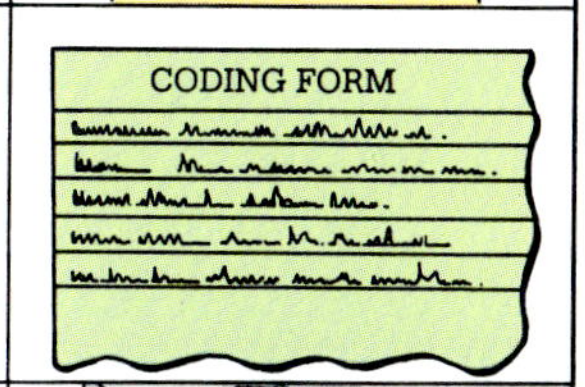
4	**EXECUTING THE PROGRAM** The set of instructions (program) is placed into the computer and the computer is directed to execute the program.	
5	**DEBUGGING THE PROGRAM** The program is checked to eliminate errors ("bugs").	
6	**TESTING THE PROGRAM** The program is tested to determine if it does what it is supposed to do.	
7	**DOCUMENTING THE PROGRAM** Write-ups, program listings, operating instructions, etc., are assembled for future program modification or for individuals who may want to use the program.	
8	**PROGRAM MAINTENANCE** The program is kept functioning at an acceptable level.	

FIGURE 6–1
Stages of program development

☐ What programming language will be used?
☐ What are the inputs and outputs?
☐ How much data must be manipulated to produce the desired output?
☐ How much will it cost?

In some cases, in order to write a program the programmer will work from detailed program specifications prepared by a systems analyst (Figure 6–2). The specifications include all input to be processed by the program, the processing required, and details of all output from the program. The programmer must be satisfied that all possible conditions have been considered and that any conditions not specified can be handled adequately. Having agreed to the specification of the problem, the programmer must then develop a strategy to be used in writing the program. In addition to the programmer's experience, strategy will depend upon the capacity of the computer, type of programming language to be used, and complexity of the problem. The process of understanding the problem is called **problem analysis**; its goal is the formal and logical presentation of the problem for a computer solution.

Problem analysis is subjective. A sure method of analysis that always provides all the information required for a solution does not exist. However, all analyses will require the programmer to recognize the problem, identify the inputs and variables of the problem, list the outputs desired, formulate a precise problem statement, and determine whether a computer is needed for the solution.

FIGURE 6–2
Whether working individually or with a team, programmers find that problem solving is a challenging part of their job. (Courtesy of TRW Inc.)

During problem analysis, the following steps are generally taken:

1 The elements in the problem are determined precisely, and all input and output conditions are specified.
2 All elements to be processed are converted into quantitative terms.
3 The operations and manipulations, expressed as steps and required to produce the desired results, must be determined.
4 The sequence of steps is ascertained.
5 The relationships among all elements that enter into the problem's solution are established.

Step Two: Program Design

Now that we know the program requirements, we must outline the program that will meet them. **Program design** is like producing blueprints for a building or the electrical schematic for an integrated circuit. **Top-down program design** is the general process of going from a large, complicated problem to a series of smaller problems, each having a greater probability of being solvable than the original problem. In other words, top-down program design breaks down complex systems into many easier-to-handle subsystems.

Consider the problem of developing a payroll system (Figure 6–3). The diagram is broken down into a hierarchy format with the most important control modules at the top. These modules are in turn broken down

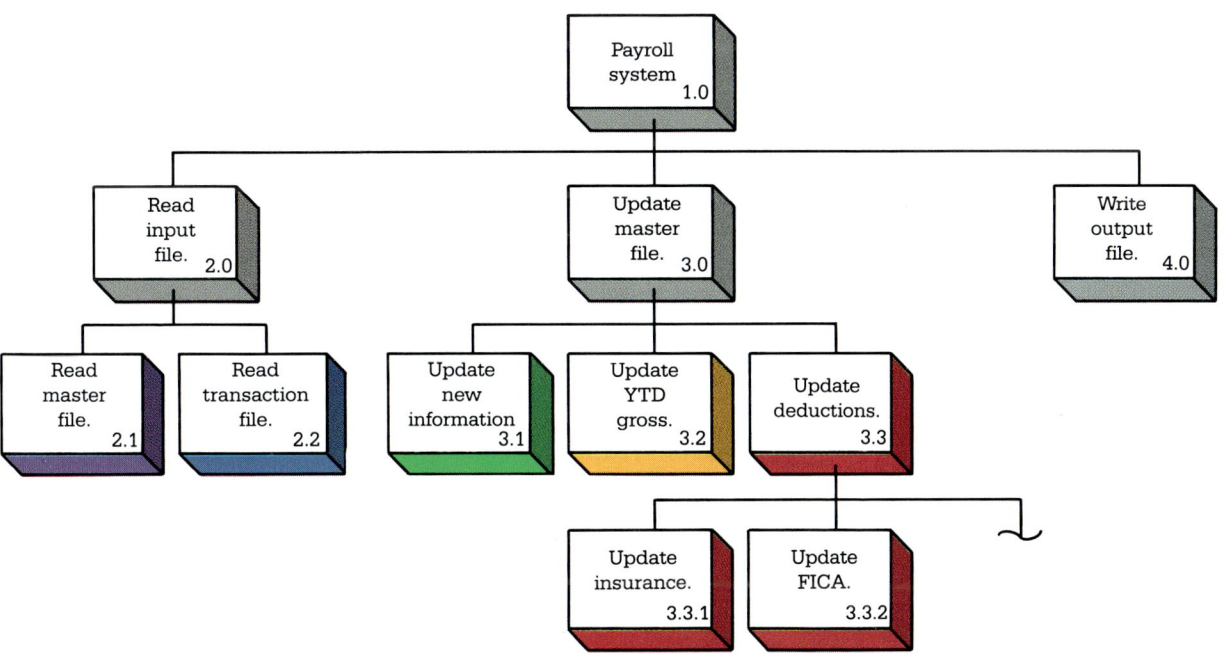

FIGURE 6–3
Diagram of a payroll system

into lower-level modules of increasing detail. Each module, with the exception of the top one, is controlled by the module above it.

Good top-down program design is achieved by following a few simple rules.

- ☐ Each module should be small and independent of the other modules.
- ☐ Each module should have only one entry and one exit.
- ☐ When a module is complete, control should pass to the module controlling it.

Modules are coded in much the same way they are diagrammed. The high-level control modules are coded first. Lower level modules are represented by dummy programs . Program coding proceeds from top to bottom, with modules of increasing detail being completed. By the time the lowest level modules are completed, the higher level modules have been fully tested.

After all elements and relationships in the problem have been studied and defined in specific terms, they must be expressed as steps the computer can perform. This sequence of steps for solving a problem is called an **algorithm**. Simply stated, an algorithm is a record or list of instructions for doing something. More precisely defined, it is a complete, logical, step-by-step plan for solving a problem.

The algorithms for many problems are rather simple, but those for scientific problems can be quite complicated. For example, the algorithm for determining if 379 is a prime number is simple: divide 379 by each of the numbers 2,3,4 . . ., 378. If any division results in a zero remainder, the number is not prime; otherwise, it is a prime number. On the other hand, the algorithm for simulating the flight of an airplane is complex and involves several thousand steps. To be useful, an algorithm must be precisely defined, finite, and effective.

Often, several different algorithms may be used for solving the same problem. Development of different methods often reflects a personal style. Some people are very clever at finding algorithms that give quick answers; others use familiar approaches that require more time but produce the same results. Among the methods commonly used to describe algorithms are flowcharts, pseudocodes, decision tables, and HIPO charts.

Flowcharts A **flowchart** is a simple, unambiguous pictorial view of how the computer will solve a problem. It is composed of simple descriptions contained in special symbols that are connected by straight lines. Most flowcharts use only five basic symbols and are easy to prepare and use. The symbols are linked in a sequential manner through the use of straight lines with directional arrows.

Programmers use standard flowchart symbols established by the American National Standards Institute. The complete set of symbols is fairly large, however, we will deal only with the most common ones. The terminal symbol is used to indicate the beginning or end of an algorithm.

The parallelogram symbol indicates either the need for information by the algorithm (input) or the availability of information in the form of an answer (output). This symbol is used to show what goes into or comes out of a procedure.

A rectangle is used to indicate processing, such as a computation. The information written in this symbol may be an English statement, an algebraic statement, or some kind of meaningful shorthand. "Calculate $Y = X/10$," "Move X to Z," and "Compute $N \cdot N + 3$" are examples of processing and would be represented in flowchart notation as

A diamond symbol is used to indicate that some type of decision is to be made. This symbol usually has one entrance and two exits.

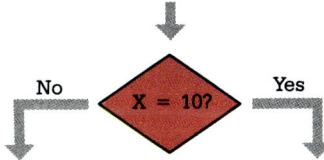

Clarifying notes can be added to flowcharts by using the annotation symbol. Note that this symbol is connected to the procedure flow by a dashed line.

Straight lines with arrows are used to connect flowchart symbols and thus indicate the direction of flow and logic of processing. The flowchart in Figure 6–4 shows a procedure for reading a value for variable Y, computing $X = Y + 27$, and printing the computed value of X. The normal direction of flow is from left to right and from top to bottom. In certain cases, however, it is not always possible to conform to the normal flow direction. Arrowheads are then included on the flow lines to indicate direction. Figure 6–5 shows a procedure that inputs three numbers, determines the largest of the three, and prints it.

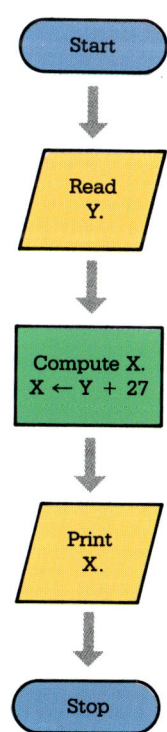

FIGURE 6–4
Procedure for a simple computation

FIGURE 6–5
This procedure inputs three numbers, distinguishes the largest of the three, and prints it.

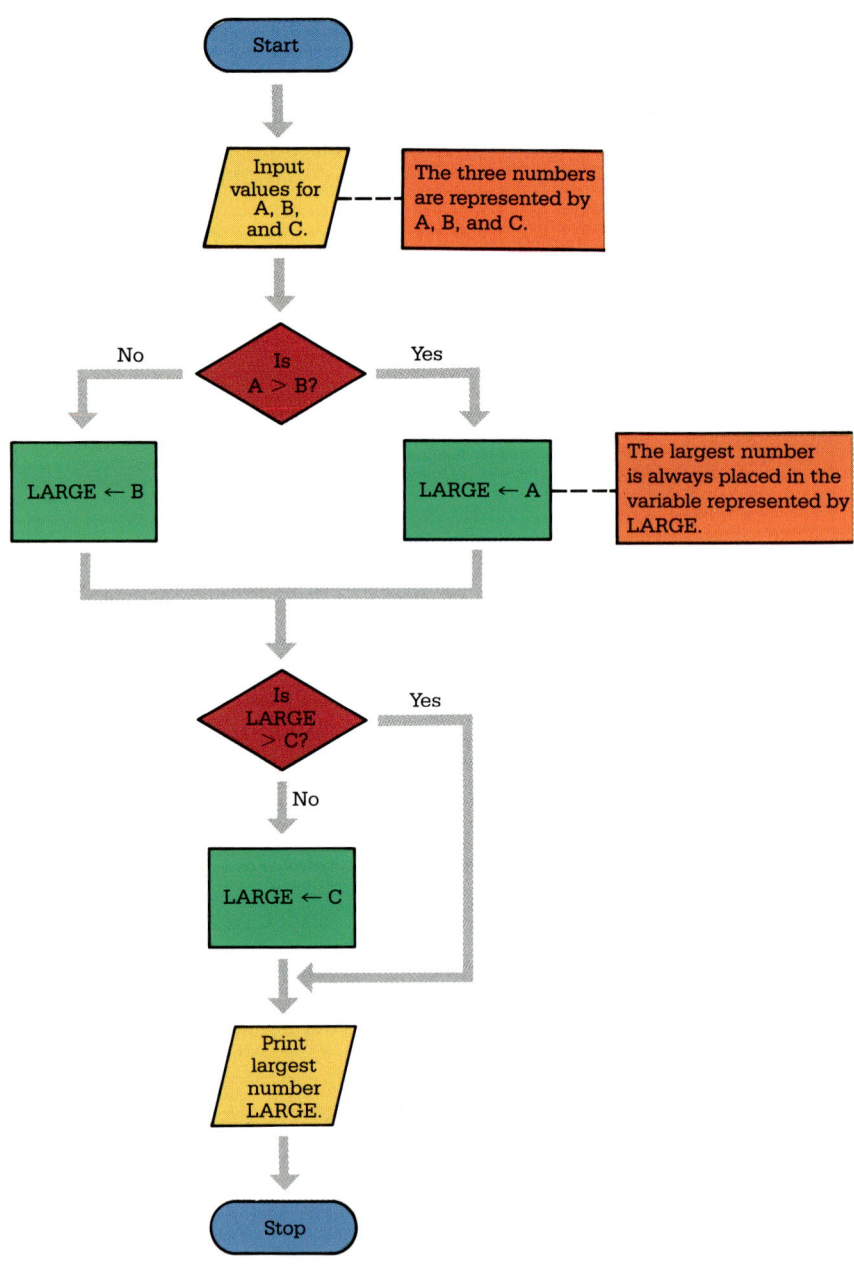

Structured flowcharts   Structured flowcharting is a method of representing an algorithm in terms of three basic flowcharting structures: sequence, selection, and looping. Each of these structures has a single entry and exit point.

The sequence structure represents the format in which instructions are executed in sequence (Figure 6–6). The selection structure provides for a choice between two alternative paths, based on a certain condition (Figure 6–7). The basic condition is stated at the top of the structured

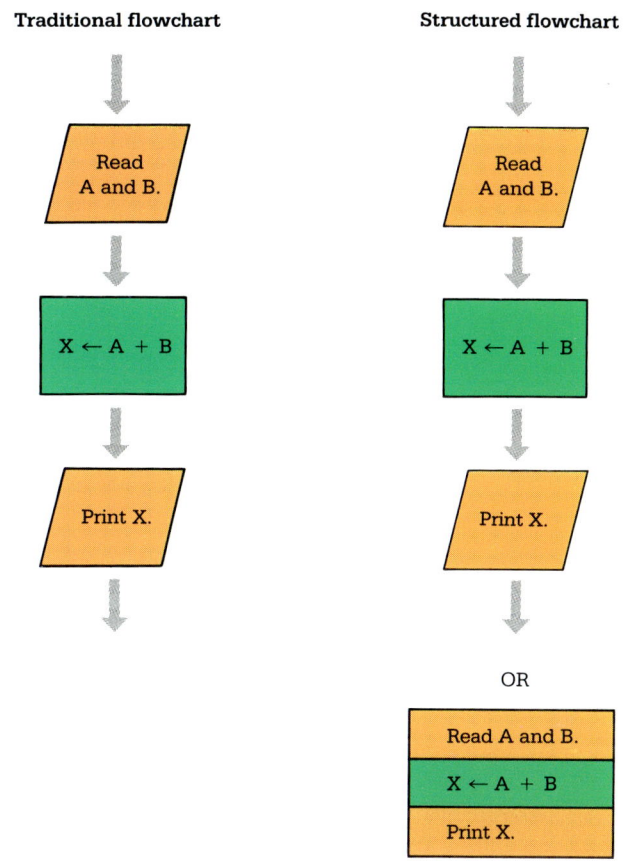

FIGURE 6–6
The sequence structure

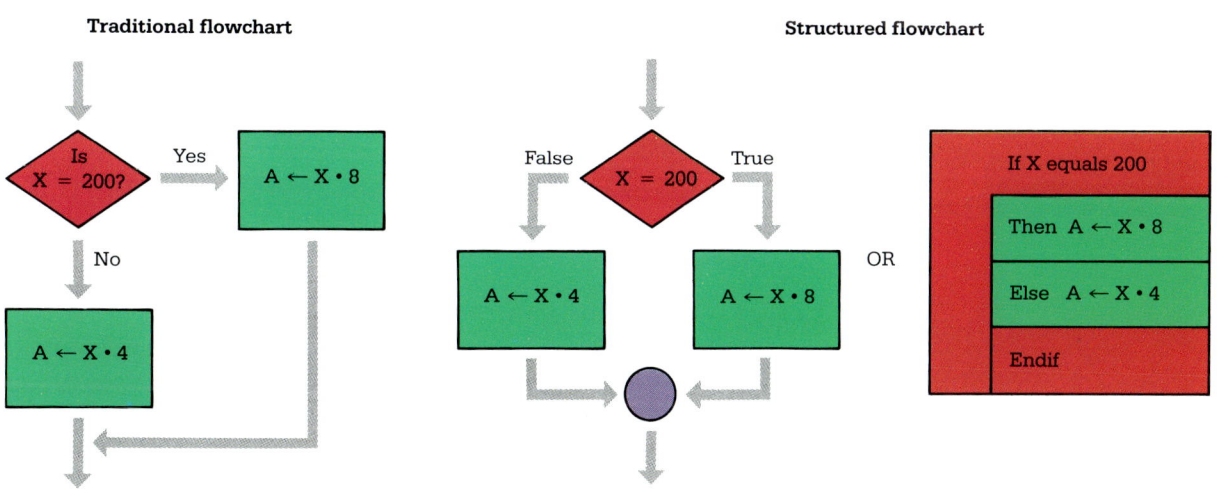

FIGURE 6–7
The selection structure

flowchart box. The ending of the flowchart is the ENDIF box. The looping structure provides for repetitive execution of a function until a condition is reached (Figure 6–8). The beginning of the flowchart for the looping structure is the DO WHILE or the DO UNTIL statement. This statement is followed by a series of actions. After all the actions have been processed in the loop, the structured flowchart ends with the ENDDO box. Let's examine how the three structured flowchart segments can be used together in constructing a structured flowchart.

The procedure shown in Figure 6–9 reads an employee's identification (ID), pay rate, hours worked, and overtime. It then determines and prints the employee's ID and wage and repeats the process for 250 employees. Figure 6–9 illustrates this procedure using both traditional and structured flowcharts.

Decision tables   A decision table is a tabular format for representing the solution to a problem and can be used as an alternative to or an addi-

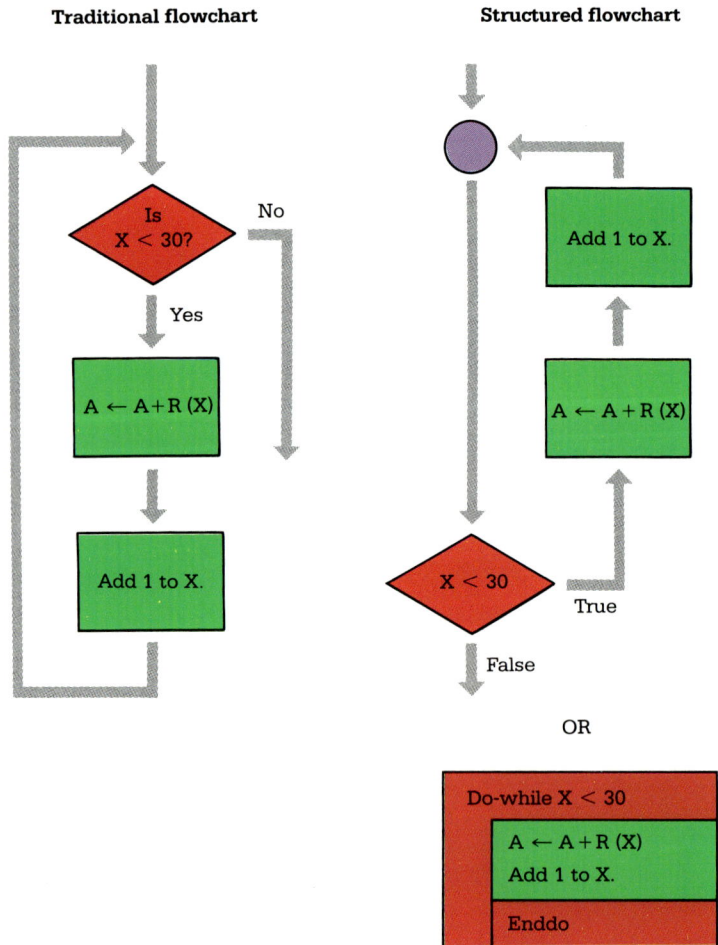

FIGURE 6–8
The looping structure

tion to a flowchart. Decision tables consist of four overlapping major parts, each represented by a rectangle within the overall rectangular shape of the decision table (Figure 6–10). The four parts are the:

☐ Condition portion (upper part)
☐ Action portion (lower part)

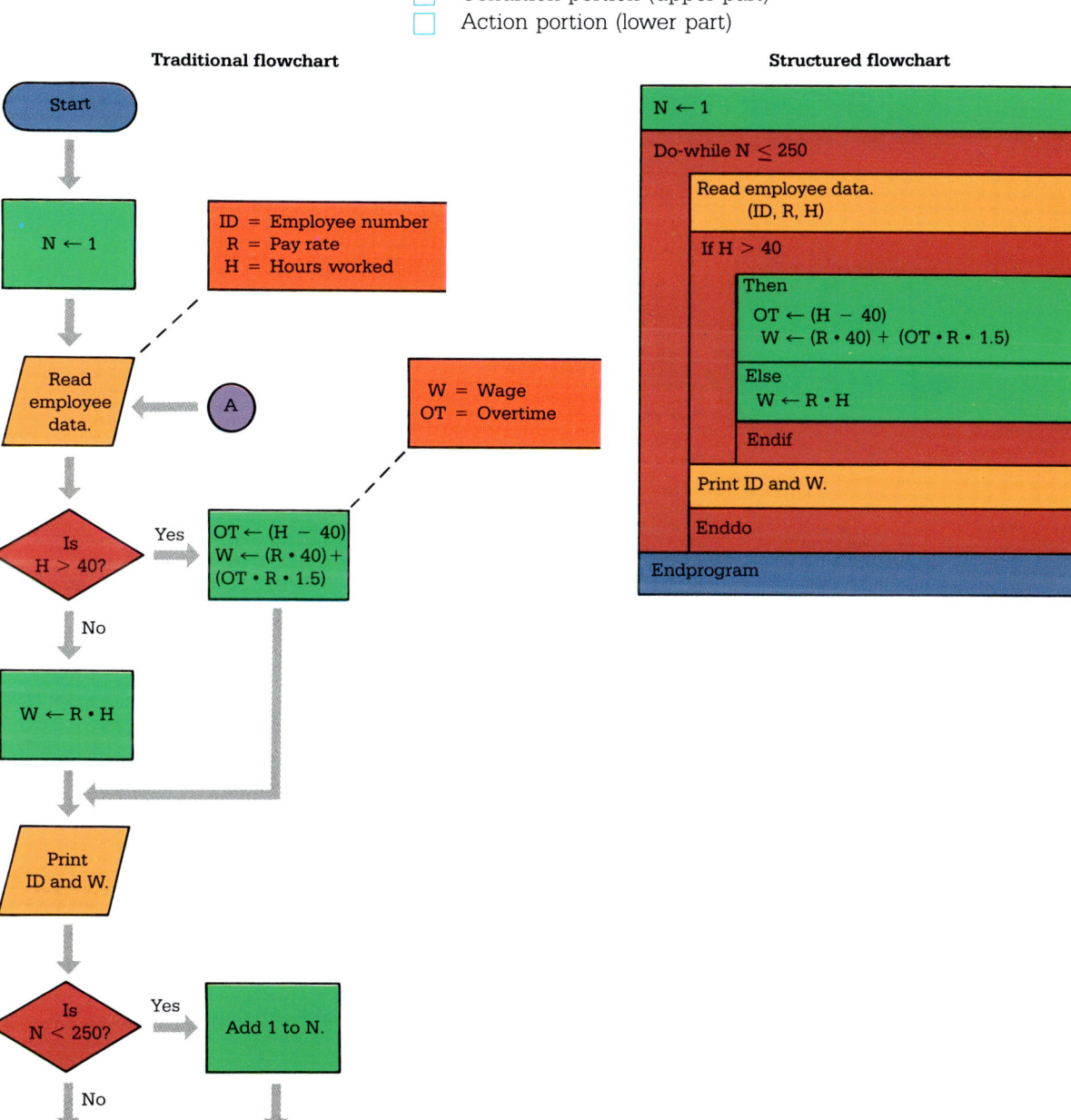

FIGURE 6–9
A wage computation procedure represented by a traditional flowchart and a structured flowchart.

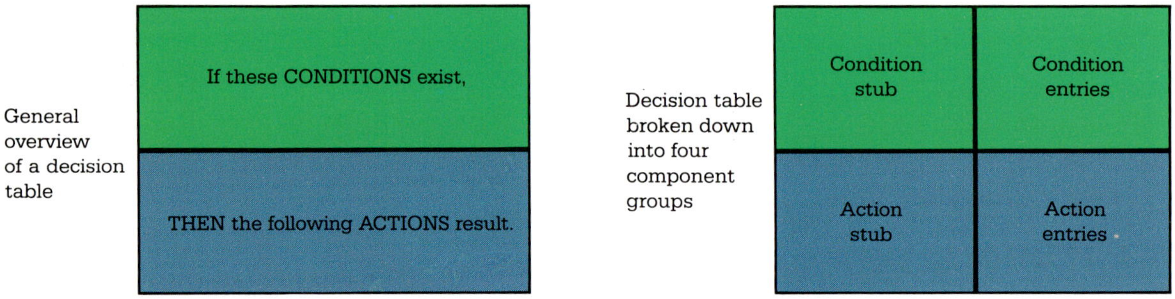

General
overview
of a decision
table

| If these CONDITIONS exist, |
| THEN the following ACTIONS result. |

Decision table
broken down
into four
component
groups

| Condition stub | Condition entries |
| Action stub | Action entries |

FIGURE 6–10
The format of a decision table. The table is divided into halves and subdivided into four sections.

☐ Entry portion (right-hand part)
☐ Stub (left-hand part)

Each column of a decision table is known as a decision rule. Because of the overlap, the upper left-hand portion of a decision table is known as the condition stub; the upper right-hand portion is the condition entry; the lower left-hand portion is the action stub; and the lower right-hand portion is the action entries in the decision rules. The appropriate action to take when a specific condition or combination of conditions exists is called a rule. The rules list the alternative values of conditions and the presence or absence of the actions to be taken. A simple example of a decision table describing a procedure for ordering low-usage products under several conditions is shown in Figure 6–11. A target inventory level has been set at 20 units of stock for items covered by this decision table. Look at the third column from the right in the decision table (Rule #6). If the weekly usage is low (less than 8 units) and the

Condition/Action	Rules							
	1	2	3	4	5	6	7	8
On hand < 20	Y	Y	Y	Y	Y	Y	N	Else
Weekly usage	> 15	> 15	8–15	8–15	8–15	< 8	—	
Local vendor available	—	—	N	N	Y	—	—	
On order > 30	N	Y	N	Y	N	N	Y	
Rush order	X		X					
Regular order		X		X	X	X		
Cancel order							X	
No action								X

FIGURE 6–11
Example of a decision table describing a procedure for ordering low-usage products under several conditions.

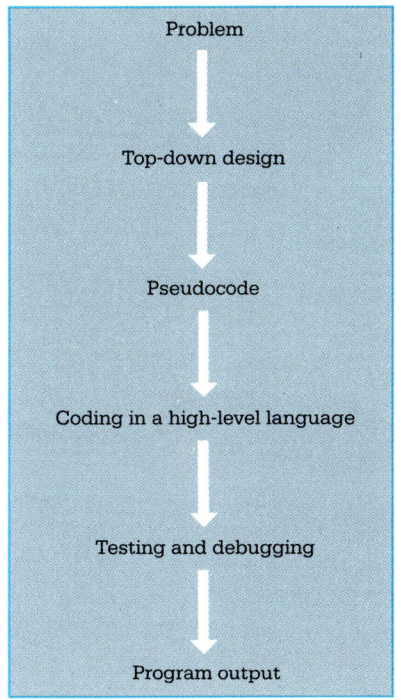

FIGURE 6–12
Role of pseudocode in program design

Problem

Top-down design

Pseudocode

Coding in a high-level language

Testing and debugging

Program output

amount on order is not greater than 30 units, then a regular order should be placed if the stock on hand amounts to less than 20 units.

To use a decision table, an individual first reads the condition stub and notes the input values for each condition. Then he or she matches these values against the condition portion of the decision rules, one rule at a time, from left to right. If the conditions do not match, the user rejects the decision rule, goes to the next rule, and checks for a match. When the rule is found that does match, the user goes to the respective action portion to find out what actions are to be performed and in which sequence. When these actions are complete, the user applies the decision table with a new set of input values for each condition.

Although they are not used as extensively as flowcharts, decision tables have the advantage of serving as a compact way to describe or specify operations. However, decision tables have disadvantages that keep them from being more widely used. Large decision tables become incomprehensible and can neither be checked nor used well. Decision tables do not reduce the labor of thinking; human beings must define, specify, and follow each chain of conditions and actions to its logical consequences.

Pseudocodes   A pseudocode is an imitation, nonexecutable instruction that aids in developing and documenting programs. Pseudocodes allow you to state the logic of the program clearly, ignoring machine constraints. Pseudocodes are often a mixture of language-oriented control key words and program-like statements used to describe an abstract design. For example, if you have not decided how to update a record, you simply indicate "update master record" at the appropriate point. Early stages of pseudocoding emphasize *what* needs to be done and essentially *where* in the overall logic structure. Later efforts expand the early logic by defining variable names, correcting logic flaws, and elaborating necessary lower level code structures. Therefore, the pseudocoding process starts with an abstract design structure and eventually stops with a set of syntax closely approximating a high-level programming language. The overall process proceeds in a top-down manner. Pseudocode basically represents the third step in the program design process (Figure 6–12).

As a simplified example of pseudocode, a sequence can assume that multiple records are read and processed until all data are handled (Figure 6–13). When processing is complete, summaries are produced and the program is terminated. Pseudocode is used to get the program logic correct at the start, before actual coding begins. There are two advantages of pseudocode:

1   Program logic is written so that others can read and understand it.
2   Program logic can be written without programming language or machine restraints.

Variable specification and initialization
Open files.
Read first record.
Do-while there are more data.
          Process data.
          Read next record.
Enddo
Wrap up processing.
Close files.
Stop

FIGURE 6–13
A typical pseudocode sequence

Thus, pseudocode allows you to write a program in structured form before writing it for a specific language or machine.

HIPO charts   HIPO (hierarchy plus input-process-output) charts were originally designed to document the hierarchical nature of a system more efficiently than flowcharts. HIPO charts consist of two parts:

1   The hierarchy chart illustrates how each program function is divided into modules.
2   The input-process-output chart expresses each module in terms of input and output.

The hierarchy chart serves as the overall organization of a program's design (Figure 6–14). Undoubtedly, the most valuable design function of the hierarchy chart tree diagram is the numbering system that enables users to locate and reference the various lower level design details. This reference logic can be maintained in paper documentation as well as subsequent source programs. The input-process-output chart describes what is done in each logical section identified in the hierarchy chart (Figure 6–15).

Like flowcharts, HIPO charts are being refined, expanded, and detailed as program development continues. The process is repeated until the function under development is logically completed. Well-constructed hierarchy and input-process-output charts will lead easily from the de-

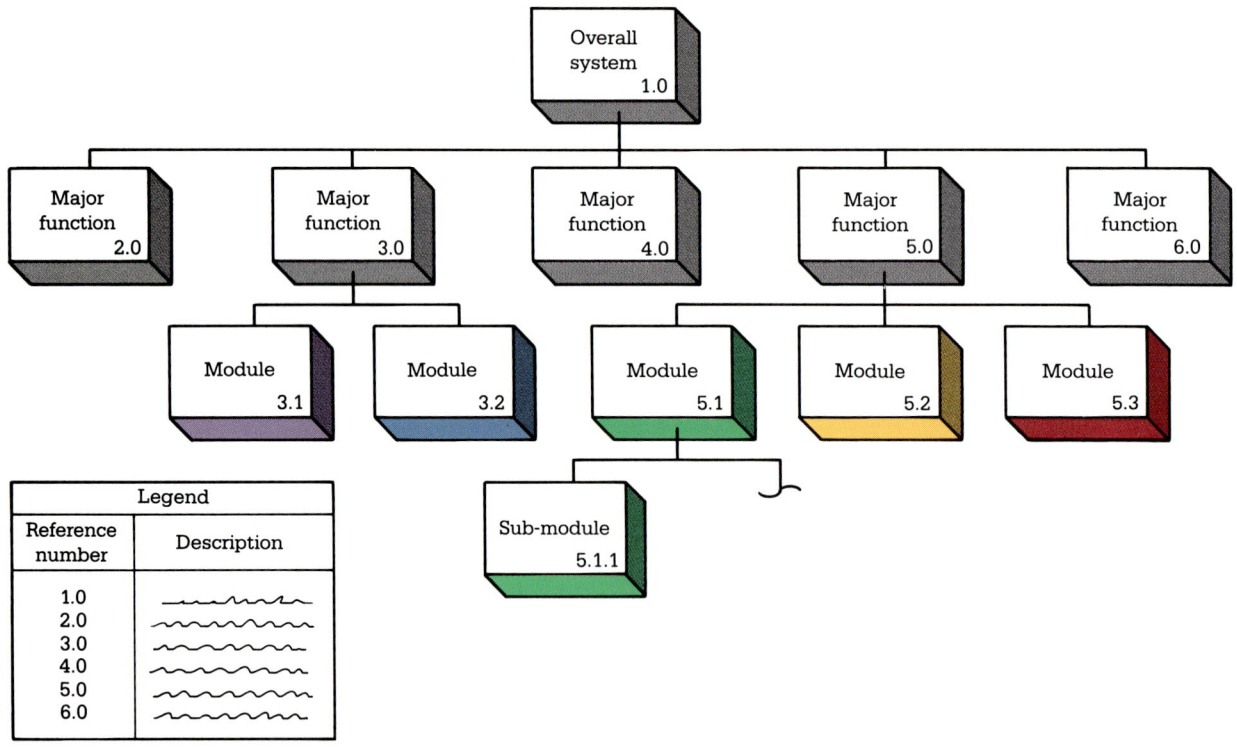

FIGURE 6–14
Example of a HIPO hierarchy chart

FIGURE 6–15
Example of a HIP0 input-process-output chart

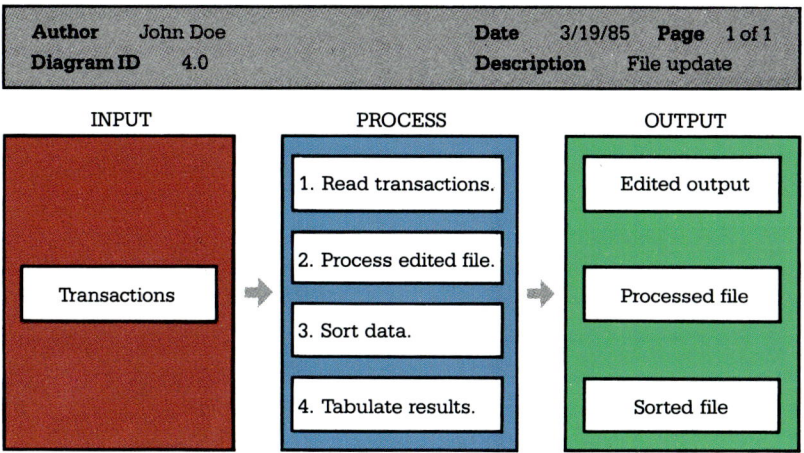

sign through final code. HIPO documentation is a good communication tool for describing the design. Other advantages are that it

☐ Generally supports the overall needs of functional design
☐ Is easier to read and maintain than a flowchart
☐ Enforces top-down and structured design concepts
☐ Supports debugging and testing activities
☐ Provides good documentation

Step Three: Coding the Program

After the algorithm has been developed, it must be changed into instructions the computer understands. The process of changing the steps in an algorithm to instructions written in a programming language is called **coding**.

Programs can be written using a variety of programming languages. Regardless of the language used, the programmer's goal is to reproduce the logic of the program described in the algorithm as economically and efficiently as possible. Some basic guidelines for writing programs follow:

1 Keep the program simple and straightforward.
2 Write the program so future changes and revisions can be made easily.
3 Use comment statements wherever possible to make the program easier to understand.
4 Use meaningful names and labels.
5 Use the simplest features feasible of whatever programming language you are using.
6 Place all inputs, data statements, outputs, program specifications, etc., in their respective groups to simplify finding them in case of change or error.

All the hardware components that make up a computer system can perform no meaningful activity without software. Selecting software is the most important aspect of establishing a satisfactory computer system. Software makes one computer a bookkeeping tool and another identical computer a financial analyst. The right software for an organization can make work easier for both managers and employees; the wrong software can convert the computer into nothing more than an interesting conversation piece.

DETERMINE YOUR NEEDS

Decide exactly what activity is to be computerized. Pre-purchase planning is necessary if a workable system with complementary software is to be found. Reviewing the operation from top to bottom will present a good view of interrelationships among activities. This process can lead to identifying the best activity to computerize. Also consider future plans for your business. Will all of the applications remain the same over the next few years, or will they change? A systems and software plan should follow the business plan very closely, taking into account planned physical expansions, new products, additional staff, and any other factors that may affect the purchase later on. This is a good time to question whether the systems and packages that will be purchased can be expanded or upgraded simply and inexpensively.

WRITING YOUR OWN SOFTWARE

Writing your own programs is possible, but it's rarely practical for business users. Few business users have time to develop elaborate software, and few have the experience to write complex programs that work efficiently. A business user can often develop simplistic programs not worthy of outright purchase, but the major software for complex applications probably should be purchased or written by a software consultant.

SOFTWARE THAT MEETS YOUR REQUIREMENTS

Once you have determined your needs, become informed about available software. *Computerworld, Creative Computing, Byte, Portable Computer*, and dozens of other computer publications provide up-to-date information about available software. Most computer stores will let you use their computers and software for a few hours. During this time, you should determine which system will meet your specific needs. Speak with associates who have experience in buying software. If possible, arrange to drop into their homes or offices to try out the application packages that might meet your needs. Your public library is another information source. Many libraries have computers and application software packages that you may use there. Then make a checklist of "must" features to help you rank different applications packages.

CANNED AND CUSTOM SOFTWARE

Most personal computers are sold with an operating system. Many vendors offer, at additional cost, general-purpose applications software such as payroll, inventory control, word processing, electronic spreadsheets, general ledger, and accounts receivable/payable. These general application packages are called canned or packaged software. Software that is written specifically for a

Software development companies are producing canned software packages for a wide range of applications, including inventory control, word processing, computer graphics, general ledger, payroll, game playing, engineering, electronic spreadsheets, and data base management.

business, either by the vendor's programmers, independent consultants, or computer store programmers, is called custom software. Compared to custom software, canned software is inexpensive, and some vendors offer a wide range of applications including administration, inventory control, medical/dental patient record keeping and billing,

electronic spreadsheet, real estate, word processing, insurance, and graphics programs.

If a business has special needs that cannot be met with a canned applications program, custom software may be needed. Get references from several sources before selecting a software house. Some small software companies set up shop, write some custom software, and then go out of business. Their customers are then stuck with custom software that doesn't work and can't be changed because the person who wrote it is no longer in business. Reliable software houses do exist, however, even though their programmers have good intentions, they may lack the experience required to solve diverse programming problems. In an effort to please a client, they may promise to deliver software within a time frame that does not include the time needed for debugging. If you have selected a reputable software house, its representatives will continue to help you until your software problem is solved.

COMPARING SOFTWARE VENDORS

Canned software packages are closely tied to the vendors that produce them. Therefore, a vend-

or's reputation must be scrutinized as well as the software package's specifications. How long has the vendor been in business, and what are its chances of staying in business? How many software packages has the vendor developed? Does the vendor offer training? Does the vendor offer a warranty arrangement? Does the vendor provide ongoing support by supplying software that reflects changes in usage? How many copies of the software package have been sold? Does the vendor have a vendor/user ''hot line'' for questions? The answers to these and other important questions can often be found in computer publications.

Comparative shopping will eliminate the risk of over-paying for your software. However, don't sacrifice performance or services for the sake of price. Visit as many vendors as possible and gather as many reviews as your time allows. Wait until consistent advice begins to emerge before selecting a software package.

BUNDLED SOFTWARE

Applications software generally may be acquired in four ways: (a) bundled with the computer; (b) purchased separately; (c) written by the user or a consultant; or (d) obtained at no charge from public domain. Bundling software has become popular with computer manufacturers who use the value-added approach of including numerous applications programs to enhance the salability of their product. This approach can save you a considerable amount of money. Some computers now include software that could cost from $2 000 to $3 000 if bought separately. The bundled packages often include a BASIC language processor, word processor, spreadsheet program, and data base manager. On the other hand, some bundled software may not be what you want or need. Perhaps the word processor is too powerful or too weak for your application. Maybe you don't need a data base manager. Therefore, bundled software is a good deal only when the individual packages are those that meet your needs. In addition, bundled software often is not supported by its original developer. Should you wish to update the program later or get help with a problem, you may find that the original software developer won't cooperate because it's not his product anymore, while the computer supplier can't or won't do anything because she didn't originate the program.

Keep in mind that buying a computer without bundled appli-cations software can be unex-pectedly expensive. As a general rule, you can allow from $1 000 to $3 000 above the cost of a personal computer system just to obtain the minimal software you will need. Over a year or so, however, the cost of quality software can more than double the original price of a personal computer system.

IS THE SOFTWARE FRIENDLY?

Applications software, like any product you buy, can have a wide range of quality. A good program is distinguished from a bad program by its ease of use. In other words, it is user-friendly.

You can recognize "friendly" software by its use of menus and dialogues. The menu is a list of activities you can perform; dialogue refers to the questions the program will display. One beneficial feature to look for provides operator instruction. If an operator isn't sure what to do next, executing the instruction function will produce a display that describes all the menu selections in detail. Thoughtfully designed business programs also have a "help" feature. An operator can type HELP and see a display on the screen explaining everything that happens at that point in the

In 1977, there were fewer than 150 computer stores. Today, there are nearly 3 000 with over 7 000 expected by 1990. In addition to computer stores, software packages can be purchased at many department stores, mail order houses, and software stores. Program World is a store that specializes in computer software; no computers are sold there. Approximately 400 stores of this kind are located throughout the United States.

program. A good business program also won't let you accidentally delete data you didn't intend to delete.

Business software should respond quickly with dialogue messages and not take a long time to process or retrieve data. Generally, if there is a noticeable response lag after data are entered, the program is not adapted properly to the machine's capabilities. However, sometimes there are other reasons why the program cannot respond instantly. For example, the computer might require several minutes to perform

TYPES OF PROGRAMMING LANGUAGES

The computer cannot even add 2 + 2 until it is directed to do so by a program. Programming involves writing a set of instructions in a sequence that produces a desired result when the sequence is executed by the computer. These instructions are stored in the computer's main memory, as are the data on which these operations are performed.

Writing sequences of instruction is called coding. Coding can take place on various levels. The different levels of coding are:

1 Machine language
2 Assembly language
3 High-level language
4 Natural language

All coding levels except machine language are symbolic and must be translated into machine language instructions. The computer operates at the level of machine coding, therefore, all other codes must eventually be translated into that form. Symbolic coding involves programming a computer to recognize instructions in a language more easily understood by the user and then translating these expressions into machine language. This coding has led to the development of different symbolic programming languages that are easy to use.

Machine Language

Machine language is the common language of a particular computer and does not require further modification before being executed. A program written in machine language is a sequence of binary numbers (1's and 0's). Once the problem is defined, the programmer codes the operation using codes the computer can interpret. Machine languages require users to have a thorough knowledge of the computer's intricate details; therefore, few people write programs in machine language.

Assembly Language

Assembly language is a low-level symbolic language used to develop programs that must go through an assembly to be converted into a machine code necessary to operate the computer. It closely resembles the computer's machine code rather than the language of a problem. Programming in an assembly language offers these advantages over machine code:

☐ All operations are given mnemonic designations. For example, the actual operation for coding the instruction "add" may be 100110. In assembly language, users need only write the mnemonic operation code ADD.

☐ All data and machine addresses in assembly commands are written using symbolic notation, thus relieving users of potential problems in allocating computer storage.

☐ Because symbols are meaningful, the program is easier to read and understand.

Use of assembly languages also has its disadvantages.

□ A line of machine language must be written for each instruction. Large programs would require thousands of lines of assembly language.

□ Assembly language requires users to know the internal operational characteristics of the computer before a program can be written.

□ An assembly language program cannot be executed directly by a computer. First, the mnemonic operation codes and symbolic addresses must be translated into a form the machine can use. This is the function of the **assembler**.

High-level Language

Unlike assembly and machine languages, which are highly dependent on a particular hardware system, high-level languages are relatively machine-independent because they relate to the procedures being coded. Therefore, a program coded in a high-level language can be executed on any computer system that has a translator for that programming language.

Programs written in high-level language are translated into the machine language of the computer by compilers or interpreters. **Compilers** translate the program, written in a high-level language called a source document, into the equivalent machine code program understood by the computer. Compilers complete their work before any computation begins (Figure 6–17). In fact, the entire machine code program is stored before any part of it is executed.

Interpreters translate each statement of a program each time the statement is executed. An interpreter's capabilities become apparent when the program contains a syntax error (misspelled word, incorrect instruction name, too many commas, etc.) because the computer signals the user that an error has been found so it can be corrected immediately. Interpreters are widely used on microcomputer and interactive time-sharing systems.

Compilers and interpreters are usually lengthy programs that can occupy a major portion of a small computer's memory. Many microcomputers have implemented programming language interpreters in ROM to provide for more user storage.

Natural Language

Natural language processing attempts to make computers understand spoken languages such as English, French, or Spanish. Natural languages are nonprocedural; they don't require users to write detailed procedures directing the computer. Instead, they allow users to tell the computer what they want. "Intelligent" compilers then translate the natural language requests into a series of operations that direct the computer.

About 80 percent of one language can be translated into another without problems, but differences in syntax make it almost impossible to

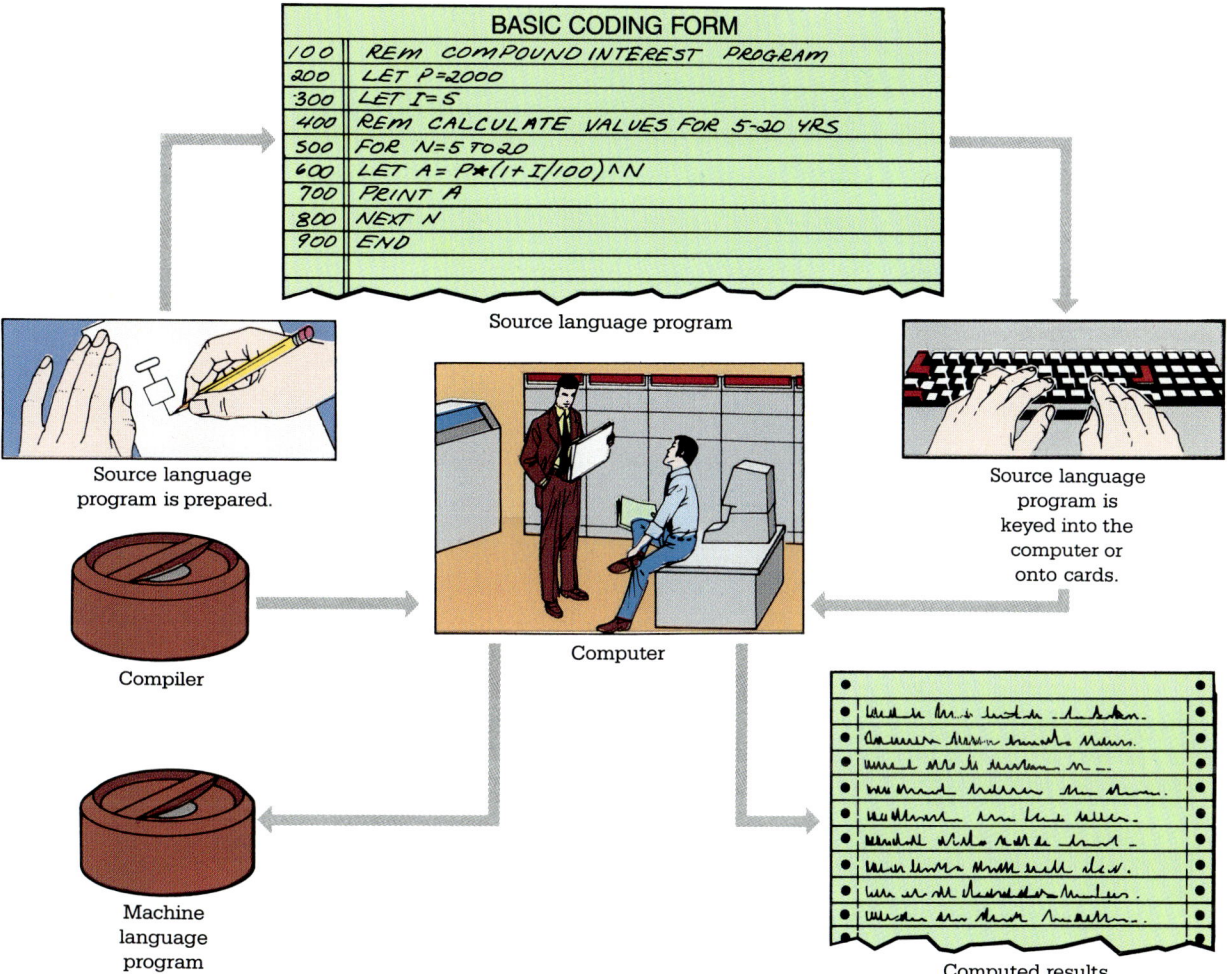

FIGURE 6–17
Creating, computing, and executing a program written in a high-level language

process the remaining 20 percent with computers. It will probably be some time before meaningful language translations can be made solely by computer.

Query languages and data manipulating languages are natural languages that allow users to interrogate and access computer data bases with English statements such as

- ☐ Show the statistics for family income and size in California and New York
- ☐ Correlate salary to years of service for all employees over age 40
- ☐ Produce a bar chart of the top 20 sales people in 1985

A QUICK LOOK AT SOME HIGH-LEVEL LANGUAGES

The major high-level programming languages are BASIC, COBOL, Pascal, FORTRAN, Ada, and RPG. These languages were developed by computer manufacturers, universities, committees, and individuals to make computers more accessible to users.

BASIC

BASIC is an acronym for beginner's all-purpose symbolic instruction code and was developed primarily for interactive computing on time-sharing systems by those with little or no computer experience. Today, BASIC is available on all time-sharing computer systems, most minicomputers, many medium- and large-scale machines, and almost all microcomputers.

The BASIC language consists of about 20 statement types such as GOTO, LET, PRINT, READ, and END. Each statement in BASIC has a number that identifies the line and specifies the order in which the statements are executed. To use BASIC, the user simply types the program (or enters it via disk or tape) into the terminal and issues a RUN command to execute it. Program answers are produced immediately.

Consider a program for computing the compound interest of an initial bank deposit of $2 000 invested at 7 percent interest for 5 to 20 years. The compound interest formula is

$$A = P \left(1 + \frac{I}{100} \right)^N$$

P is the principal (amount originally invested); I is the yearly rate of interest; N is the number of years; and A is the amount (P + I). A BASIC program for solving this problem is shown below.

```
100 REM***COMPOUND INTEREST PROGRAM***
200 LET P = 2000
300 LET I = 7
400 REM***CALCULATE VALUES FOR 5-20 YEARS***
500 FOR N = 5 TO 20
600 LET A = P*(1 + I/100) ^ N
700 PRINT "IN";N;"YEARS, THE AMOUNT WILL BE";A
800 NEXT N
900 END
```

COBOL

COBOL is an acronym for common business oriented language and is internationally accepted as the programming language for general commercial and business use. It is a high-level compiler language in which the source program is written using statements in restricted English but in readable form. A program coded in COBOL bears little resemblance to machine code. For example, an accounting program might contain the COBOL statement: ADD RECEIPTS TO STOCK ON HAND. The COBOL compiler would analyze each word of the statement separately and then generate several machine code instructions to carry out the calculation. The compiler would perform the following analysis.

- ADD becomes an operating instruction.
- RECEIPTS is a location of data.
- TO directs attention to what follows, (i.e., STOCK ON HAND).
- STOCK ON HAND represents data in storage.

Each COBOL program has four major divisions:

1 Identification—lists the programmer's name, program name, outputs of compilation, date, location, and security classification of the compilation
2 Environment—identifies the equipment needed for compiling the source program and for executing the machine language
3 Data—describes the files and records that the object program is to manipulate or create
4 Procedures—tells the computer the steps to be performed to solve the problem using data described in the data division

COBOL uses many reserved words that have special meaning to the COBOL compiler and must be used according to COBOL language rules. There are about 250 reserved words that are an inherent part of COBOL and are not available for use as data or procedure names. In the statement ADD OVERTIME TO NORMAL HOURS, the reserved words are ADD and TO; they instruct the COBOL compiler to generate the machine code necessary to perform addition. OVERTIME and NORMAL HOURS (defined in the data division) are names or labels referring to units of data.

Because of its similarity to English, a COBOL program can be read easily by nonprogrammers. Since COBOL programs are relatively machine-independent, they can be compiled and run on many different machines.

Pascal

Pascal, named after the famous French mathematician Blaise Pascal, was developed in 1968 by Niklaus Wirth of Zurich, Switzerland. Originally used in universities because of its simplicity, precision, and readability, Pascal is now widely used in business and science.

Pascal is a structured language requiring certain regularities of format and program design. The term "structured" has many other connotations, mostly having to do with the way programs are designed, written, and run. Structured programs are generally composed of blocks of code which can be viewed as complete units independent of the program in which they are used. Pascal was the first major new language developed after structured programming was introduced.

A Pascal program is made up of one or more of these blocks. A heading names the block and gives the parameters it uses. Every block has two main parts—one for definitions and one for program logic. The part for definitions may have up to five specific sections that describe everything before the program logic is presented. The sections specify labels, constants, data types, variables, and subroutines.

The program logic, in what is called the statement, is the actual algorithmic expression of the block in program code. Thus, data definitions in Pascal are segregated from the algorithm. As a result of Pascal design features, programs written in this language tend to be more straightforward in design, making them easier to code, debug, and maintain. The following is a Pascal program that adds two numbers and prints the result.

```
program add (input, output);
var
  first, second, sum: integer;
begin
  read (first, second);
  sum: = first + second;
  write (sum)
end.
```

The first line of the program contains the word *program*—the first word in all Pascal programs. It is followed by *add*, which is the name of the program. After the name comes the relationship between the program and its environment. The word *input* indicates that the program will request data; *output* indicates that the original will generate results. There are three instructions: (a) *read (first, second)*; (b) *sum: = first + second*; and (c) *write (sum)*. These instructions will be executed sequentially one after the other. The words *begin* and *end* act as brackets around an instruction sequence. (This program contains only one such sequence and therefore only one begin-end pair.) More complicated programs contain many instruction sequences, each bracketed by *begin* and *end*.

Unless otherwise specified, program instructions are executed left to right and top to bottom. Thus, program *add* takes two integers from the data and assigns them to *first* and *second* respectively, then adds these two values together, places the result in *sum*, and prints the value of *sum* in the output.

FORTRAN

An acronym for formula translation, FORTRAN is a high-level language for scientific and mathematical use. FORTRAN source programs are written using a combination of algebraic formulas and English statements of

LOGO has been called the "educational language of the future" with good reason. One explanation for its increasing popularity in the classroom is that LOGO is more than just another computer language; it also represents a philosophy of education. Developed by Seymour Papert, LOGO is a first cousin of LISP (list processing), an artificial intelligence language. It combines some of LISP's programming techniques with learning theories. LOGO's most common educational applications have been teaching geometry and designing graphics by moving a turtle around the display screen in response to keyboard commands. The language can also be used to compose music, manage data, build sentences, write poetry, and practice arithmetic.

a standard but readable form. As with other programming languages, the source program written in FORTRAN defines the operations to be performed.

FORTRAN consists largely of mathematical notations similar to those used in algebra. For example, the mathematical expression

$$y = 3x^3 - 4x^2 + 12x - 34$$

is represented in FORTRAN as

```
Y = 3.*X**3 - 4.*X**2 + 12.*X - 34
```

The symbol for multiplication is an asterisk (*), and the symbol for exponentiation is a double asterisk (**). Other arithmetic operators in FORTRAN are addition (+), subtraction (−), and division (/).

Consider the following problem. An airplane flying at altitude A passes directly over a point P. If its speed is S, compute its distance from point P at times T = 1,2,3 . . . . . . 60 seconds after the pass. The distance traveled by the airplane after passing over P is S × T, and the required distance is D. The formula

$$D = \sqrt{A^2 + (S \times T)^2}$$

can be used to compute the required distance. This is a sample FORTRAN program

```
C    AIRPLANE DISTANCE COMPUTATION
     S = 1.0
     A = 3.0
     I = 0
10   I = I + 1
     T = I
     D = SORT (A**2 + (S*T) **2)
     WRITE (6,20) T, D
20   FORMAT (F5.0,F10.3)
     IF (I .LT. 60) GOTO 10
     STOP
     END
```

An examination of this program points out that FORTRAN may be more useful to mathematicians and engineers than to programmers seeking business solutions. Nevertheless, FORTRAN is used by many businesses to solve commercial problems.

Ada

Ada is a programming language for numerical and systems programming applications. Developed at the initiative of the U.S. Department of Defense (DOD) to satisfy programming needs of military and aerospace systems, Ada was designed in France and evaluated by many industrial and military application programming teams. It is a general purpose language that may become a very popular DOD programming language during the late 1980s and 1990s.

Aimed at reducing cost and improving reliability of large programs such as those required to control military systems, Ada is similar to Pascal and easy to read. The following procedure reads two numbers, computes their sum, and prints the results.

```
Procedure ADD
  X, Y, Z: INTEGER;
begin
  GET (X);
  GET (Y);
  Z: = X + Y;
  PUT (Z);
end ADD;
```

The first line of this program specifies that this program is a *procedure* named *ADD*. The second line declares the three identifiers *X, Y,* and *Z* to be integer variables. These two lines together constitute the declarative part of the procedure and are followed by a sequence of executable statements enclosed by the words *begin* and *end*. The statement sequence contains two input statements which read data from an input medium into *X* and *Y,* an assignment statement which computes the sum of *X* and *Y,* and an output statement which prints the result.

RPG

RPG (report program generator) is a high-level programming language designed to process business data and provide business reports. It facilitates preparation of computer programs by those who want to concentrate more on the problem to be treated by the computer system than on the details of specific procedures for solving the problem.

RPG programs are written on specification sheets. The RPG compiler reads the program specifications written in the RPG symbolic language and produces an object program in machine language that can be used to perform a particular application. Preparing an RPG program is not the same as preparing one using BASIC, FORTRAN, or COBOL. The logic of an RPG program is predetermined and the user is concerned with only four basic considerations:

☐ The general nature of the data files to be processed
☐ The specific nature of the input data
☐ The specific nature of the output data
☐ The calculations that must be performed on the input data to produce the output results

RPG is a powerful and quick language for updating files and producing reports. It is not suitable for scientific applications, but commercial users who process business applications on small-scale computers have found it to be an extremely valuable language.

SUMMARY

- ☐ Programming is the process of producing a set of instructions for a computer to make it perform some specified task. The set of instructions produced is a program.

- ☐ The stages required in developing a program are defining the problem, designing the program, coding the program, executing the program, debugging the program, testing the program, documenting the program, and program maintenance.

- ☐ Here are the steps taken to solve a problem: (a) User studies the problem and prepares a plan of action. (b) Programmer decides what steps the computer must take and specifies input and output. (c) Plan of action is coded into programming steps. (d) Instructions are keyed into the computer. (e) Inside the computer, the program is translated into machine language by a compiler, interpreter, or assembler. (f) The program is executed by the computer, and output is generated.

- ☐ Top-down program design is the process of breaking a large, complicated problem down into a series of smaller easier-to-solve problems.

- ☐ An algorithm is a set of rules or a plan for the solution of a problem. Algorithms can be presented as flowcharts, pseudocodes, decision tables, or HIPO charts.

- ☐ Structured flowcharting is a method of representing problem solutions in terms of three flowchart structures: sequence, selection, and loop.

- ☐ Decision tables serve as a compact way to describe or specify operations. Because large decision tables can become incomprehensible, they are not used as often as flowcharts.

- ☐ Pseudocode is a code, using English, that allows program logic to be expressed in an easily readable manner.

- ☐ HIPO (hierarchy plus input-process-output) charts were designed to document the hierarchical nature of a system in a more efficient manner than flowcharts.

- ☐ The physical equipment that makes up a computer system is called hardware. Programs that instruct and guide the operations of the computer and peripheral devices are called software.

- ☐ Two basic types of software are systems software and applications software. Systems software include language translators, text editors, and operating systems. Applications software are programs developed to solve a single problem (e.g., a payroll or chess program).

- ☐ Writing sequences of instructions is called coding. Coding can take place at four different levels: machine language, assembly language, high-level language, and natural language.

- ☐ Major high-level languages include BASIC, COBOL, Pascal, FORTRAN, Ada, and RPG.

REVIEW QUESTIONS

True or False

1 An algorithm is another name for a computer program.

2 The size of a flowchart symbol, not its shape, determines its meaning.

_____ **3** A set of instructions that controls the computer is called an algorithm.

_____ **4** A flowchart is a verbal description of how the computer will solve a problem.

_____ **5** Once a computer program has been written, translated, and stored in computer memory, it cannot be modified by the programmer.

_____ **6** Flowcharts are usually drawn after the problem has been coded and run on the computer.

_____ **7** It is not possible to use the computer as an aid in developing computer programs, i.e., helping the programmer code and check out his problem.

_____ **8** A set of instructions must be prepared before computer processing can take place.

_____ **9** A flowchart shows the relationship of one part of the program to another.

_____ **10** A flowchart may be drawn before the problem is analyzed.

_____ **11** Developing programs for computer systems is expensive. In fact, over a long period of time, it may cost more to develop application software than it originally cost to purchase the computing hardware.

_____ **12** The recommended procedure in preparing a program is first to code the program in a programming language, then to prepare the flowchart for documentation purposes.

_____ **13** Since program debugging is often a time-consuming task, it is normally done only if time permits.

_____ **14** A diagnostic message from a compiler or assembler often indicates that the program contains incorrect logic or a possible program mistake.

_____ **15** A program is generally considered to be free of mistakes when a comprehensive set of test data has been run, producing correct results.

_____ **16** A HIPO chart is used to provide an orderly approach to program development.

_____ **17** A decision table is a technique used to debug programs.

_____ **18** Program flowcharts evolve from decision tables.

_____ **19** A HIPO chart is a special type of decision table.

_____ **20** Pseudocode means the same thing as compiler code.

_____ **21** The hierarchy chart is one part of a HIPO chart.

_____ **22** The basic theory of top-down design is to break large programs into smaller, more manageable components.

_____ **23** The concept of pseudocode involves solving a problem by successively refining English statements into computer code.

_____ **24** Writing programs in machine language code requires a thorough knowledge of the computer being used.

_____ **25** Two types of symbolic languages are assembler languages and high-level languages.

_____ **26** A program written in symbolic language is called machine code.

_____ **27** The source program is the program that is executed by the computer.

_____ **28** An assembler is used to translate assembly language programs into code that the computer can understand and execute.

_____ **29** Assembler languages are considered high-level languages.

_____ **30** High-level programming languages require an extensive knowledge of HIPO charts.
_____ **31** COBOL is mathematically or scientifically oriented.
_____ **32** FORTRAN is an assembler language.
_____ **33** The entire collection of systems programs is called the operating system.

Short Answer

1 An _____ is a set of rules or a plan for the solution of a problem.

2 The process of understanding the problem is called _____.

3 A _____ is a pictorial view of how the computer will solve a problem.

4 _____ is the process of converting the steps in the algorithm to a set of instructions written in a programming language.

5 The process of running a program on a computer is called _____ _____.

6 Regardless of the programming language used to write a program, it will ultimately have to be converted to _____ _____.

7 The forms, algorithms, program listings, and problem statements associated with a program are commonly called _____.

8 Error messages are also called _____.

9 The objective of _____ _____ is to keep the program functioning at an acceptable level.

10 _____ _____ _____ is the process of going from a large, complicated program to a series of smaller problems, each having a greater probability of being solvable than the original problem, i.e., breaking down complex problems into many easier-to-handle subsystems.

11 A _____ _____ is a tabular format for representing the solution to a problem.

12 _____ is an imitation, nonexecutable instruction used as an aid for developing and documenting structured programs.

13 _____ _____ is a method of representing problem solutions in terms of three flowcharting structures.

14 _____ is a plain language alternate to flowcharting.

15 The four levels of producing programs are _____ language, _____ language, _____ language and _____ language.

16 Top-down programming essentially means proceeding by refinement from the highest level down to the _____ _____.

17 A _____ language program must first be translated into a machine language program before it can be executed.

18 Major high-level languages are _____, _____, _____, and _____.

19 A program that is easy-to-use is sometimes referred to as a _____ _____ program.

7 COMPUTER GRAPHICS

OUTLINE

COMPUTER GRAPHICS APPLICATIONS

COMPUTER GRAPHICS FOR BUSINESS

INPUT AND OUTPUT DEVICES

GRAPHICS SOFTWARE

DESIGNING EFFECTIVE BUSINESS GRAPHICS

A COLORFUL FUTURE FOR BUSINESS GRAPHICS

WordStar—King of the Word Processing Systems

OBJECTIVES

1. Explain the importance of computer graphics.
2. Identify some of the areas where computer graphics are used.
3. Identify the three basic types of graphics hardware systems.
4. Identify several input and output devices used with graphics systems.
5. Identify some of the future uses of business graphics.

hy do many people relate better to pictures than to words? One theory is that pictures are processed differently in the brain. The human brain is divided into two hemispheres, with the left side doing the analytical work and the right side doing the perceptual work. Because pictures are initially processed by the right hemisphere, then passed to the left side for analysis, more of the brain is involved in handling pictures than words and numbers. Processing by both sides of the brain may account for the increased understanding and better recall of pictorial information.

The tabular report shown in Figure 7–1 and the graph shown in Figure 7–2 illustrate the difference a graphical presentation can make. To determine the health of the company shown in the tabular report would require a great deal of analysis. Are sales improving? What's happening to profits as a function of sales? How does the inventory relate to sales and profits? The answers to these questions quickly reveal themselves in the simple linear chart in Figure 7–2. In a matter of seconds, you see that sales are relatively flat in the second half of 1985, and inventory increased steadily before finally leveling off. As inventory rose, sales leveled off and profits began to slide. You were able to spot important trends that would have taken you much longer without the use of graphics. By using your brain's power to visualize, you were able to speed up your understanding

Month	Monthly Sales	Inventory	Profits
1	78	25	7
2	84	30	10
3	96	33	8
4	85	26	11
5	97	39	15
6	90	33	13
7	97	42	18
8	110	49	24
9	98	41	27
10	102	54	32
11	109	49	28
12	97	56	32
13	102	54	25
14	99	61	27
15	112	64	30
16	117	59	23
17	102	65	27
18	125	58	25
19	117	62	30
20	130	57	27
21	140	60	30
22	110	55	25
23	119	61	22
24	130	50	27

FIGURE 7–1
Table of data values for sales, inventory, and profits.

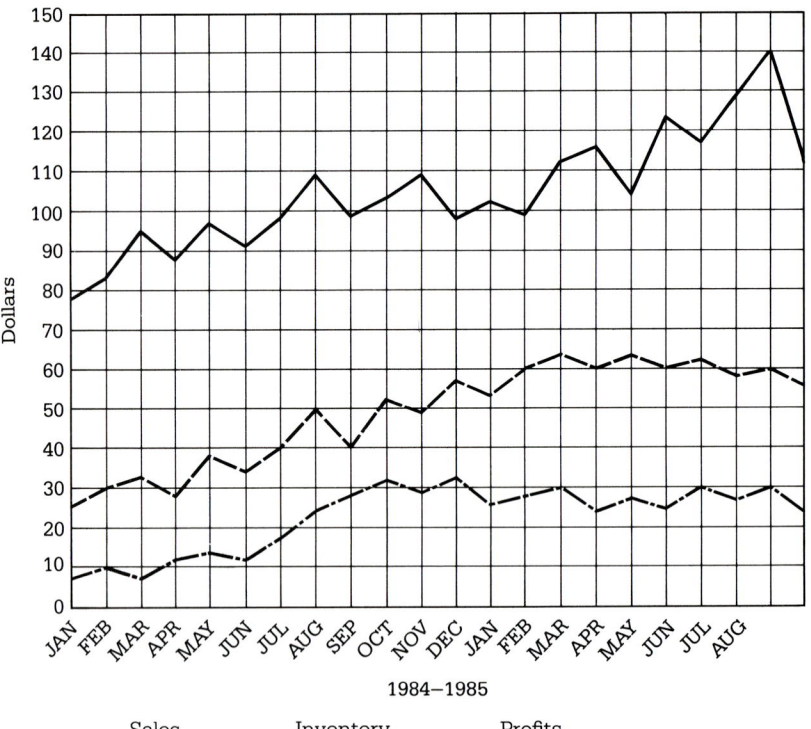

FIGURE 7–2
A graphic representation of the data values shown in Figure 7–1.

because the chart presented you with information extracted from the data of the written report.

Based on your own experience in reading the two versions of the company's report, you should understand why graphics is the fastest growing area in computer software. Computer graphics displays make the conveying of information faster, easier, and more interesting. They enhance meetings by making individuals sit up and take notice; they cut through the verbiage of lengthy reports to show results concisely. Displays become easier to understand with the addition of color (Figure 7–3).

COMPUTER GRAPHICS APPLICATIONS

Computer graphics technology has moved so rapidly in the past few years that it has outpaced our ability to apply it. The kind of knowledge needed to produce professional, high quality computer imagery is very sophisticated, therefore, well trained people are always in demand. Among other duties, to generate a picture, a programmer must give the computer the: measurements, colors, and reflective properties of the objects in the environment; point of view of the imaginary camera (close up, zoom, etc.); and locations of any light source in terms of X (horizontal), Y (vertical), and Z (depth) coordinates. Creating effective, sophisticated graphics from the ground up is a costly, time-consuming process. For example, the animation in *Tron*, a 1982 Disney film, took 15 minutes per frame to produce.

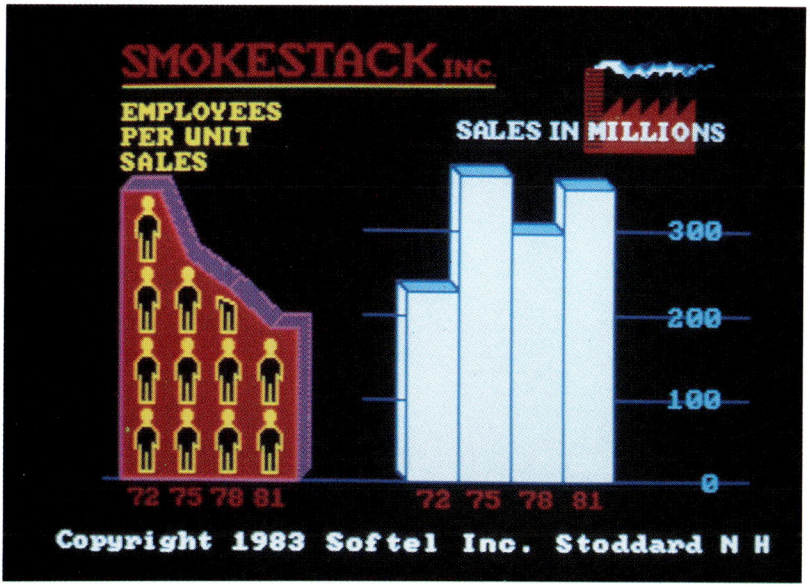

FIGURE 7–3
The use of color in this bar graph enhances the viewer's ability to gather pertinent information. (Courtesy Lang Systems and Softel)

From this very brief description, you can see that the average person has neither the time, training, or equipment to produce his or her own professional quality graphics. More good computer graphics software packages are needed so that the average person can simply follow written documentation or on-screen commands to produce useful graphics. The following discussion will give you an idea of how computer graphics is used in various fields.

Medicine

Computer graphics systems are used to present biomedical information for research, diagnosis, and treatment planning. Perhaps one of the greatest medical breakthroughs has been the development of computerized axial tomography scans (CAT or CT), three dimensional computer images of the human body's internal structures. CAT scans provide doctors with a noninvasive method of diagnosis on which to base their treatment of tissue-related diseases such as breast cancer. Nuclear magnetic resonance (NMR) scanners are also being used in some hospitals for the same purposes.

Computer graphics is also used in interactive surgical planning. By manipulating the three-dimensional image of organs shown on the computer screen, surgeons can plan and test various procedures before they enter the operating room. This capacity to try various surgical solutions to risky procedures has made computer graphics an invaluable aid.

CAT scans and interactive surgical planning are only two of many ways that computer graphics is used in the medical field to save time, money, and lives (Figure 7–4). Nearly 25 percent of the examinations in radiology departments of major hospitals are digitally formatted so that the information can be processed by a computer or computer-controlled device. This percentage will rise to 50 percent by the late 1980s, according to Dr. Samuel J. Dwyer, a professor of diagnostic radiology at the University of Kansas Medical Center.

Engineering

Executives at General Motors predict that by 1990 nearly all the new machines in their manufacturing and assembly plants will be controlled by computer. Computer-aided design enables engineers at General Motors and other plants to use computer capabilities to create, transform, and display pictorial and symbolic data (Figure 7–5). Engineers use CAD to analyze the structural designs of buildings, bridges, and spacecraft. What is the maximum stress a building can withstand? What is the most efficient design for a bridge? How can a spaceship be made even more durable? CAD helps engineers answer these and many other questions necessary for designing safe, comfortable, and utilitarian equipment for human use. It also organizes and transforms masses of often unintelligible raw data into meaningful information essential for manufacturing.

Not only do engineers design cars and trucks while sitting at graphics terminals, they also use the computer to evaluate the structural characteristics of their designs. The computer makes it possible to put to-

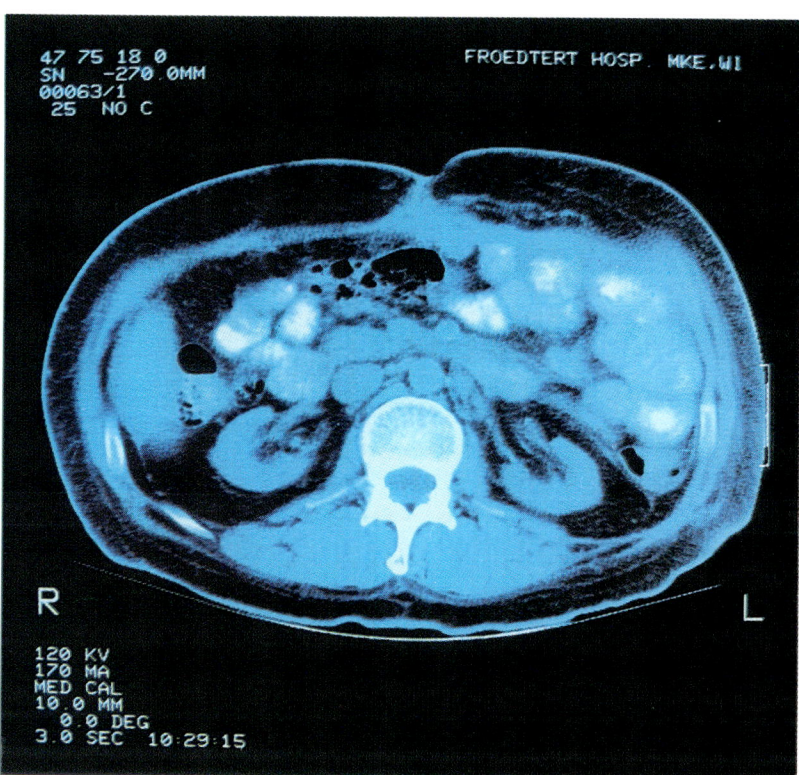

FIGURE 7–4
Computer axial tomography (CAT) is a nonsurgical means of examining the body through the external application of X rays. A CAT scanner consists of an X-ray tube and a detector, mounted on opposite sides of a patient and rotating around the patient's body, snapping scores of X-ray pictures in a matter of minutes. A computer processes the individual snapshots and produces a cross-sectional view of the patient's body on a video screen. (Courtesy of General Electric Co.)

gether mathematical models of the vehicle's various components and then run the models through computer simulated road tests long before actual test cars are manufactured.

One of the newest and most important fields in computer graphics is computer-aided design/computer-aided manufacture (CAD/CAM). CAD/CAM applications combine design and manufacturing techniques by involving conceptualization, design, and dimensioning of an object interactively on a display terminal and then transferring it directly to the manufacturing process. CAD/CAM systems are used by mechanical engineers to generate mechanical drawings, by topographers to generate maps, and by architects and other professionals to generate test models that can later be built or manufactured.

Another example of the use of CAD/CAM is the development and manufacturing of the printed circuit (PC) board layout required for electronic devices. PC boards can be designed on display terminals with components shown in the desired location and interconnections automatically routed for optimum circuit function and manufacturability. In

FIGURE 7–5
Engineers use graphics terminals to design products. (Courtesy of General Electric Co.)

addition to full computer-aided design, sophisticated CAD/CAM systems perform design rule checks and provide machine readable output suitable for manufacturing the finished PC board (Figure 7–6). This output is then used as input to the automated equipment to manufacture PC board blanks and drilling boards, perform the photolithography, and automate the loading of components on the PC board.

Sophisticated CAD/CAM systems can cost as much as $600 000, but despite the cost, the number of systems in use is growing by 30 percent annually. Because of their contribution to increased productivity, the systems typically pay for themselves within two years.

Aircraft Simulation

Simulations are models of real world systems used to solve problems and evaluate strategies for operating the final product. Because of the seemingly endless list of interacting variables that comprise events in life, aircraft and spacecraft simulations, used to train pilots and astronauts, are among the most difficult software to create. These simulations must be sufficiently realistic to provide all the visual cues necessary for pilot training, and they must be generated fast enough to simulate motion.

These complete environment simulators are usually mounted on hydraulic legs to simulate movement. They include a large screen, like a windshield, on which a mind-boggling array of graphics is generated. All of the instruments of a modern jet cockpit are there to make the simula-

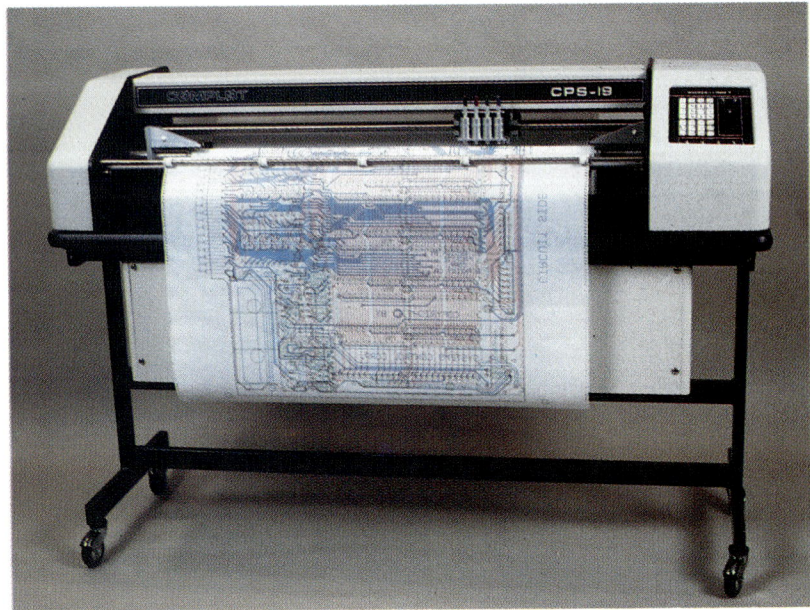

FIGURE 7–6
The pattern for an electronic circuit board was first drawn using a display terminal; the results were output on a plotter. Through photographic techniques, this drawing is used to produce the printed circuit board. (Courtesy of Bausch & Lomb, Houston Instrument Division)

tion as close to reality as possible. Figure 7–7 shows a Boeing 747 flight simulator. These sophisticated, expensive simulators are so realistic that the Federal Aviation Administration equates them to flying an actual aircraft.

Architecture

Geometric modeling techniques and computer graphics systems can save architects time, money, and aggravation. Rather than performing the tedious and expensive task of building scale models so that clients have a visual representation of results, a three-dimensional computer graphics data base of information about the structure can be used. Computer graphics also offers animation, a visual aspect model builders cannot produce. Viewers can fly around the building and actually go through it. Buildings can be moved around the site to show how they would best be positioned. Should it face Main or Broad Street? What landscaping would be most appropriate? Does an aerial view of the building show that it blends well with neighboring architecture? These and many other questions can be answered in a precise, visually exciting manner with computer graphics.

Computer Animation

Computers have been used to produce the animation in films such as *Tron, Buck Rogers, Star Wars*, and *Close Encounters*. The computers must be programmed with complex formulas on the nature of light, optics, and the geometry of perspective. The computer then calculates what the image would be on a point-by-point basis and displays it line-by-line on a CRT screen. An animated sound movie requires 1 440 separate pictures for each minute of running time (Figure 7–8). The more

FIGURE 7–7
Computer controlled flight simulators are used by the military and all major airlines to train and familiarize pilots with new aircraft. The realistic window scene is a moving computer generated image. Pilots will spend many hours using flight simulators before they touch the controls of an actual aircraft. (Courtesy of Eastern Airlines and Boeing Co.)

 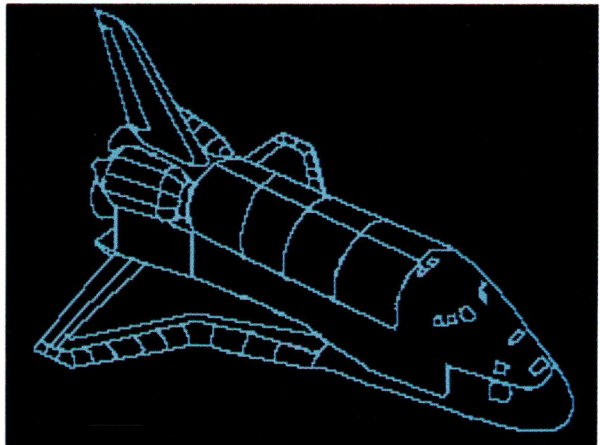

FIGURE 7–8
Computer-generated animation

complex a three-dimensional animated picture is, the more expensive it is to create. Some portions of *Tron* were so complicated that they required several scene coordinators to implement them. In *Close Encounters*, a camera followed actors as they, supposedly, were followed by UFOs. Months later, technicians used a computer to reproduce the camera's motion on a special effects stage, and the UFOs were added to the screen.

Computers are also being programmed by cartoonists to eliminate the tedium of drawing by hand the thousands of frames necessary for animating even a typical short cartoon. Computer animation is being used in advertising to sell everything from jeans to cars. As you can see, the bright, high resolution graphics produced by computer animation add visual pleasure to our lives.

Computer Art

Computer art, the result of creative interaction between an artist and a computer, has become an increasingly appealing art form to all types of people. The artist controls originality and composition through input parameters which tell the computer exactly what to do and how to do it. Good computer art combines logic, precision, and an artist's eye for beauty. Museums and galleries feature computer art exhibits.

Microcomputers have put electronic paint brushes in the hands of professional painters and hobbyists alike. Using a microcomputer system, a graphics tablet, or other input device, a person can produce a wide variety of colorful drawings. The computer controlled graphics tablet is an ideal tool for the computer artist. It is a magnetic bit pad which digitizes signals created by touching a magnetic pen to the tablet surface. The tablet consists of the bit pad, an overlay grid, magnetic pen, and software. It has commands that clear the screen, change color, recall and store the picture, add/delete background color, and insert boxes, straight lines, frames, windows, and so on. The magnetic pen is used to draw on the screen and execute any of the commands. The computer draws when the pen is actually touching the surface of the tablet. When the pen is close to the surface, crosshairs appear on the video screen to indicate location. Manipulating the pen is like writing with an ordinary pen; with a little practice, you can write cursive and draw complicated pictures with ease (Figure 7–9).

COMPUTER GRAPHICS FOR BUSINESS

The information explosion has sent managers at every level scurrying to make sense of the fragments of computerized information bombarding them from all sides. Management of information has become a large part of the typical business manager's job, and there are a number of ways he or she can avoid information overload.

The use of graphs and charts provides a method of condensing data and making it more comprehensible. A single page of charts can represent several pages of text or tabular data. Increasingly, computer graphics are replacing or supplementing paper charts in a wide variety of business applications. Many large companies use computer-generated graphs to monitor the performance and financial status of each division. The trends shown in the graphs often alert division managers to potential problems before they become critical.

Other business graphics applications include market analysis, sales analysis and forecasting, project management, training programs, portfolio analysis, inventory and production monitoring, sales targeting, product planning, site selection, investment analysis, financial planning, forms generation, and sales and management presentations. Business graphics systems are also used to create slides and transparencies for presentations (Figure 7–10). The use of graphics in a presentation helps the speaker to communicate better with the audience. In addition, a speaker who uses graphics is perceived as more professional and effective.

Computer-generated graphics for business applications can take many forms, including: pie, bar, and line graphs; maps; layouts; scatter diagrams; flowcharts; and organizational charts (Figure 7–11). The type of chart chosen depends largely on the relationship to be shown. For example, a government agency could use a pie chart very effectively to spot employment by industry throughout a city or state. Computer graphics capabilities are by no means limited to the types of graphs described here. Some of the more sophisticated graphics systems can generate three-dimensional images, conics (circles, ellipses, and arcs), shaded or patterned areas, and many special symbols (Figure 7–12).

Three basic types of graphics hardware systems are

1   Standalone graphics systems
2   Graphics terminals connected to computers
3   Time-sharing graphics terminals

FIGURE 7–9
The computer controlled graphics tablet is an ideal tool for the computer artist. This drawing of Indian chief Geronimo was produced using a graphics tablet. (Courtesy of Image Resource Corp.)

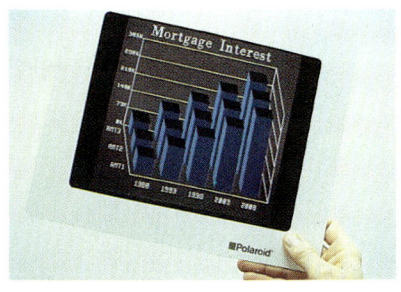

FIGURE 7–10
A 20 cm × 25 cm (8 in × 10 in) overhead transparency prepared on a computer graphics system and output on a Polaroid color camera (Courtesy of Polaroid Corp.)

What's faster than a speeding typewriter, corrects errors in a single keystroke, and produces unlimited original documents without manual intervention? Answer: a word processor.

Word processors are computer systems and/or programs that assist in the generation and handling of written text. They help achieve high levels of productivity because they allow easy, efficient editing and formatting of text. Tasks that would be very time-consuming using conventional typewriters are expedited and additional capabilities that exceed those of the standard typewriter are offered.

WordStar is a popular screen-oriented word processing system with integrated printing. Initial entry of text and alteration of text previously entered are displayed directly on the screen.

The editing function

WordStar's editing function is used to create and alter documents stored on disk. Features include video editing, automatic disk buffering, on-screen text formatting, powerful editing commands, flexible find and replace commands, help system, page break display, precise control of text format, and hyphen help.

A portion of the document being entered or corrected is always

Microminiaturization of circuitry has made it possible to place microcomputers directly in the office. Microcomputers have become as much a part of the office as the telephone. This operator is using the WordStar word processing system to produce a report.

shown on the display screen; additions and corrections are immediately displayed. Text entry is accomplished merely by typing the desired text; command functions such as cursor motion or deletion of text are quickly accomplished.

Automatic disk buffering

The size of a document is limited by disk capacity, not the amount of random access memory (RAM) in your computer. Text is brought into RAM as required, with no operator intervention or concern.

On-screen text formatting

Text is displayed on the screen as it will appear when printed, thereby facilitating review and

correction before printing. On-screen text formatting is accomplished with the aid of functions such as word wrap, automatic margination, justification, line spacing, centering, and paragraph reforming.

Word wrap Paragraphs may be entered at high speed without striking the ENTER key. When a word exceeds the right margin, WordStar automatically moves the word being entered to the next line and justifies and redisplays the line just completed. The ENTER key is used only to indicate the end of a paragraph, blank line, or other points where a permanent line break is desired.

Automatic justification With word wrap in effect, each completed line is automatically adjusted to fit the left and right margins, justified (right-aligned) unless the user has selected ragged-right format, and, optionally, double spaced or triple spaced. A line of text can be centered between the left and right margins with a keystroke command.

Paragraph reform Text from the cursor position to the end of the paragraph may be reformed on command to change the margins from ragged right to justified

```
A:TEST.DOC  PAGE 1 LINE 7 COL 12        INSERT ON  LINE SPACING 2
                            < < <   M A I N   M E N U   > > >
       --Cursor Movement--      ! -Delete-  !  -Miscellaneous-      !    -Other Menus-
^S char left ^D char right      !^G char    !^I Tab   ^B Reform     !(from Main only)
^A word left ^F word right      !DEL chr lf !^V INSERT ON/OFF       !^J Help   ^K Block
^E line up    ^X line down      !^T word rt !^L Find/Replce again   !^Q Quick  ^P Print
       --Scrolling--            !^Y line    !RETURN End paragraph   !^O Onscreen
^Z line up    ^W line down      !           !^N Insert a RETURN     !
^C screen up ^R screen down     !           !^U Stop a command      !
L----!----!----!----!----!----!----!----!----!----!----!----!----!----!----!----!----------R
```

WordStar is a popular screen-oriented word processing system with integrated printing. Both initial entry of text and alterations of text previously entered are displayed directly on screen.

or vice versa, alter line spacing, or clean up after alterations.

In addition to the basic cursor motion, scrolling, text deletion by character, word or line, and insertion or overtyping functions—WordStar's editing commands include the following:

- ☐ Find or find and replace text
- ☐ Move, copy, or delete a block of text
- ☐ Set or clear a variable tab stop
- ☐ Set or move to a place marker
- ☐ Write to and read from additional files

Find and replace commands

Searching operations and substitution operations can be done once, n times, globally (on the entire document), on whole words only, and ignoring case.

Help system

A menu of commands appears at the top of the screen during editing, or it may be suppressed for additional text display area. When the first character of a two-character command is entered, the menu automatically changes to show all commands that begin with the key entered. Additional explanations of various topics can be called up by selecting from a Help Menu.

Page breaks

Within certain limitations, the page breaks that will occur at printout are indicated on the screen during editing, and they change appropriately in response to every insertion or deletion.

Control of text format

WordStar remembers which

spaces and carriage returns were typed by the operator and which were inserted by the word wrap or paragraph reform operation.

Hyphen help

The WordStar system can also identify desirable places to divide a word between lines with a hyphen. At each occurrence, the operator may decide whether to hyphenate and optionally adjust the hyphen position.

The printing function

The print function features concurrent printing—one document can be printed while another is being edited. Print formatting features include page formatting, pagination control, microspace justification, and special effects such as boldface and underlining.

149

A **standalone graphics system** usually includes a microcomputer or minicomputer with internal storage, auxiliary storage, a graphics display terminal with keyboard, lightpen, or other input device, and an output device such as a plotter or printer (Figure 7–13). Some systems also include a digitizer, camera system for making slides, or computer output microfilm (COM) unit.

Graphics display terminals, output devices, and graphics software can be added to minicomputers or mainframe systems. In many installations, the software resides in the central computer, while the graphics terminals are placed in the end-user departments. In this type of system, a printer or other hard-copy device is not necessary at every terminal. Generally, output devices can be shared by several users. Equipment capable of making slides is often located in a central graphics facility to serve the entire organization.

The third type of system, a time-sharing service, requires users to supply a display terminal and a printer or plotter (Figure 7–14). The graphics software is provided by the service bureau. Many businesses use time-sharing systems to try out business graphics before investing in in-house graphics hardware and software.

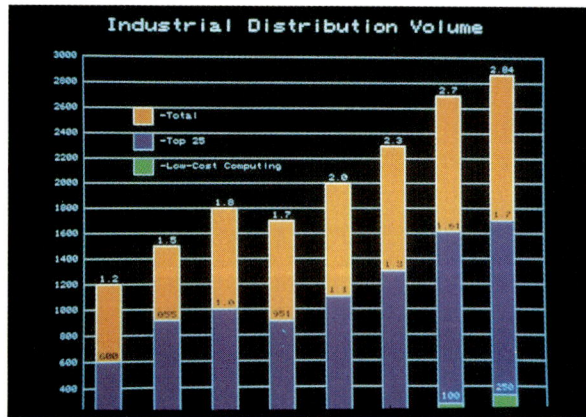

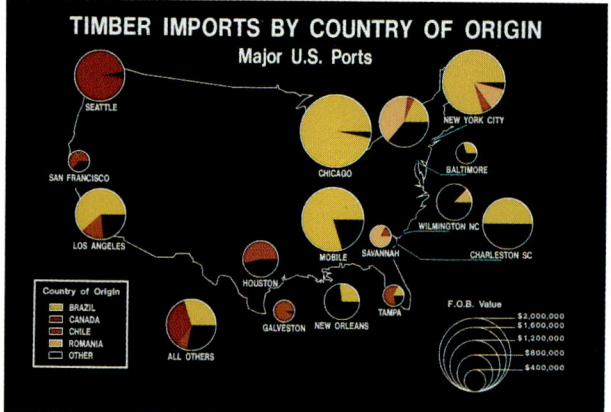

FIGURE 7–11
Typical graphic displays for business applications (Courtesy of Matrix Instruments, Inc. and DICOMED Corp.)

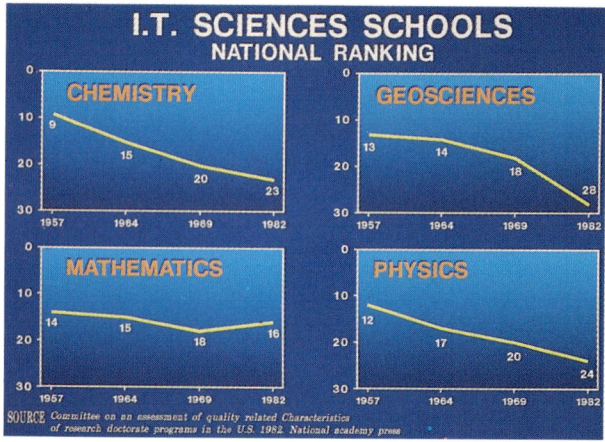

INPUT AND OUTPUT DEVICES

Input devices are the users' tools for creating results with a graphics system. An input device captures data and makes them available to the graphics program. The program processes the input data and determines the resulting effect, if any, on the visual display. Hard-copy output devices are used to produce plots, printouts, photographs, color slides, or transparencies. Some input devices (light pen, alphanumeric keyboard, mouse, trackball, and joystick) and output devices (dot matrix printers, ink jet printers, and color cameras) used with computer graphics systems were discussed in Chapter 3; additional devices will be introduced here.

Graphics Input Devices

Cursor pad   A cursor pad consists of five keys: one each to move the cursor up, down, left, or right; and one that returns the display cursor to a predefined home position. The display cursor is repositioned by pressing the key that corresponds to the desired direction. It will then move in the

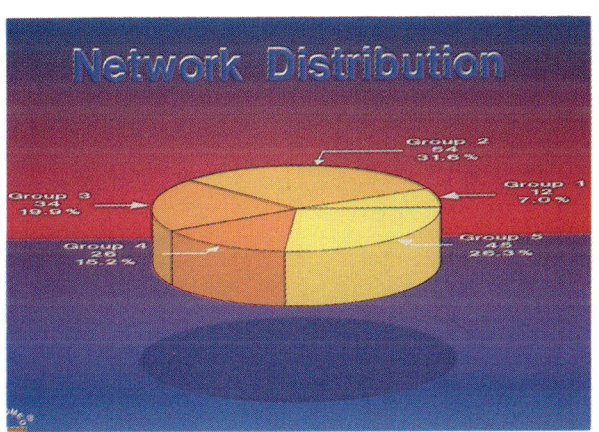

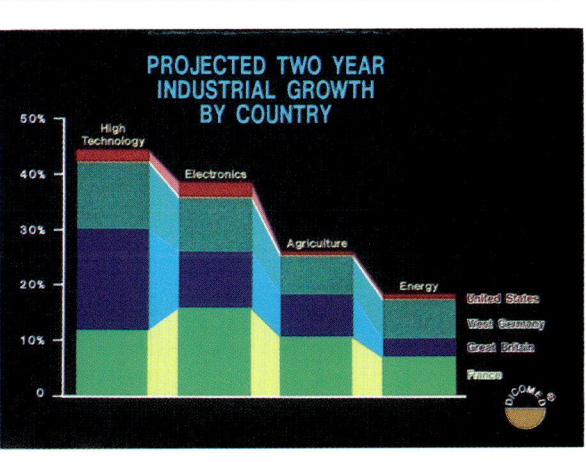

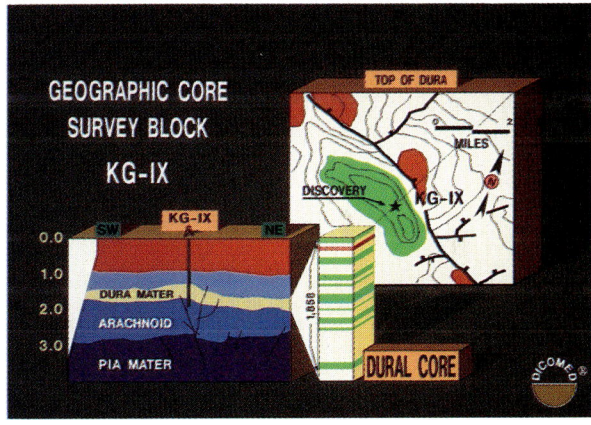

FIGURE 7–12
Typical three-dimensional displays for business applications (Courtesy of DICOMED Corp.)

desired direction a prespecified number of units. Effective cursor control can also be provided by two dials, one for vertical motion and the other for horizontal motion. A widely used configuration consists of two dials mounted on the side of a graphics terminal keyboard (Figure 7–15). These

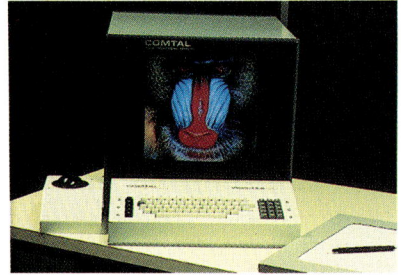

FIGURE 7–13
Standalone graphic systems

FIGURE 7–14
User display terminals and output devices connected to a service bureau time-sharing service

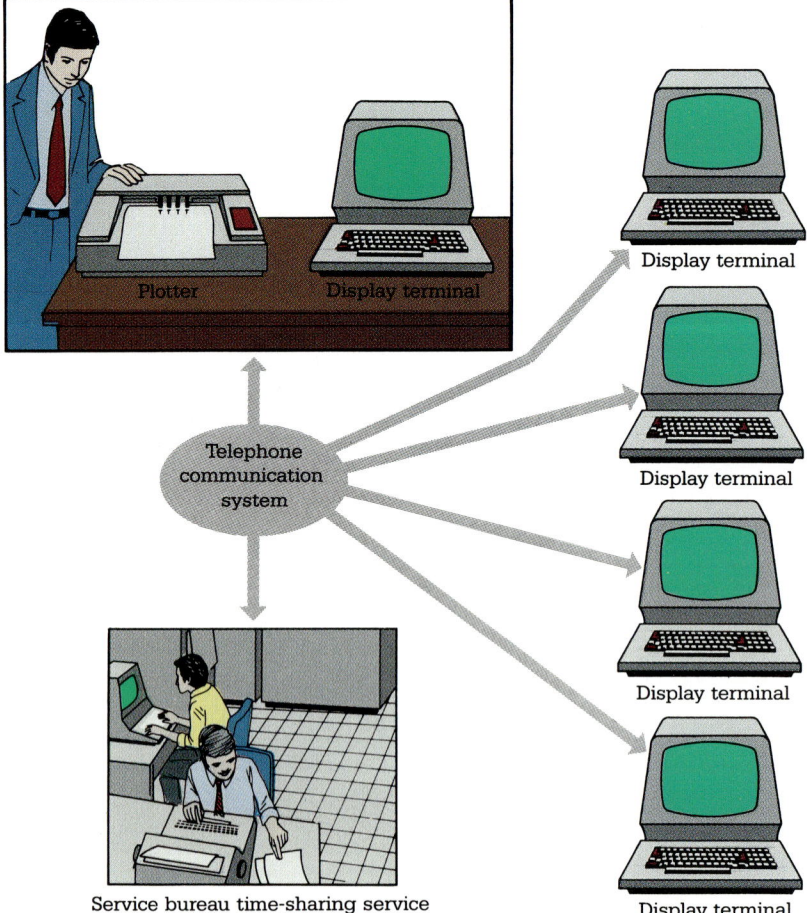

Service bureau time-sharing service

dials are referred to as **thumb wheels** because the toothed edge of each dial is easily rotated by the operator's thumb. Thumb wheels are ideal for entering accurate cursor movement along straight lines, but are less useful moving the cursor in a diagonal direction or along a curved path.

Touch-sensitive panel   Sets of horizontal and vertical wires, each mounted in a thin plastic sheet and combined into a grid separated by a third clear plastic sheet, compose the elements of a **touch-sensitive panel**. Depending on the resolution desired, the wires are positioned from one-half to one inch apart. The panel is then mounted on the face of the screen. When a spot on the panel is touched, the grid intersection nearest the spot is detected and decoded (Figure 7–16).

Digitizing tablet   A **digitizing tablet** consists of a small surface, typically 28 cm (11 in) × 28 cm (11 in), underlaid by a fine grid of wires. When a stylus or similar tool is placed on this surface and the activating button is pressed, the grid location is read and transmitted back to the graphics device. If the drawing surface is larger than a 28-cm (11-in) square, the device is called a digitizer table or digitizer board. Digitizer tables can be as large as a traditional drafting board (Figure 7–17).

Function keys   Special keys, called **function keys**, execute specific procedures. A typical application is a key associated with a particular graphics entity. The entity can be preprogrammed, then called up at various screen locations by simply striking the key.

FIGURE 7–15
Thumb wheels (to the right of the keyboard) on a graphics terminal (Courtesy of Tektronix, Inc.)

FIGURE 7–16
A touch-sensitive panel (Courtesy of Control Data Corp.)

FIGURE 7–17
An operator using a digitizing tablet (Courtesy of Control Data Corp.)

Graphics Output Devices

Line printers   Although advances such as the Figure 7–18 graph produced by an ink jet printer have made them outmoded, line printers may be used to display limited graphics by placing characters at strategic page locations or by superimposing alphanumeric characters for a half-tone effect.

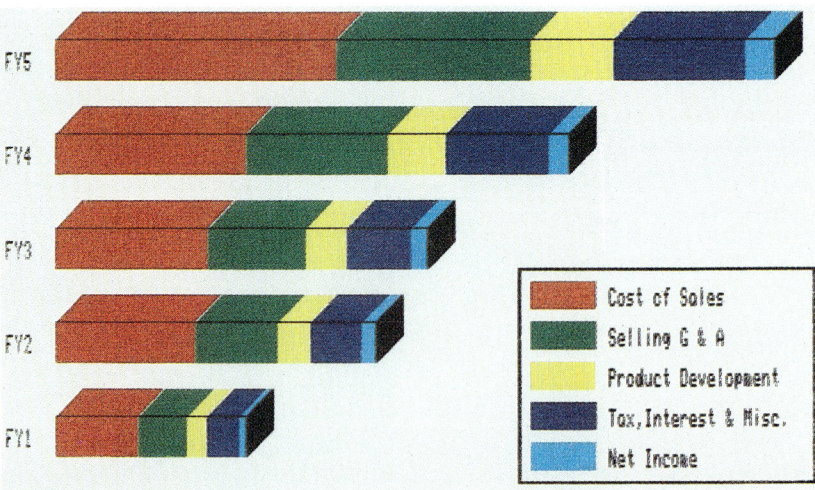

FIGURE 7–18
Chart produced by an ink jet printer (Courtesy of Ramtek, Inc.)

GRAPHICS SOFTWARE

As business reliance on graphics increases, the level of quality and user-friendliness of the software increases as well. Graphics software serves one of two purposes: (a) applications software converts data into graphical formats; and (b) device drivers provide an interface between a computer or terminal and an output device.

Applications software may be independent of other devices or designed for specific peripheral devices. Graphics software provided by computer or terminal vendors can be used only on the vendor's equipment; software provided by independent software companies can be either dependent on or independent of other devices.

For business graphics applications, users tend to look for general purpose, independent software that can be used by nonprogrammers. This software is available for all systems, from large scale to microcomputers, and it is easy to use. Generally, the operator just has to type in some data and press a button. The system then produces accurate professional graphics such as bar graphs, pie charts, and line graphs. Some software even enables the operator to plot several sets of data on the same graph, perhaps in different colors, so comparisons can be made.

DESIGNING EFFECTIVE BUSINESS GRAPHICS

A good graphic delivers its message in a clear, concise manner, and producing an effective diagram is the responsibility of the person who prepares the material for input to the computer. In this section, you will learn some of the factors that determine the effectiveness of a diagram—simplicity, visual style, color, and careful selection of charts and graphs.

Simplicity Whenever possible, charts and graphs should be kept relatively simple. A diagram should contain no more than one thought or concept; therefore, do not have all of the data you've collected placed onto a single diagram. For example, if all of your statistics are indicated in millions of dollars, use a single statement as a subhead (millions of dollars), thus eliminating the need to show all of the zeros and dollar signs as part of your scale values.

Visual style Legibility is extremely important in the design of a diagram. The right style and size of typeface eases readability and contributes to viewer retention.

Use of color Selecting correct color combinations for a diagram can be difficult. Colors affect the perception of the material being presented, therefore, you should avoid using colors that are too similar. A speaker should never have to define varying shades of the same color on a graph.

Selecting your chart or graph The right chart is essential to getting your message across. Figure 7–19 shows different types of graphs and

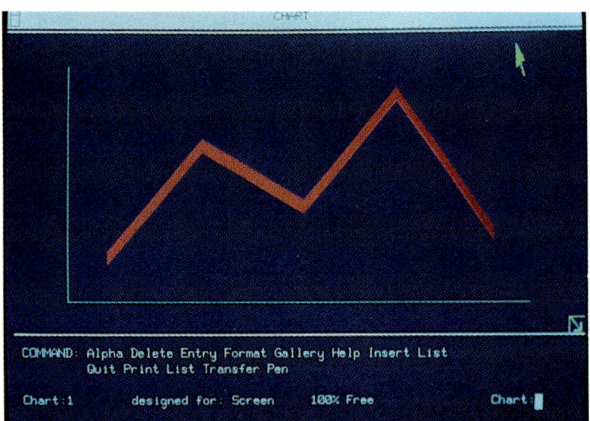

Line graph

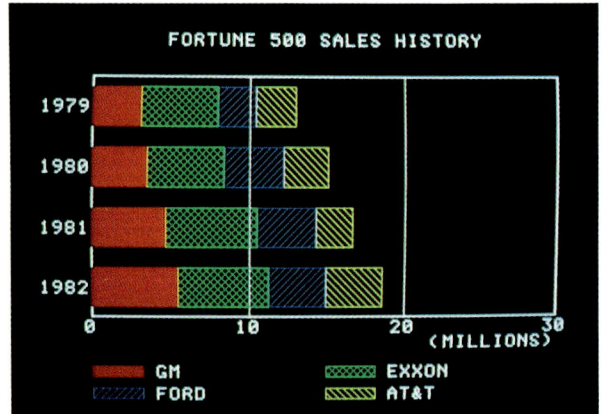

Horizontal bar graph

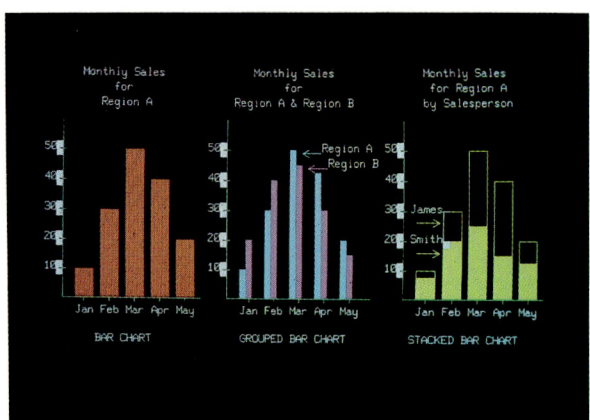

Vertical bar graph

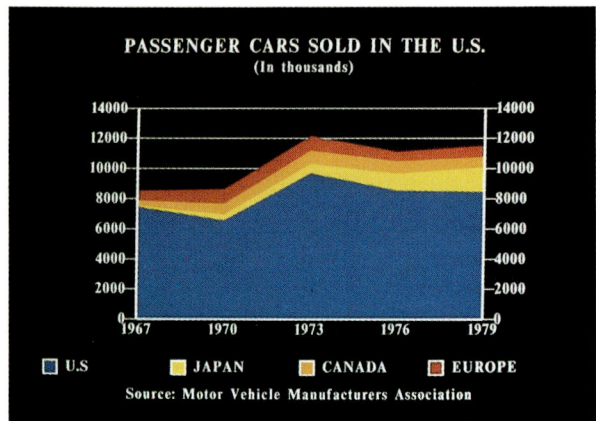

Area graph

FIGURE 7–19
Various types of graphs and charts (Courtesy of Radio Shack, A Division of Tandy Corp., Samarai, and Image Resource Corp.)

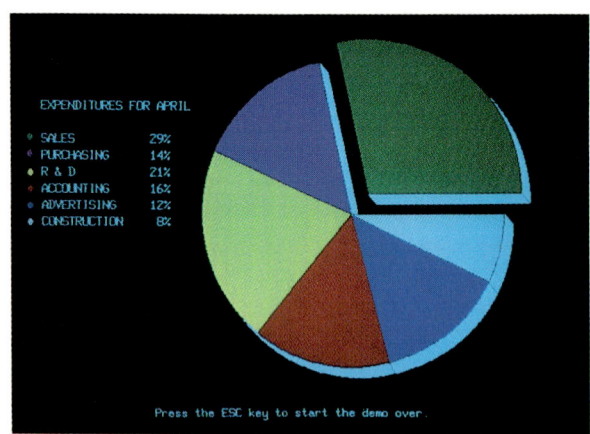

Pie chart

charts. The most common graph is the vertical **bar graph**, offering a clear comparison between two or more items. The horizontal bar graph is a variation that better emphasizes differences among data results. The **line graph** uses lines plotted across a grid to reveal trends easily. Care should be taken not to display too much data (too many lines too close together) in this format. A variation of the line graph is the **area graph**. This graph fills in the areas between the lines with color. A **pie chart** is used to represent portions of a whole.

A COLORFUL FUTURE FOR BUSINESS GRAPHICS

Computer graphics offer new opportunities for acquiring and interpreting information. Business managers, educators, government officials, engineers, medical personnel, artists, architects, and the average citizen can all expect to be affected by the impact of computer graphics.

The computer graphics field is changing at a tremendous rate. As technologies improve, the application areas using graphics will become broader. The market is expected to grow at a rate of approximately 50 percent per year through 1989. During the same period, standalone business graphics systems are expected to experience an annual growth rate of 80 percent. In 1975, the first annual computer graphics show was held in Philadelphia. The show attracted ten vendors and a few hundred visitors. In the summer of 1984, a computer graphics show in Minneapolis attracted over 350 vendors and 20 000 visitors, and filled 68 times the space of the 1975 show.

Because owners of personal computers make up the largest percentage of computer graphics users, the standard television receiver is the most common display device. As new techniques are developed, we can expect the quality of video images to improve. The price of graphics systems should continue to fall, and as it does, the number of applications will increase dramatically.

Word processing is already being affected by computer graphics. Editing a document can be done by identifying the area to be moved and pointing to where it should be moved. Graphics such as charts and graphs can be added to the text of a document without resorting to cutting and pasting.

In business, graphics will become a standard part of the management reports used for market research, analytical studies, project planning, forecasting, and training. Management and analyst work stations will produce graphic displays using touch and voice activated graphics. Executives will have most graphics prepared on paper or projection screens that can display information available from a graphics data base. Graphics data bases, graphics data base management software, and data communications networks will provide access to large quantities of diverse information. New sources of information, such as NASA's Landsat satellite, will provide opportunities for energy exploration and natural resource management.

SUMMARY

☐ Computer graphics displays make conveying information faster, easier, and more interesting, and they can save time and money for many types of organizations.

☐ Computer graphics was first used in the automotive industry by General Motors and now includes applications in medicine, engineering, aircraft simulation, architecture, computer animation, computer art, education, and video games.

☐ The three basic types of graphics hardware systems are: standalone graphics systems; graphics terminals connected to a computer; and time-sharing graphics terminals.

☐ Computer-aided design/computer-aided manufacture (CAD/CAM) represents the largest segment of the computer graphics industry. Computer-aided design uses computer graphics capabilities in product and manufacturing engineering as an aid in design, drafting, and documentation. Computer-aided manufacture involves the use of computers in a variety of manufacturing processes.

☐ Business graphics has emerged as a significant part of the computer graphics field. The uses for business graphics include market analysis, sales analysis, forecasting and targeting, project management, training programs, portfolio analysis, inventory monitoring, and generation of forms.

☐ Business applications of computer graphics include bar graphs, line graphs, pie charts, layouts, flowcharts, and organizational charts.

☐ Input devices are users' tools for creating results with graphics systems because they capture data and make them available to the graphics program. The program processes the input data and determines the resulting effect, if any, on the visual display terminal.

☐ A good graphic presents its message in a clear, concise, simple way and features an appealing visual style and appropriate color. It reflects the proper selection of the types of graphic that best suit the situation at hand. Each graphic should contain only one thought. The advantage of using color should offset the cost.

☐ The applications for computer graphics are expected to expand by 50 percent annually through 1989, and standalone business graphics systems are expected to expand 80 percent each year during the same period.

REVIEW QUESTIONS

True or False

_____ **1** Video games are an application of computer graphics.

_____ **2** CAD means computer-aided documentation.

_____ **3** Computer-aided design enables users to create, transform, and display pictorial and symbolic information.

_____ **4** A good graphic presents its message in a clear, concise, simple way and features an appealing style and appropriate color.

_____ **5** The use of graphics can make complicated information easier to understand.

_____ **6** One of the most important fields in computer graphics is CAD/CAM.

_____ **7** A mouse is an input device.

_____ **8** A joystick is an output device.

_____   **9**   A graphics output device is used to display or record an image.
_____   **10** A graphics program is a computer program that lets the
                 computer produce graphics.
_____   **11** A digital plotter produces drawings with lasers.
_____   **12** The applications for computer graphics are expected to expand
                 by 5 percent annually through 1989.

Short Answer

1   _____ _____ is a general term that describes the
        presentation of drawings on a display screen.

2   The use of _____ enhances the viewer's ability to understand
        visual presentations.

3   The price of computer graphics systems has _____ dramati-
        cally during the past few years.

4   _____ _____ uses computer graphics as an aid
        in designing, drafting, and documentation.

5   Computer graphics was first used by _____
        _____ in the automotive industry.

6   _____ _____ involves the use of computers in a
        variety of manufacturing processes.

7   One of the greatest medical breakthroughs of the past decade has been
        in producing three-dimensional computer images of the human body's
        internal structures. This technology is called _____
        _____ _____.

8   _____ _____ involves the use of computers in
        producing the animation in movie films.

9   Art form produced by computing equipment is called _____
        _____.

10 _____ graphics has emerged as a significant part of the
        computer graphics field.

11 The three basic types of graphics hardware systems are
        _____, _____, and _____.

12 An _____ device captures data and makes it available to a
        graphics program.

13 Joysticks and light pens are _____ devices used with
        computer graphics systems. Ink jet printers and visual displays are
        _____ devices.

14 A _____ _____ is a flat input device that can be
        connected to a computer. By moving a stylus or mouse over the tablet, a
        user can draw a picture that will be sent to the computer.

15 Pie charts, bar charts, and graphs are examples of _____
        _____.

16 Graphics _____ is used to convert data into graphical
        formats.

17 _____ is the abbreviation for computer-aided design/
        computer-aided manufacturing.

18 The Macintosh, a microcomputer introduced by Apple Computer, Inc. in
        1984, is designed to simplify working with graphics. The Macintosh
        system is called a _____ graphics system.

OUTLINE

OBJECTIVES

1 Understand the essence and
benefits of distributed processing.

2 Explain the purpose and operation of a time-sharing computer
system.

3 Describe a real time system.

4 Explain the functions of a data
base management system and
the role it plays in a data base
environment.

5 Describe the importance and
use of electronic spreadsheets.

6 Understand the basic functions
of an operating system.

7 Explain the concepts of
multiprogramming and
multiprocessing.

ADVANCED SYSTEM CONCEPTS

L ook around your school's library and you will see that information is made available to you on disks, microfilm, and in books. How this information is managed and brought to you reflects the concerns about information storage and retrieval in larger systems. In this chapter, we'll take a look at a few of the newer methods for processing information.

DISTRIBUTED PROCESSING

A **distributed processing system** is a set of independent but interacting computer systems or data bases situated in different locations (Figure 8–1). The function of a distributed processing system is to process some jobs at the point of user activity, while transmitting other jobs to a centralized facility. For example, a chain of department stores might

FIGURE 8–1
Distributed processing systems consist of one centralized and several smaller computer systems. Their function is to process some user jobs or tasks at the point of user activity, while permitting other jobs to be transmitted to a centralized facility.

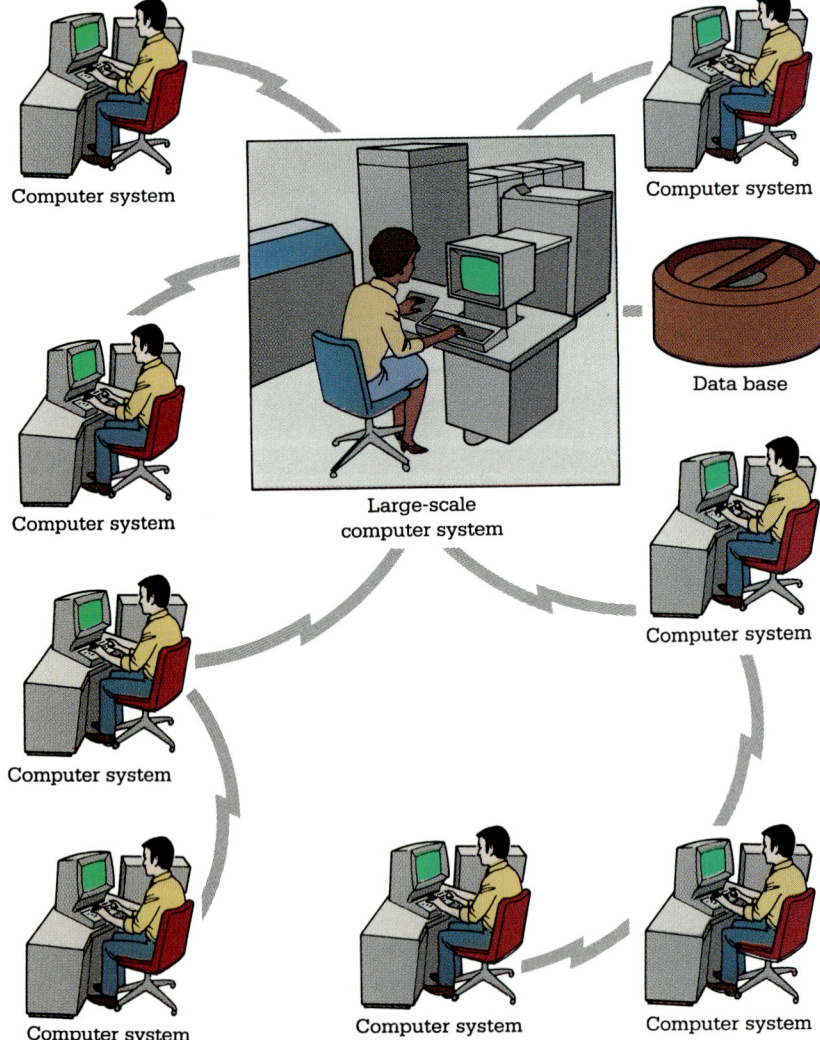

Computer system

Computer system

Data base

Computer system

Computer system

Large-scale
computer system

Computer system

Computer system

Computer system

Computer system

have a small computer system, connected by communications equipment to a large-scale computer system, located at several stores. Local processing tasks such as payroll, inventory control, and sales forecasting may be performed at each of the stores, while data for centralized accounting and management reporting are transmitted to the store's main office computer system for processing.

Distributed processing is not restricted to systems having a large-scale centralized computer system. A network of interconnected microcomputer systems is also a distributed system (Figure 8–2). Distributed processing can occur without a data communication system. For example, a weekly payroll can be processed at each of five sales offices by minicomputer systems. A diskette, disk pack, or tape reel containing changes to basic employee data may be transported by mail or courier from each sales office to corporate headquarters for weekly updating of the company's master employee file.

In a distributed processing system, less information is transmitted to the central computer system than would be necessary if all processing were done by the central system. Consequently, communication costs are lower and the central computer workload is reduced. Distributed processing takes the computer to the job rather than the job to the com-

FIGURE 8–2
Distributed processing systems are not restricted to systems with a large-scale centralized computer system. This ring network consists of several interconnected microcomputer systems.

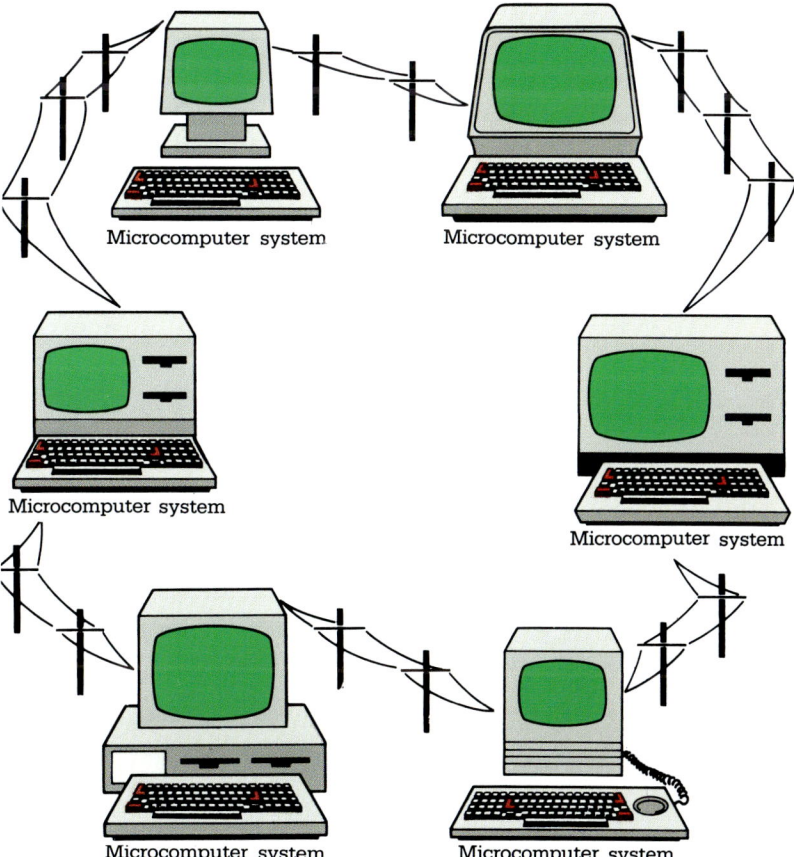

puter, yet a remote computer system, such as a satellite computer, can access a larger host computer system and communicate with larger corporate data files.

Another example of distributed processing may be found in a banking system. The bank's host computer system maintains central customer accounts while smaller satellite minicomputer systems hold branch accounts and control the branch teller terminals. The two basic structures of distributed processing networks are a star network, with end user computers connected to a large central computer, and a ring network, where local systems are tied together on a more equal basis.

TIME-SHARING SYSTEMS

Time sharing is the simultaneous use of a computer system from multiple terminals to reduce the time needed to solve problems and to economize by sharing costs. Time sharing is especially useful in scientific, engineering, and educational environments. Eventually, information systems will become the largest users of time-sharing systems. Doctors, lawyers, and other professionals will retrieve information from large data banks specific to their fields.

The principle of time sharing is based on having enough computer system capacity for multiple users because each terminal is active only a fraction of the time. Many time-sharing systems can accommodate several hundred terminals. Consider a system with 20 terminals. The computer picks up orders from one user, works on that problem for perhaps one-twentieth of a second, and stores the partial answer. It then moves to the next user, receives the orders, and works on the second problem for one-twentieth of a second before moving on in turn to the other 18 users. When each user's problem is completed, the result is printed on the appropriate terminal. The computer system accomplishes this work so fast that the user feels the system is working full-time on his or her project.

In a typical time-sharing system, the users communicate with a central computing facility via remote terminals which may be located several feet or miles away. Data communications between the computer and the terminals are accomplished by a common communications network such as telephone lines or microwave links. A terminal is usually a typewriter, teleprinter, or visual display device.

The time-sharing computer system includes not only the same equipment found in conventional computer systems, but also a communications processor, direct access storage device, and user terminals (Figure 8–3). The communications processor, usually a separate, smaller digital computer, routes data communications between the computer and user terminals. A direct access storage device is required to store the user's programs and to act as intermediate storage. These data must be available to the computer system as rapidly as possible. Inadequate magnetic drum or disk storage will dilute performance to the point where system response is low.

FIGURE 8–3
A basic time-sharing network

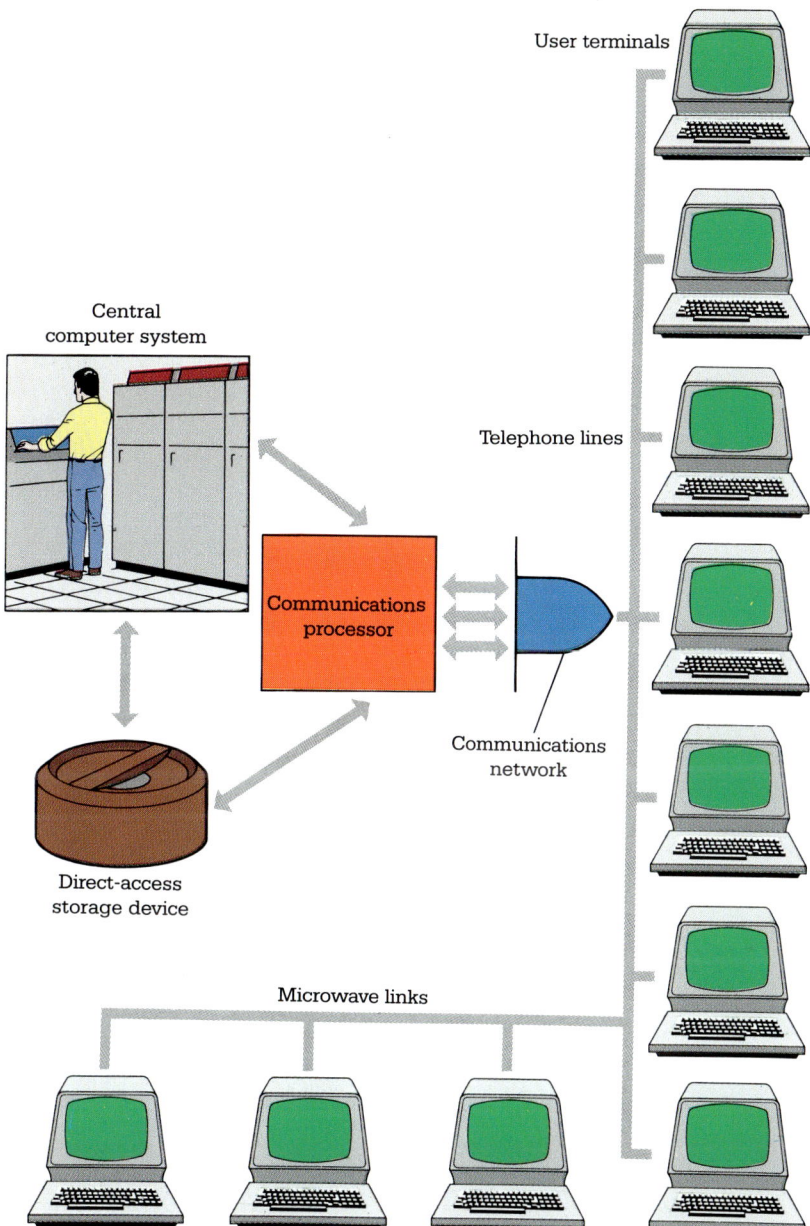

All time-sharing systems follow a similar pattern. First, the user dials the computer using a normal telephone exchange network to establish contact with the computer system. When contact is made, the user will be asked to provide identification with some special code or number and to select the programming system to be used. If the program being used is already written and stored in the time-sharing system program library, the user requests to execute the program. If, however, a new program is being developed, the user will type the program in a programming language such as BASIC. Once the program is entered, the user will tell the computer to execute the program. After the program is executed, the results are transmitted to the user's terminal. The user also has the option of storing this newly created program in the time-sharing system program library for future use.

REAL TIME INFORMATION PROCESSING

Real time describes a system capable of action at a speed commensurate with the time of occurrence of an actual process. An example of a real time system is an airline reservation system, in which each reservation must be processed by the system immediately after it is made so that a complete, up-to-date picture of available seating is maintained by the computer at all times (Figure 8–4).

Many department stores, insurance companies, and banks use real time systems. Banks use these systems to: (a) send transactions from branches to a central computer installation; (b) check customers' balances and produce statements; or (c) process customer transactions online. Real time data processing equipment also controls dissemination of the New York Stock Exchange trading data, runs stock units, and even communicates with member subscribers over the Exchange's Telephone Quotation service. Trading information is sped to the exchange's computer center via direct electronic signals from data readers on the trading floor. The system prints sales on exchange units across the United States in as little as one-half second after a special reporting card is read on the floor.

Common elements of all these applications of real time systems include a file to store information, a computer to process it, and communications lines and terminals to provide access to or for someone located remotely. Real time systems normally require the use of: (a) data communications equipment to feed data into the system from remote terminals; (b) direct access storage devices to store large volumes of incoming data; and (c) computers capable of executing the programs needed to validate data and control the input at the same time it is being used. The impetus for acquiring real time systems is the need for immediate information so that users can make judgments based on the most recent data.

DATA BASE TECHNOLOGY

The organization, storage, and management of vast amounts of information create such problems that departments are often established to handle these specific functions. With the development of computer systems and sophisticated mass storage technology, data management has become an important application of computers. The problem of maintaining large amounts of information in a central storage location is not perplexing; however, locating and extracting specific pieces of information from that huge storehouse often is. This situation is further complicated when several specific bits of information are needed simultaneously and their relationships to one another explored.

In the mid-1970s, data base management systems were confined to the exclusive domain of the business management information system department. Requests for the extraction of information required special programs written for the specific request. Department managers often had to wait up to six months for one job request to make its way to the

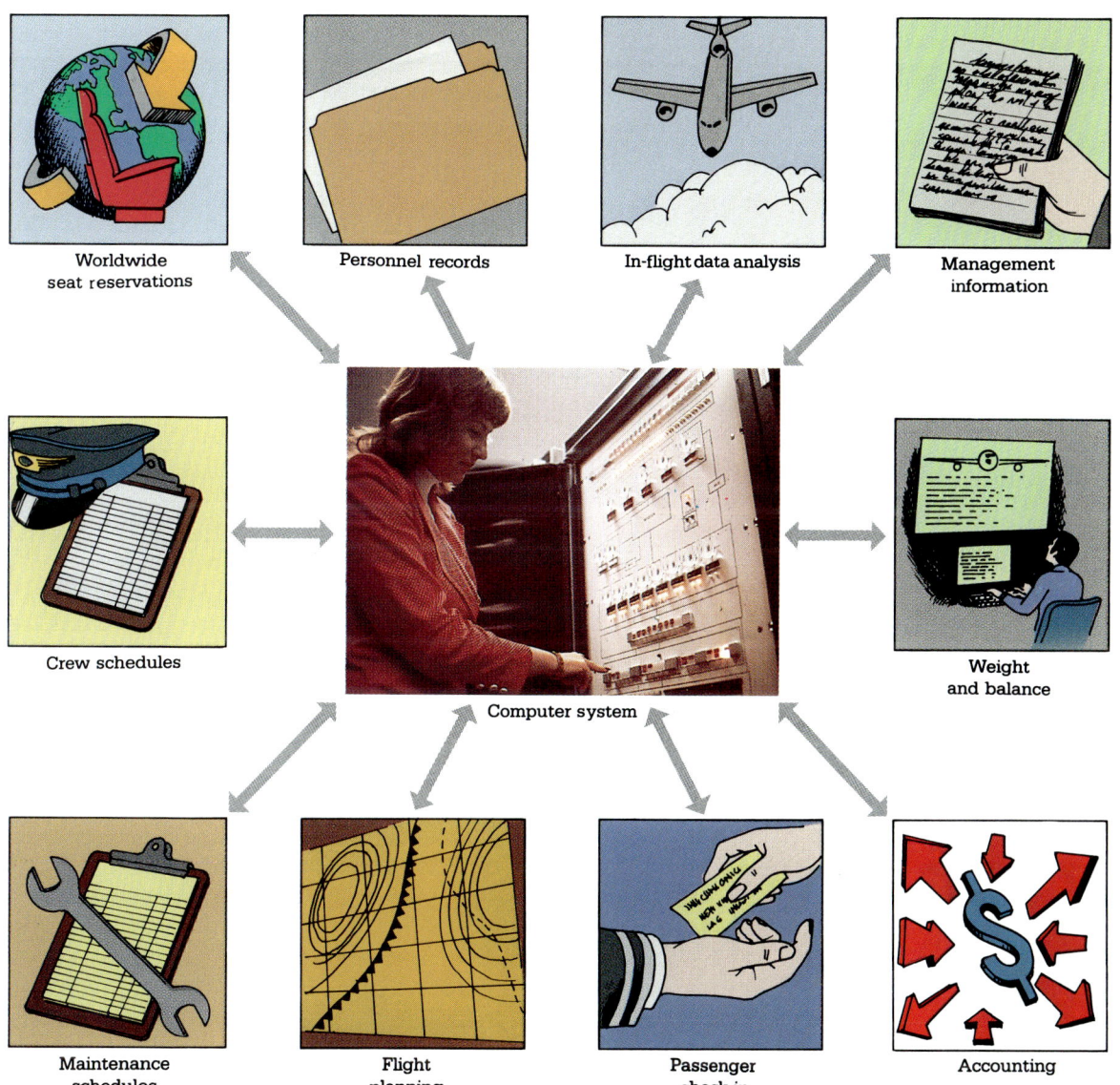

Worldwide
seat reservations

Personnel records

In-flight data analysis

Management
information

Crew schedules

Computer system

Weight
and balance

Maintenance
schedules

Flight
planning

Passenger
check-in

Accounting

FIGURE 8–4
Real time application. Computer systems used by airlines control a worldwide reservation system, provide information for management, control stocks, schedule flights and their crews, print out maintenance schedules, and fulfill a variety of other functions. (Courtesy of Eastern Air Lines)

top of the queue; once there, the information was either too late or incomplete.

In those days, the most used data base structure was the hierarchical structure. These fixed systems required extensive planning and tailoring to a particular application. Once the system was set up, the end user was locked into the structure forever because these large computer systems were too expensive to arbitrarily alter to suit individual changes.

Because these early data base management systems often created corporate chaos and programming nightmares due to their inflexibility, microcomputer data base management systems got off to a slow and rocky start. By 1984, however, the efficiency of microcomputer data base management systems improved to such an extent that over one million were in use.

The Data Base Concept

The easiest way to understand the concept of a data base and of data base management is to visualize a large general filing department. Within the filing department, information is contained in groups of filing cabinets and organized by subjects such as history, math, science, and art. The collection contains letters, documents, periodicals, and illustrations. Each collection is housed in files that have several drawers holding file folders. The file folders contain the documentation or, in some cases, references to where the documentation can be found. Extensive directories enable a user to access required information. Each user of the department may have different requirements for the information, but the collections provide all the current and historical information needed.

A computer data base management system attempts to duplicate this condition within a computer system composed of a central processing unit, main and auxiliary storage, and the necessary input/output terminal units. The system provides a data structure where information can be stored and accessed for many applications. For example, all information regarding employees is contained in a data base file marked EMPLOYEE. The payroll program accesses this file for information regarding the employee: name, social security number, salary rate, and deductions. While performing its own function, the payroll program also updates the EMPLOYEE data base file with current information from a payroll period. Therefore, any other programs needing employee information will have the most recent data.

The user of a data base management system usually requires information specifically relating to his or her business. Therefore, the system permits creation of the files containing the information to encompass any desired set of data. Information may be accessed by asking for it in any way that does not confuse the computer. Most systems have rules for the retrieval of information called ''selection criteria.''

Once the information has been accessed from the system files, the data base management system has the ability to sort it in a useful manner. In many cases, the data may be sorted several times, each time by a different criterion. For example, a data base may be asked to select all the

In a few years, a small antenna on your rooftop could give you access to hundreds of millions of pages of information every day. The amount of information that could be delivered by high-power satellites to homes and businesses is virtually unlimited. The high-powered multichannel satellite technology needed for direct broadcast satellites will be available by 1986. An information utility could be launched in the United States within a few years; by the end of the decade, the utility could operate worldwide.

people named Wilson, and the selection may be sorted by zip code, sex, and color of hair. Nonnumerical information can be counted, and the system could tell us that there are N number of people named Wilson living in an area. The data base system also performs calculations of numerical data selected from the records. For example, the total wages, hours, and taxes can be obtained from the information in the EMPLOYEE file discussed earlier.

Sharing data is one of the major reasons for using a data base system. The data base can be accessed by multiple users at the same time. The data does not have to be stored more than once to be used for multiple purposes. Sharing data also allows new applications that operate on existing data to be developed at any time.

Files Because a data base is an organized, integrated collection of data centrally stored for access, retrieval, or update, its files have similar characteristics and can be combined or separated in storage. Files can be divided into various types of lower level structures. The division of a file is called a record, which can be further divided until a field, the lowest level data element, is obtained.

The data base organization consists of logical and physical arrangement of files, records, and their substructures. The locations of these organizational entities can be expressed in terms of their actual (physical) and apparent (logical) positions in the system storage devices. Consider the records R_1 and R_2. Although they are physically separated, records R_1 and R_2 are logically contiguous, if they are always processed in the sequence indicated by their subscripts.

Data independence In data base systems, data independence makes it possible for applications to have different views of the same data. From the system's standpoint, data independence makes it possible for the storage structure and accessing strategy to be modified in response to the installation's changing requirements, but without the need to modify functioning applications.

Data dictionary An index to all the items in an organization's data base is called a **data dictionary**. A data dictionary is actually a data base containing information about the data base. It lists the types of information in the data base, which programs use which data, which user groups require which reports, and which entities of each type exist in the system.

Data Base Organization

The primary means of defining data base organization is by specifying the arrangements of records in a file. The basic types of record organization are sequential, linked list, random, and inverted.

Records in the sequential structure are stored in positions relative to one another based upon a certain sequence. This sequence is usually ordered according to an explicit attribute, called a key, or by an implicit characteristic, such as arrival into the system. In the linked list organization, each record is directed to its successor by a pointer, and the logical and physical structures are seldom identical. Typical of the various kinds of list organizations are the simple and ring structures. Records in the random organization are stored in random fashion relative to their logical and physical storage locations, which are either directly available or obtainable by computational methods. The inverted structure is a special type of data organization that is grouped relative to the index terms that describe the information. Associated with each index term is a reference, usually a storage location, to all the records to which the term applies.

Data Base Operations

A limited set of ancillary operations can be performed upon the data base; these include file maintenance and file creation. File maintenance involves updating the data files by adding, deleting, and modifying information. File creation provides data for a previously structured file. This is frequently accomplished by updating an empty or obsolete file. In performing both operations, various fundamental functions are necessary to manipulate the data. These include sorting and merging, which is the combination of two or more files into one.

Distributed Data Base

A **distributed data base** is one that is spread throughout the computer systems of a network. Ordinarily each data item in these systems is stored at its most frequently used location, but it remains accessible to other network users. Distributed systems provide the control and economy of local processing with the advantages of information accessibility over a geographically dispersed organization. These systems can be costly to implement and operate, however, and they can suffer from increased vulnerability to security violations.

Data Base Management System Categories

A **data base management system (DBMS)** is a collection of related programs for loading, accessing, and controlling a data base. The data base is independent of the programs that use the information, and a system may have several data bases within one data base management system. Hierarchical, network, and relational data base management systems are three DBMS models that have achieved widespread popularity.

Hierarchical data base management system (HDBMS) In a HDBMS, data are organized like an inverted tree with a series of nodes connected by branches (Figure 8–5). These nodes and branches form what is described as a parent-child relationship; each parent may have many children but each child may have only one parent. Data go through the tree from top to bottom until they reach their appropriate destination. The hierarchical structure assumes that certain data are more important

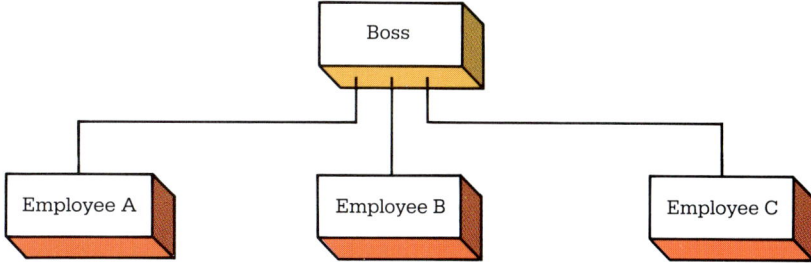

FIGURE 8–5
Hierarchical data base structure

than other data; therefore, these systems are created to work within a specific application.

Network data base management system (NDBMS)   In a NDBMS model, data are organized similarly to those of a HDBMS except that each node may have more than one branch, so that data can come from several different sources (Figure 8–6). In the network structure, records are linked by a complex system of pointers that frequently must be updated, making the network model more flexible than the hierarchical one. A disadvantage to the network approach is that some structures begin to have pointers going off in all directions. Such a structure can be difficult to comprehend, modify, or reconstruct in case of failure.

Relational data base management system (RDBMS)   The most fundamental property of a relational data base management system is that data are presented to the user as tables. Thus, the data consist of rows and columns, with the rows corresponding to traditional data base records and the columns representing fields within the records.

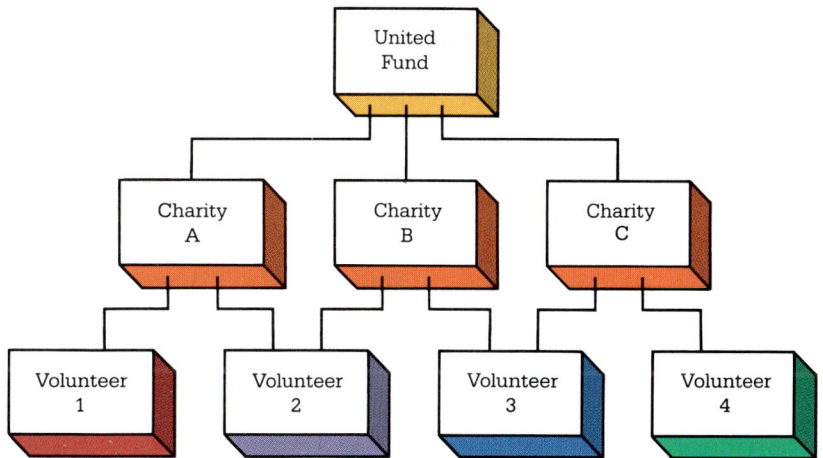

FIGURE 8–6
Network data base structure

The following is a relational data structure for employee information.

Row (or record)	Column (or field)		
	Employee number	Name	Department
1	632107	Smith	Manufacturing
2	431605	Wilson	Accounting
3	552108	Wineburg	Manufacturing
4	563270	Brown	Sales
5	333407	Nelson	Advertising
6	443167	Jeffery	Manufacturing

This table shows three facts about each employee (employee number, name, and department), each in a separate column of the table. The table has only six rows (records), one for each employee. Such a data base for a company large enough to require a data base would have many more rows.

A join is an RDBMS operation capable of combining relational tables. Other relational operations are selection, creating a subset of all the records in a table; and projection, creating a subset of all the columns in a table. The results of any relational operation always produce new tables. This makes it possible to provide very powerful and concise languages for the manipulation of relational data structures.

The relational data base organization has these advantages over the hierarchical and network schemes:

☐ Tabular representation is easy for users to comprehend and implement in the physical data base system.
☐ Conversion of other types of data base structures into the relational scheme is relatively easy.
☐ Access control to sensitive data is straightforward.
☐ Operations are easy to implement, thereby making the creation of new relations easy to do.
☐ Modifications to relational structures are easier to make than those to hierarchical or network structures.

Data Base Languages

Users access a data base via statements in some form of data base language. Applications programs may use a conventional language like BASIC, COBOL, or Pascal; a terminal user may use a specially designed query language that makes it convenient to express requests in the context of a particular application.

In relational data base systems, a language that explicitly provides selection, projection, and join operations is called a relational algebraic language; an example is SQL. Relational algebraic languages work with sets of records; that is, they work on tables as a whole. Another relational language is called relational calculus language. This language is less procedural than relational algebraic languages are. Any operation of either algebraic or calculus languages results in a new table. This means that composite expressions can be constructed in which the result of one operation becomes the operand of another.

MANAGEMENT INFORMATION SYSTEMS

Since information is the key to the successful control and operation of any organization, managers are allowed access to the computer systems in which many firms store information. In many organizations, this access is accomplished by using a **management information system (MIS)**. A computer system that aids the management process is often called a computer based management information system (CBMIS). In this book, the acronym MIS means CBMIS.

In a typical MIS, all data are collected and sorted in a data base. Special software, called **data base management software**, is used to aid in the organization and retrieval of data stored in a data base. The person who performs data base management tasks, such as the design and management of data base applications, is called the **data base administrator (DBA)**. The DBA acts as an interface between systems analysts and operational personnel. The major responsibilities of this position are the design and implementation of the data base, establishment of procedures for accessing the data base, and coordination of data sharing. Therefore, the DBA must possess a thorough understanding of software technology, data base management systems, access methods, and storage devices.

The objective of an MIS is to provide a means for an organization's information to be integrated and updated for purposes of planning, decision making, and control. An MIS is an on-line, real time information system consisting of the following resources:

- ☐ Centralized data base consisting of an organization's information resources
- ☐ Comprehensive set of data on the organization, its operating structure, and the competitive environment
- ☐ Capability for updating and retrieving information from the data base
- ☐ Plan or model to be used for decision making, using the information in the data base
- ☐ Plan or model to be used in organizational planning activities
- ☐ Checklist to be used to monitor the organization's performance

Management can use an MIS for many purposes; however, operational, long range, and tactical planning are the most widely developed areas for which MIS's are used. The information necessary for planning is derived from market research, internal statistics, competitive analysis, and known operational characteristics of the organization.

Imagine yourself as a manager with a computer-controlled visual display terminal on your desk. You must order the raw materials required to make 5 000 popcorn popping machines. If you order too few, there will not be time to reorder. If you order too many, your raw material costs will be high, resulting in a lower profit on product sales. You need some information on the actual production costs of the machines your company produced in previous years. An accurate purchase order of materials is essential, and the only way an accurate one can be produced is by determining actual manufacturing requirements. You turn to the MIS and type in the machine product code number to obtain manufacturing information. The computer searches the data base, extracts previous manufacturing information, and displays quantities, costs, and required raw materials. You use this information to instruct the computer to perform a few simple computations to estimate the raw materials required to manufacture 5 000 machines. Satisfied, you use this information on your purchase order as the required raw materials.

The system just described represents the typical MIS found in many businesses. As computer costs decline and management systems become more sophisticated, the use of MIS's will grow. Since many organizations are geographically dispersed, remote locations use the office's central computer to transmit data. To reduce expensive data communications costs, a distributed processing network is often used.

ELECTRONIC SPREADSHEETS

Electronic spreadsheets are the most popular business application for microcomputer systems (Figure 8–7). In minutes, electronic spread-

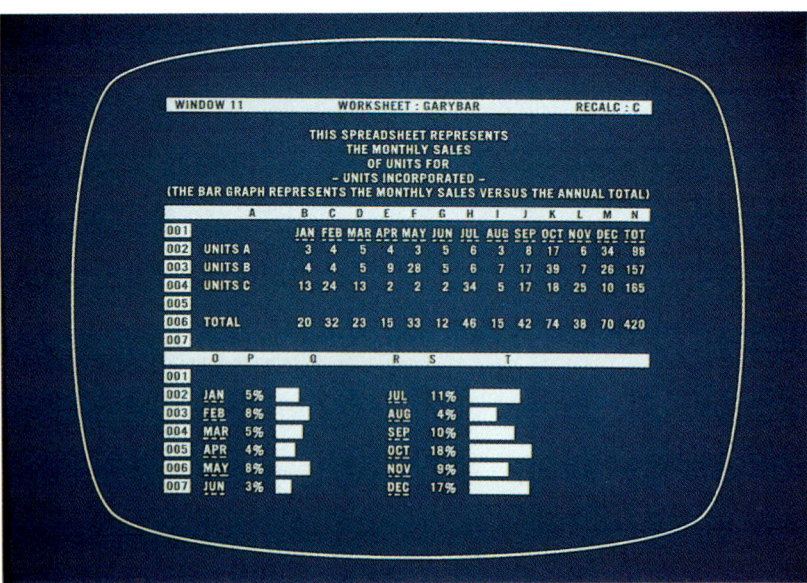

FIGURE 8–7
A typical screen display from a spreadsheet program (Courtesy of Genigraphics)

sheets can perform complex financial analysis tasks that would take days to perform manually.

VisiCalc, the first electronic spreadsheet, is responsible for much of the present proliferation of business microcomputers. Several million spreadsheets, including VisiCalc, Lotus 1-2-3, and Supercalc, are now being used in large and small businesses.

These spreadsheets are popular for several reasons. In the past, manual ledger sheet analysis was a tedious task facing many accountants. In order to submit a five-year forecast, the manager of a company had to make a ledger sheet for the company controller that assumed values for categories such as sales revenues, overhead costs, interest rates, repeat business, and cost of materials. If repeat business was projected at 80 percent instead of 75 percent, the manager would have to recalculate all values affected by the change in the repeat business category. Such a change could affect every value on the spreadsheet. Because the tools used to perform this massive recalculation usually consisted of nothing more than an eraser and a calculator, very few accountants would make more than two projections per category.

An electronic spreadsheet transforms the display screen into a huge ledger sheet (Figure 8–8). By simulating the rows and columns of a ledger sheet, it permits a user to work with a large series of interrelated values. When a user changes a given value on the spread sheet, the program automatically recalculates in seconds any other affected values. Without such a program, these recalculations could take hours. The spreadsheet job not only enables calculations to be performed more quickly, it also encourages more projections to be assessed.

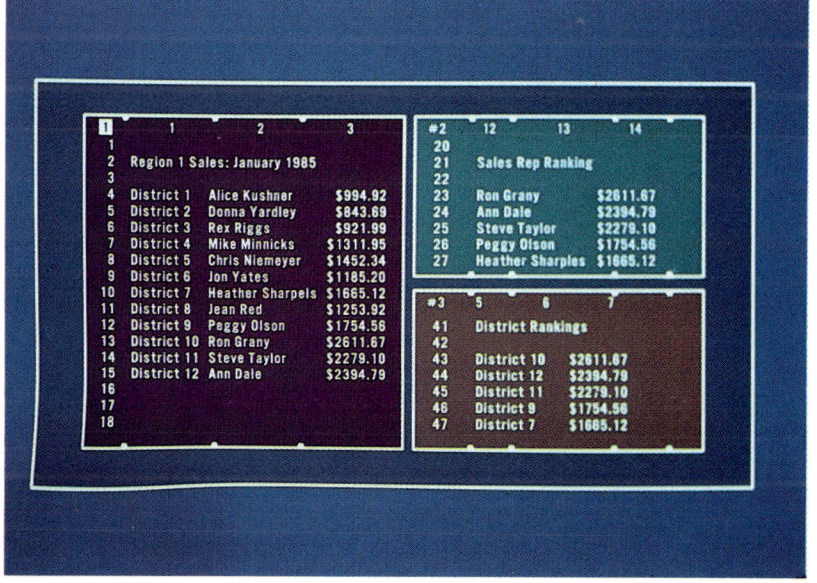

FIGURE 8–8
Typical split screen display from a spreadsheet program (Courtesy of Genigraphics)

Although originally intended for accountants, electronic spreadsheet programs are now being used by anyone needing to juggle figures. Spreadsheet programs have become popular with department managers for producing budgets, action and profit plans, sales forecasts, payroll, accounting, and real estate analysis. Other common uses for electronic spreadsheets include: currency conversion, expense reports, engineering applications, business plans, job cost analysis, sales projections, budget consolidation, cash flow projections, and income statements.

OPERATING SYSTEMS

An information processing system must efficiently apply all its resources: hardware, information, and human. These resources represent a considerable investment and must be used efficiently. Human resources must be relieved of tasks that computer systems can perform.

An operating system (OS) is a collection of control, processing, and data management programs specifically designed to manage the resources of a computer system and to facilitate the creation of programs and control their execution (Figure 8–9).

Through the use of operating systems, computer users delegate part of the burden of improved information processing efficiency to the computer, which reduces the time lag between jobs by automatically calling in programs and data as required. The management of jobs, tasks, and data are the three major management functions of an operating system.

The management of jobs is an external interface, i.e., the function of managing the transfer of jobs into and out of the processing streams. A **job** is a specifically defined set of work such as producing an inventory report, processing a payroll, or compiling a program. The management of tasks is an internal function, i.e., the management of carrying out the internal tasks necessary to complete jobs. A **task** is an element of work that

FIGURE 8–9
Makeup of an operating system

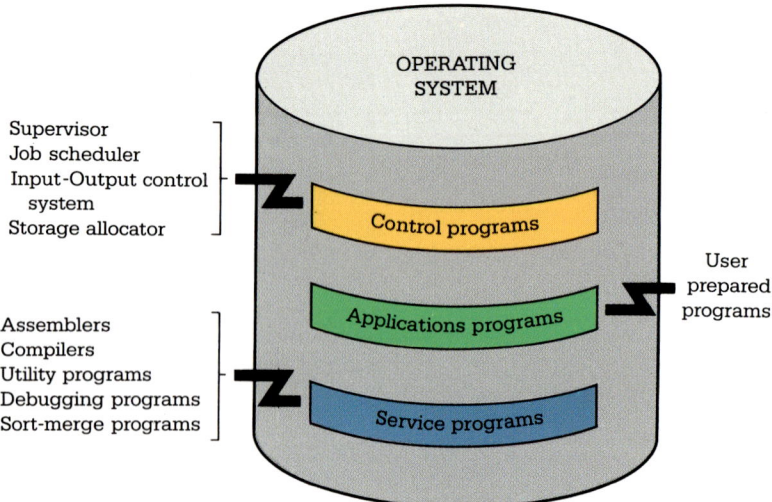

is part of the process of getting the job done. Loading a program into computer storage is an example of a task. The transfer of data elements and information between auxiliary storage devices and main storage is called data management.

To achieve the high efficiencies of which present information-processing systems are capable, an operating system should be able to handle these functions:

- ☐ Scheduling and performing input/output and related functions for programs
- ☐ Interpreting human operator commands and/or control cards that describe the work to be done
- ☐ Handling requests for the allocation of system resources
- ☐ Monitoring the execution of processing programs
- ☐ Protecting the various programs from one another

In general, the more sophisticated the computer system, the more complex the operating system required to manage its use. The philosophy behind the functions of the operating system is that the computer should perform those operator tasks it can do faster and more accurately, and the computer should be kept operating as continuously and effectively as possible.

Operating System Components

An operating system consists of two types of programs: control and service (Figure 8–10). **Control programs** supervise the automatic loading of jobs into and out of the library, schedule jobs for computer processing, initiate actual processing, and handle the termination of all jobs on the computer. **Service programs** consist of language processors, utility programs, and other operating system support programs.

Control Programs

Control programs, which ensure that activities take place correctly and in proper sequence, consist of the following programs: supervisor, interrupt handler, job scheduler, input/output control system, storage allocator, and operator communicator.

The supervisor program controls the other components of the operating system. The remaining programs have interrelating functions. The interrupt handler processes all interrupts to the system, and the job scheduler establishes the order in which jobs are to be processed. Activating the proper input/output and storage units of the computer system in compliance with the requirements of the program being executed is the function of the input/output control system (IOCS). The storage allocator distributes the storage facilities of the computer system to the jobs being processed, and the operator communicator handles communications between the operator and the computer and causes system status messages to be displayed on the computer console.

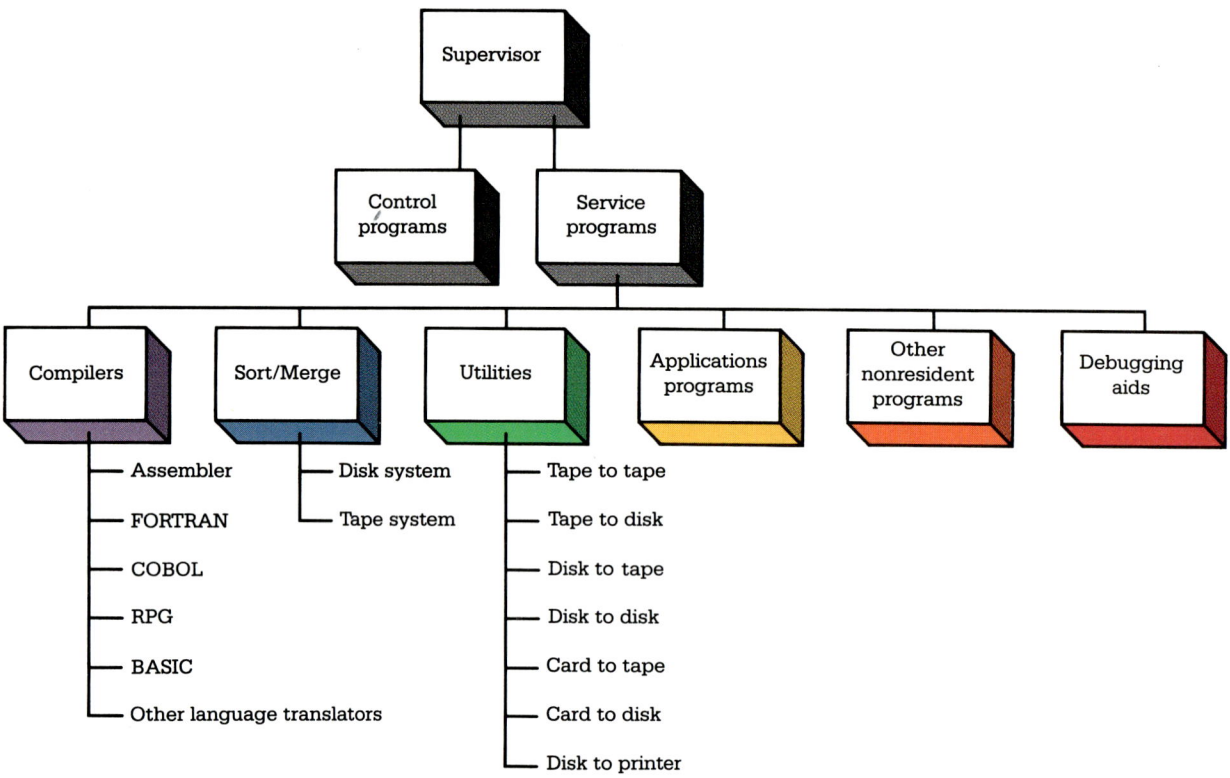

FIGURE 8–10
Components of an operating system

Additional operating system software is required for computer systems with such features as time-sharing, multiprogramming, virtual memory, or remote processing. In all cases, operating system software provides the computer user with a workable system for facilitating multiple operations.

Service Programs

Service programs are usually supplied by the computer manufacturer and consist of:

    □   Language translators, such as assemblers, BASIC interpreters, Pascal, COBOL, and FORTRAN compilers
    □   Utility routines, such as disk-to-tape, and tape-to-disk

Service programs, along with any user-prepared applications programs stored in the computer system, are collectively called the program library. Each program stored in the library is given an identification name. A program directory is maintained by the operating system; users, as well as the operating system, may access these programs by referencing the program name. Many computers provide security access by establishing different levels within the program library that are authorized only to certain individuals. The **library manager** is the program that inserts programs into the library, maintains a directory of these programs, and retrieves programs.

Other types of service programs include library maintenance routines, diagnostic software, sort and merge programs, and job reporting software. Library maintenance routines can add, delete, or copy programs from the various program libraries in auxiliary storage. Diagnostic software sends the user error messages when conditions make it impossible for the computer to process a job.

CP/M and MP/M

For years, **CP/M** (control program for microcomputers) has been a standard for the microcomputer industry. It is probably the most widely used disk operating system in the world. CP/M is a collection of programs, residing on a system diskette, that are loaded automatically when the computer is turned on. Another operating system is called **MP/M** (multiprogramming monitor for microcomputers). MP/M is a multiprogramming version of the CP/M operating system from Digital Research, Inc.

The purpose of CP/M, or any operating system, is to execute user commands and allow convenient use of all hardware resources provided by the computer. For example, CP/M will send text to the printer, read and process information from the keyboard, and display information on the display screen. In addition, it will perform such internal chores as managing disk or storage space. As soon as the computer is turned on, the operating system installed inside the computer's storage begins monitoring the keyboard for commands from the user so it can activate the desired applications programs. Once an applications program is executed, that program takes over the storage of the computer and all further interaction is with that program. When an applications program is completed, CP/M takes over again and waits for the next command. A simple way to view CP/M is as an ever present servant, ready to obey commands and manage the computer's resources when the user is not in the midst of executing an applications program.

CP/M provides specific commands for executing programs, manipulating files, and transferring information among the devices connected to the computer. One main advantage of CP/M is that all CP/M compatible software and files can be shared by users. Because of its compatibility as a standard operating system, CP/M will probably be used as long as the processors on which it resides are manufactured. Because improvements can always be made, CP/M and MP/M will continue to evolve, but new versions of these systems are usually compatible with previous ones.

The UNIX System

UNIX, an elegant and powerful computer operating system developed at AT & T's Bell Laboratories, is one of the world's most successful operating systems. Over 80 percent of the universities in the United States use

RUN "APPLICATION"

Local area networks (LANs) represent one of the keys to the automated office. At the heart of the automated office concept is the ability of diverse office devices to share information. Within limited distances, LANs are hardware and software systems which undertake this job of interdevice communications in a cost-effective manner, by offering ways to establish an electronic mail system and to share common data bases, costly printers, Winchester disk drives, and business software.

Home information systems are on their way. What entertainment was to television in the 1970s, information will be to the home computer of the 1980s. Interactive communication between data banks and homes is already taking place in many areas.

In 1979, The Source Telecomputing Corporation became the first company to offer computer networking services to small computer users. For varying fees to users throughout the United States and Canada, the Source makes a number of computer data banks available 24 hours a day. A sampling of the data services available on The Source include

- ☐ U.S. and international airline schedules
- ☐ Business and financial information
- ☐ Restaurant guides
- ☐ Discount shopping service via electronic mail order catalogs

- ☐ Educational programs and games
- ☐ Classified ads and bulletin boards
- ☐ Political campaign reports
- ☐ News and sports information
- ☐ Travel club information (tours, etc.)
- ☐ Weather bulletins and forecasts

Another telecomputing company of special interest to small computer users is CompuServe. CompuServe makes the full text of several large daily newspapers available by computer, allowing network users to compare different treatments of the same story. It also facilitates selective reading of various papers without the user actually having to subscribe. Like those who use The Source, CompuServe customers receive a diverse selection of information and home entertainment services that run the gamut from stock updates to clubs organized around various interests. CompuServe also features an electronic mail

capability enabling customers to communicate nationwide.

Invented in Great Britain, Viewdata is an information system under development in some parts of the United States. Viewdata ties together the services of home telephones and television sets. Used in Canada and Europe for several years, Viewdata can receive everything from travel advice and recipes to educational and financial information. Viewdata users can also send and receive electronic mail, and purchase goods and services. A simple decoding device enables all home computers to be easily tied in to the Viewdata system. Users telephone a local number and select the desired information from pages of data that can be displayed on home TV screens.

The subscriber narrows his or her selection step by step by choosing a number from each successive page to get more and more detailed information. For example, a traveler wishing to find a room in San Diego could begin by typing the number corresponding to the San Diego index page. From the listing that would appear on the screen (A), the subscriber would select the number opposite *Accommodations* and then enter this new number into the system. From the new listing that would appear, the traveler would select the number for *Hotels*, and once again key this number into the system (B). By following this refining process, the traveler would arrive at *San Diego Hotels*, which would likely be a listing several pages long giving hotel names, locations, phone numbers, and tourist information (C).

Using computerized network systems involves no special skill by subscribers. CompuServe, for example, stores all its information as pages—one page being the information that can be displayed on the screen at one time. Each page has its own reference number or address. To retrieve information, users' computers must be connected to a modem (a device that encodes and decodes computer signals sent over telephone wires) that links their machines with the network's mainframe computer. Once on-line, users consult a general index and follow the simple directions that show how to key in choices. With a little practice, most subscribers of The Source and CompuServe quickly become adept at finding the information they want.

(A)

```
SAN DIEGO
  KEY NUMBER FOR
  CATEGORY YOU WANT
  1. GENERAL INFORMA-
     TION
  2. HOW TO GET THERE
  3. THINGS TO KNOW
  4. ACCOMMODATIONS
  5. RECREATION
  6. WHAT TO SEE
```

(B)

```
SAN DIEGO
  ACCOMMODATIONS
  KEY NUMBER FOR
  CATEGORY YOU WANT
  1. HOTELS
  2. MOTELS
  3. CAMPSITES
  4. TOURIST HOMES
  5. TRAILER PARK
```

(C)

```
SAN DIEGO
  HOTELS
  KEY NUMBER FOR
  CATEGORY YOU WANT
  BLUEBEARDS HOTEL
  25 PACIFIC AVENUE
  STEPS FROM
    WATERFRONT
  350 ROOMS, COLOR TV
```

UNIX and it is becoming available on microcomputer systems. As a matter of fact, if you are going to use a computer, the chances are increasing daily that you will use a UNIX system.

The UNIX system is an interactive operating system: you type commands; the system obeys the commands and displays appropriate responses; and so on. Compared to other operating systems, particularly microcomputer operating systems such as CP/M, UNIX offers greater freedom of action and more comprehensive services. The UNIX system is a multiprocessing operating system; therefore, you can edit a file, print out another file, and check the spelling of a third file, all at the same time. UNIX is also a multiuser operating system whereby it allows many users to share the resources of one powerful computer system.

The UNIX system maintains a file system where users can store and retrieve information in named chunks called *files*. The system uses a directory of file names indicating where the files can be found in the file system. Understanding how to use the capabilities that the file system offers is perhaps the most important part of using the UNIX system effectively. The system contains a command interpreter, called the *shell,* that listens to your terminal and accepts and interprets the commands you type. The shell interprets the commands and causes the system to perform the work you want.

The UNIX system comes equipped with a large number of program tools to help users get started with useful applications right away. Among these tools are text editors, text formatters, spelling checkers, syntax checkers, text rearrangers, program debugging aids, interactive arithmetic calculators, phototypesetter text formatters, and programming languages such as C, Pascal, BASIC, COBOL, and FORTRAN.

The MVS System

The multiple virtual storage operating system (MVS) is IBM's operating system for its large mainframe computers. Logically, up to 9 999 concurrent tasks may be supported on MVS, but the practical limit is more like 300 to 400 concurrent interactive users, each in its own storage area.

Because MVS is such a large operating system, it is able to perform a variety of functions, such as:

- [ ] Supervisor (providing controls needed for multiprogramming)
- [ ] Master scheduler (responsibility for starting the system and communicating with the operator)
- [ ] Job entry subsystem (allowing work to be entered into the system and printed output to be returned to the user)
- [ ] System management facility (collecting information to account for system use, analyze system performance, and charge users for system resources)
- [ ] System activity measurement facility (recording system events for later reporting)
- [ ] Time-sharing option (providing users with interactive editing, testing, and debugging capabilities)

☐ Data management (handling all input/output and file management activities)

☐ Telecommunications (providing access to MVS by remote terminal users)

☐ System support programs (providing linkage editing, loading, and other support functions)

☐ Utility programs (providing utility functions such as copying files and performing catalog updates)

☐ Service aids (providing dump formatting, tracing, and other functions useful to the systems programmer)

MULTIPROGRAMMING AND MULTIPROCESSING

The difference between the speed at which a computer is able to perform calculations and the speed at which even the fastest input/output devices operate is vast. In the time it takes a printer working at 1 200 lines a minute to print one line, a computer could perform 10 000 additions. Multiprogramming was developed to relieve this imbalance and to increase computer use.

Multiprogramming is the concurrent execution of two or more programs simultaneously residing in the internal storage unit of a computer (Figure 8–11). Its basic principle is that the programs in internal storage share the available CPU time and input/output units. Each program is written to be completely independent. While input/output operations of one program are being handled, the CPU is essentially idle and can handle some non-input/output processing of another program at the same time. For example, a program to read data from punched cards and transcribe them to disks will only require use of the computer for a small fraction of the program's running time. The remainder of the time represents input/output transfer time during which other programs can use the CPU.

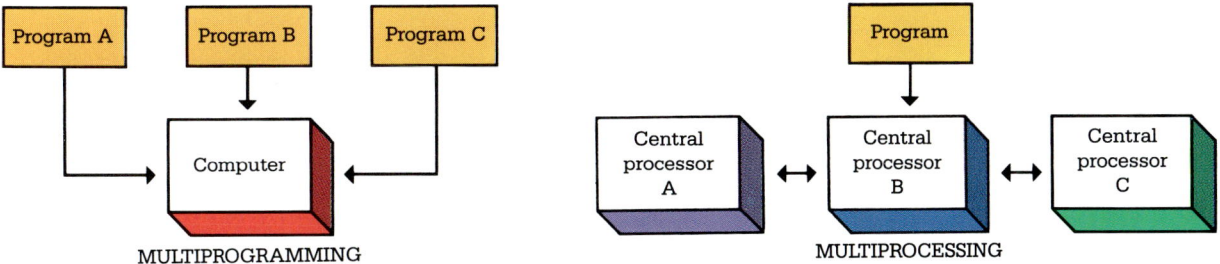

FIGURE 8–11

Multiprogramming and multiprocessing configurations. Multiprogramming is a technique used to increase the use of a computer system by running two or more programs concurrently in the same computer. Each program is allotted its own place in storage and its own peripherals, but all share the central processing unit. Multiprocessing is the simultaneous execution of a program by multiple central processing units under common control.

Benefits gained from multiprogramming include the elimination of off-line equipment normally used to transcribe data onto a faster medium for input. While this activity is proceeding, using limited numbers of input/output devices and little processing time, other more productive programs can use the remaining input/output devices and CPU time.

Some operating systems for medium or small computer systems permit one foreground program and one background program to be executed concurrently. Other systems can control two foreground programs (of different priority) and one background program. In either case, if more than one program requires the CPU at a given time, the priority assignments determine which program receives attention first.

Multiprocessing is the simultaneous execution of two or more sequences of instructions by multiple central processing units under common control (see Figure 8–11). A computer system operating in a multiprocessing configuration contains two or more interconnected CPUs, each with its own arithmetic and logic units and each capable of independent operation. Such a system must be able to interpret and execute its own programmed instructions. In addition, facilities must be available to transfer: (a) data from one CPU to another; (b) data and instructions to and from internal storage; and (c) data and instructions to and from a common auxiliary storage device. Multiprocessing offers computer processing capabilities that are not available when only one CPU is used so that many complex operations can be performed at the same time.

DATA COMMUNICATIONS

We live in the midst of a vast electronic universe in which information is transmitted at the speed of light. Data communications, also called telecommunications, combines computer capabilities with high-speed electronic communications to transmit characters (information) via electrical currents, light beam pulses, or radio waves. The signals are perceptible to computers, terminals, and other electronic equipment, but the information conveyed by the signals is interpretable to humans only when presented on paper or a visual display. The ultimate function of data communications is to transmit signals correctly from one machine to another, over short or long distances, as a method of human communication.

Data transmission is not limited to human language information transfer. Although much of data traffic is apparently decipherable when decoded, information transfer is not complete. For example, while you can recognize the numbers in a transfer of payroll information, you cannot understand their significance unless you know the format for each field or group of numbers transferred. That format definition is stored in the receiving computer. Assuming the sending and receiving parties agree about the definition of each information field, the definitions themselves do not have to be transmitted; however, the data transmitted must be totally accurate. Therefore, data transmission is the transfer of information according to a predefined format.

A **data communications system** consists of terminals, computers, and communications links that connect the various elements of a data processing system. A system may be as simple as a terminal in an executive's office connected to a computer in another part of the building, or it may be as complex as a worldwide network of interconnected computers and terminals (Figure 8–12).

The Computer's Role in Data Communications

The function of data communications is to transport information to and from the user at a terminal. There is always a computer in the path between terminals. To manage the flow of information over communications lines, computer systems have communications programs that establish the necessary dialogue with the terminal operator and handle various management functions in the transmission system.

Computer systems move data at the rate of 100 million bits per second. Medium-speed voice communications facilities, such as telephones, move data at less than 10 000 bits per second—10 000 times slower than the computer. Most people read at less than 50 bits per second and type at about 15 bits per second—or nearly 1 000 times slower than the transmission line. These figures prove that a communication problem exists among computers, transmission lines, and humans. Fortunately, a number of techniques can be used to balance these differences. These techniques include multiplexing and time sharing, in

FIGURE 8–12
Data communications system

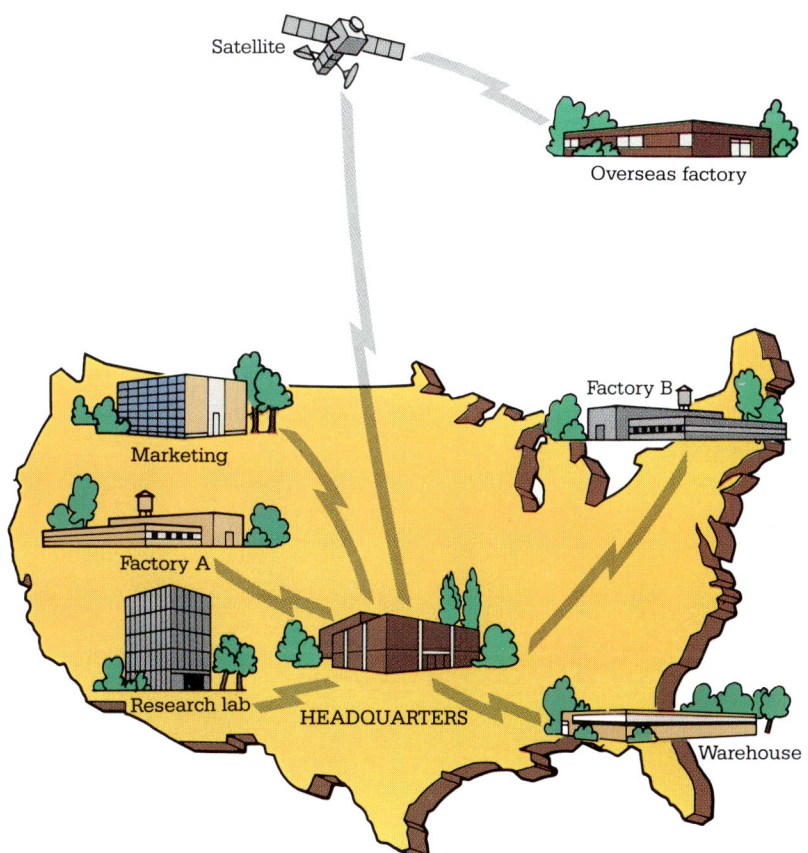

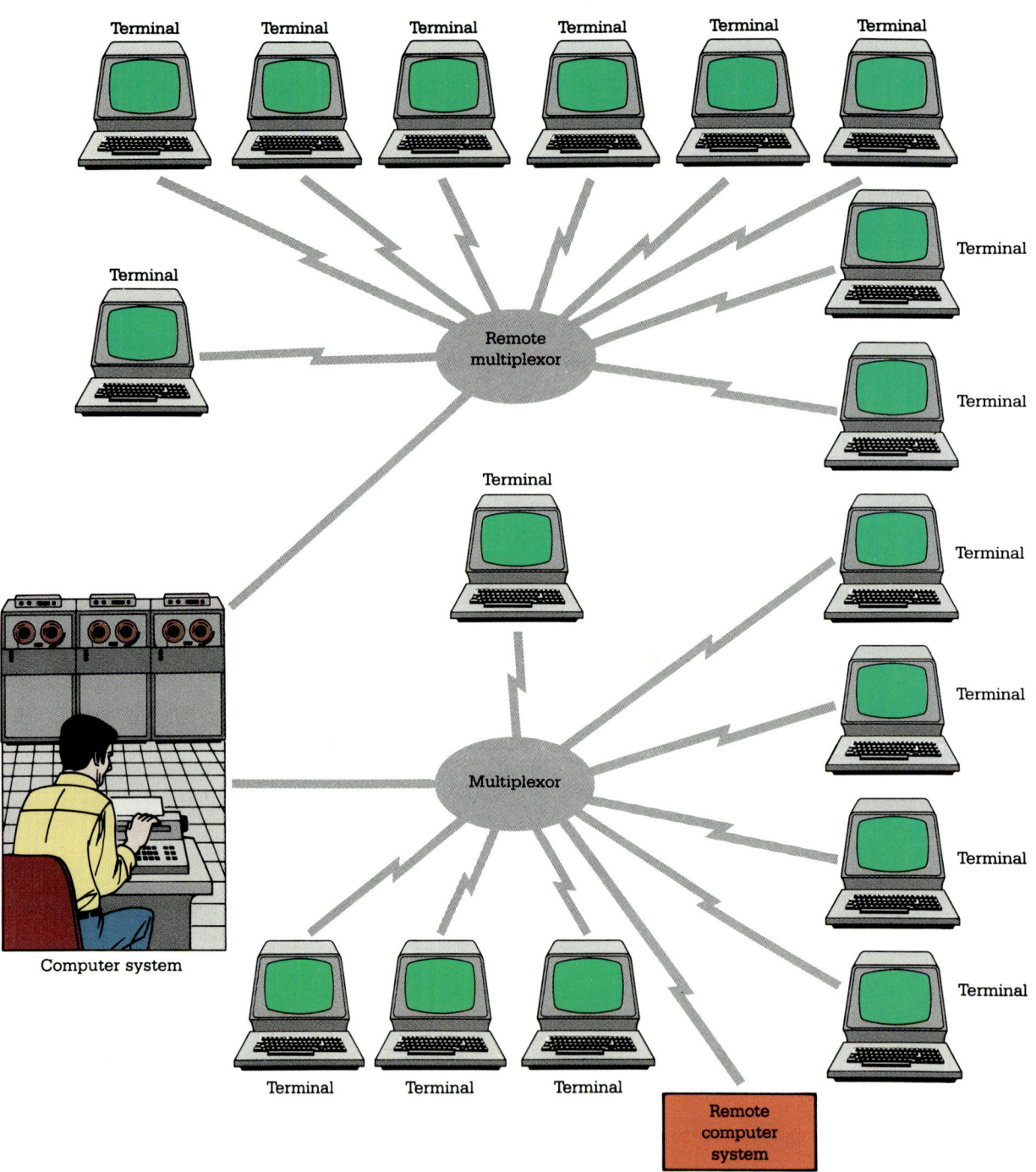

FIGURE 8–13
Data communications system with distribution services

which many terminals share a single computer, and remote multiplexing, in which many terminals share a single data communications line (Figure 8–13). Remote **multiplexors** condense many slow speed devices onto one higher speed communications line.

Data Communication Links

The bulk of data traffic, mostly generated by computer systems, is currently carried asynchronously over the telephone network, but synchronous communications links are designed specifically for data traffic. Various transmission media used for data communications include wires, cables, coaxial cables, microwave transmission, communication satellites, waveguides, lasers, fiber optic cables, and digital networks.

Modems and Acoustic Couplers

Communication between remote terminals (Figure 8–14) cannot take place without **modems**, or **data sets**, that encode and decode the computer's serial bits into frequencies that can be transmitted over standard

FIGURE 8–14

Modem's relationship with a communications network. The modem at the computer end converts the electrical signals sent by the computer to tones that can be carried over the communications link. The modem at the terminal end reconverts the tones back to electrical signals that activate the terminal. When the terminal sends data to the computer, the modems function identically, but in the reverse direction.

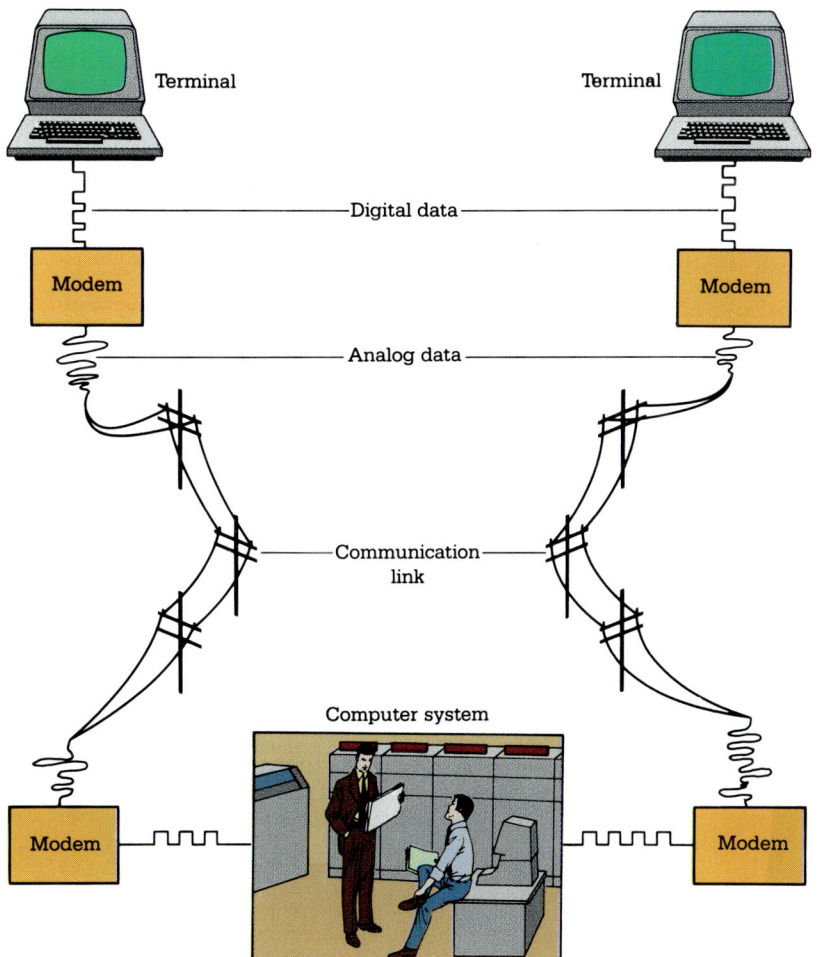

telephone lines. Modem is an acronym for modulator/demodulator. Two modems, one for each computer, are needed for data communications over telephone lines. The two types of modems are direct-connect modems and acoustic couplers. A direct-connect modem is a hard-wired device that plugs directly into a modular telephone jack. An acoustic coupler modem uses a pair of rubber cups that fit over a traditional telephone handset to send and receive signals.

COMPUTER NETWORKS

A **computer network** is a collection of computers and terminals connected by a communications system. A centralized, or star, network is characterized by a central computer with several terminal devices connected to it (Figure 8–15). Distributed networks consist of several computer systems connected via local communications facilities or direct connection with the communications system (Figure 8–16). A ring network consists of direct connections between computers at local sites without contact through a central computer.

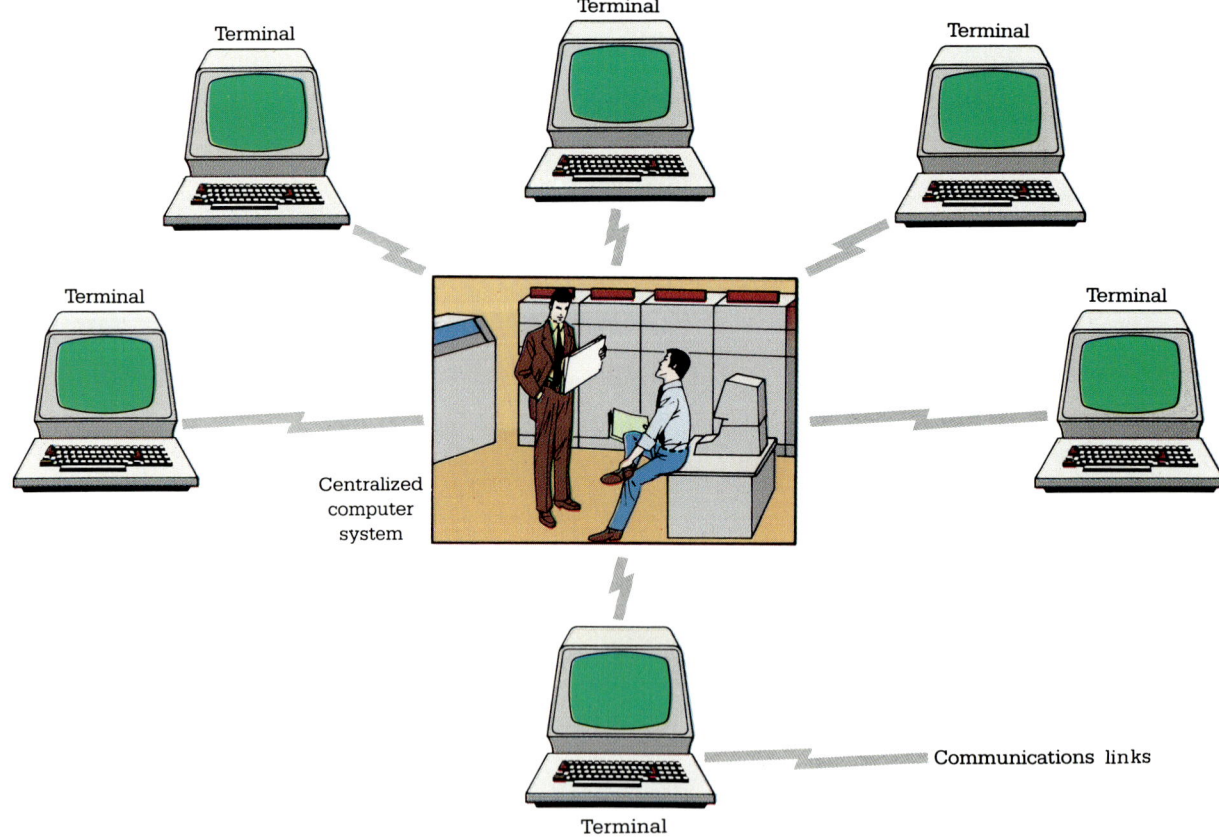

FIGURE 8–15
Centralized computer network

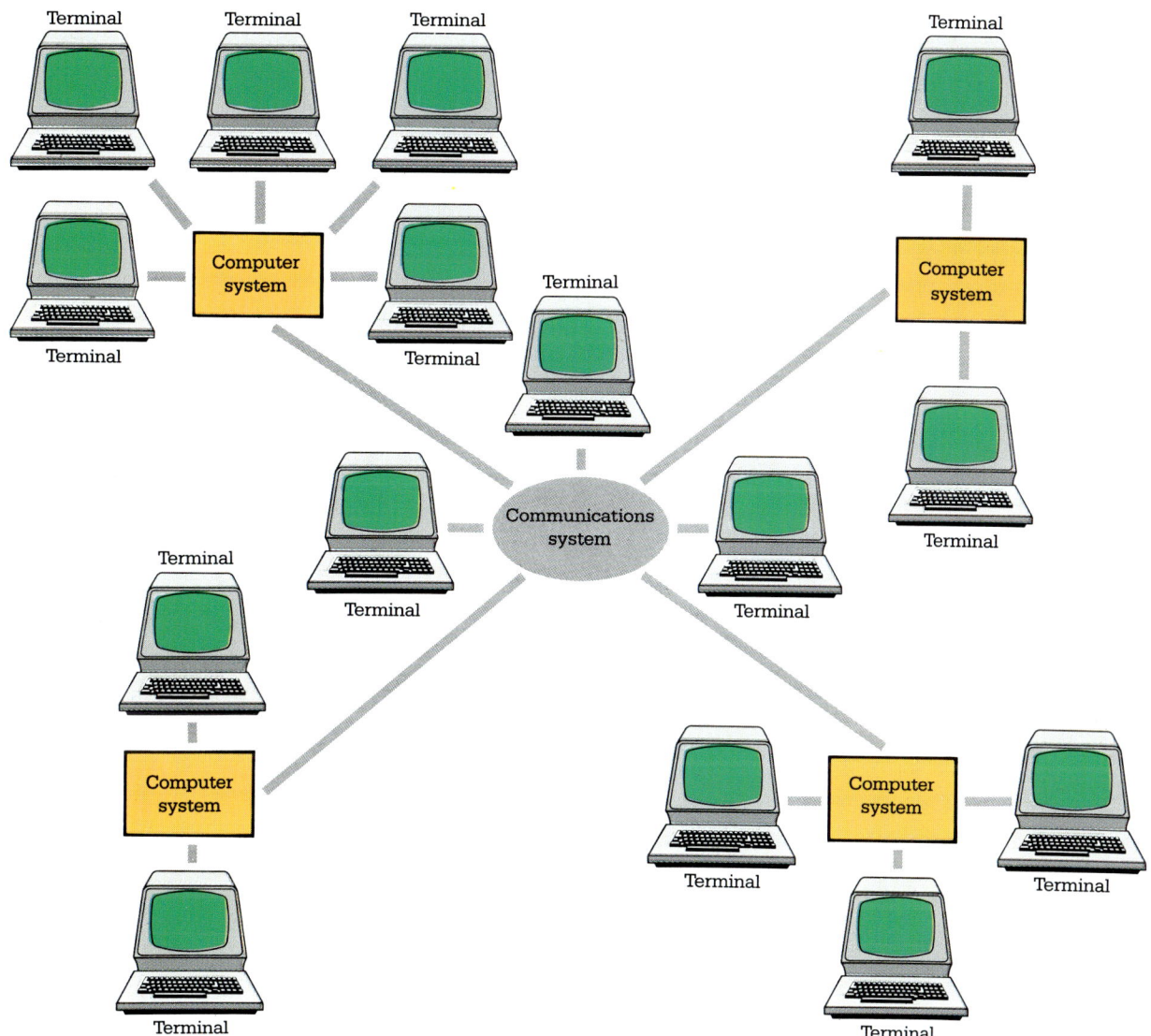

FIGURE 8–16
Distributed computer network

Computer networks provide a cost effective method for distributing high-speed computer services to a large number of users. Global computer networks using international data bases may soon make information available to everyone. Computer networks are already popping up in unlikely, but convenient, locations. For example, supermarkets equipped with automated teller machines enable customers to withdraw cash, make deposits, and check their balances with participating banks.

Two fast growing time-sharing communications networks are those offered for personal computer users through CompuServe and The Source. For a fee, these information utilities make the resources of their

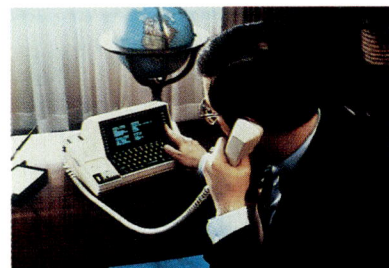  

FIGURE 8–17
Teleconferencing participants may be located throughout the world. Data terminals are connected via the telephone network. (Courtesy of Bell Laboratories, and TRW, Inc.)

large mainframe computers available to owners of modem-equipped small computers. Stock and weather information, encyclopedia data bases, access to numerous on-line clubs, and hundreds of other services are offered to subscribers.

Teleconferencing is another network capability that uses the telephone as a medium for voice transmission, the television for video, and the computer for data transmission services (Figure 8–17). More than 20 million business meetings are held every day in the United States. Because business travel accounts for a large portion of a company's budget, those firms equipped with proper teleconferencing equipment can save travel, time, and money.

SUMMARY

☐ Time sharing is the simultaneous use of a computer system by multiple terminals. A time-sharing system makes computer capabilities available to many users by apportioning small slices of time to each on a rotating basis.

☐ A real time system controls an on-going process and delivers its output by the time it is needed for effective control. Airlines use real time systems to provide immediate reservations for passengers. Banks use real time systems to send transactions from one branch to another.

☐ Electronic spreadsheets are the most popular business application for microcomputers. A complex financial analysis task that takes days to perform manually can be accomplished in minutes with a spreadsheet program.

☐ The primary purpose of an operating system is to reduce the cost of running application programs by increasing the use of the various computer system components, thereby avoiding lost time.

☐ In general, the more sophisticated the computer system, the more complex the operating system required to manage its use. An operating system has two types of programs: (a) control programs that supervise automatic loading of jobs in and out of the library, and schedule, initiate, and terminate processing jobs; and (b) service programs that consist of language translators, utility routines, mathematical routines, special subroutines, sort/merge programs, and programmer aids such as trace and dump routines.

☐ Multiprogramming is the concurrent execution of two or more programs simultaneously residing in the internal storage unit of a computer where they share available CPU time and input/output units. Each program is written as a completely independent program.

☐ Multiprocessing is the simultaneous execution of two or more sequences of instructions by multiple central processing units under common control.

☐ Data communications combines computer capabilities with high-speed electronic communications to transmit characters (information) via electrical currents, light beam pulses, or radio waves.

☐ Computer networks, including star, distributed, and ring networks, provide a cost effective method for distributing high-speed computer services to a large number of users.

REVIEW QUESTIONS

True or False

——— 1 Time sharing refers to sharing off-line equipment with several users.

——— 2 Terminals are input/output devices to a time-sharing computer system.

——— 3 Real time refers to current time rather than historical time.

——— 4 An airline reservation system is an example of a real time system.

——— 5 Real time systems are never used in banks because of the low volume of check processing required.

——— 6 Processing all student programs on the evening computer shift is an example of real time processing.

——— 7 One of the advantages of data base systems is that duplication of data is minimized.

——— 8 The auxiliary storage devices used on most data base management systems are magnetic tape systems.

——— 9 In a relational data base system, data are stored in the form of "relations" in a number of tables.

——— 10 A data base administrator is responsible for establishing and managing a data base.

——— 11 In a network data base management system, the structure permits the multidirectional connection of nodes.

——— 12 A superior–subordinate or parent–child relationship exists in a hierarchical data base management system.

——— 13 A data dictionary is an index of all items in a data base.

——— 14 A key is the field that determines the position of a record in a sorted sequence.

——— 15 An electronic spreadsheet transforms the display screen into a ledger sheet.

——— 16 Electronic spreadsheets were originally designed to be used by graphic artists.

——— 17 By the end of 1986, every other office worker will use some form of electronic spreadsheet.

——— 18 Lotus 1-2-3 is an electronic spreadsheet program.

——— 19 An operating system is a program that has been operating properly for a long period of time.

_____ **20** In general, the more sophisticated the computer system, the more complex the operating system required to manage its use.

_____ **21** The main objective of an operating system is to maximize the use of auxiliary storage devices.

_____ **22** A key feature of the operating system concept is a supervisory or control program which is in storage at all times.

_____ **23** The control program provides automatic transition from one job to another.

_____ **24** One of the main purposes of the operating system is to replace computer operators.

_____ **25** UNIX and BASIC are both considered operating systems.

_____ **26** The operating system tends to isolate the user from the hardware.

_____ **27** CP/M is a disk operating system widely used with microcomputers.

_____ **28** Data communications involves transmission and processing of data over a communications system.

_____ **29** A data communications system consists of computers, terminals, and communication links.

_____ **30** The primary purpose of modems is to improve the transmission of data over the telephone network.

_____ **31** An acoustic coupler uses a telephone handset to connect a digital terminal to a computer system.

_____ **32** A centralized collection of data is called a file.

Short Answer

1 In a distributed processing system _____ (less, more) information is transmitted to the central system than would be necessary if all processing were done by the central system. Consequently, communication costs are _____ (lower, higher) and the central computer workload is _____ (reduced, expanded).

2 A network of interconnected microcomputer systems is called a _____ processing system.

3 In a typical time-sharing system, the users communicate with the central computing facility via remote _____.

4 _____ _____ storage devices are used in time-sharing systems to store the user's programs.

5 In a time-sharing system, the _____ _____ gathers and routes all data communications between the computer and user terminals.

6 A _____ _____ _____ is a data base that is spread throughout a computer network.

7 In a network data base management system, data records are linked by a complex system of _____.

8 _____ _____ implies that the data and the applications programs that use them are independent and may be changed without changing the other.

9 Three types of data structures used in data base management systems are _____, _____, and _____.

10 A _____ _____ _____ _____ is a collection of related programs for loading, accessing, and controlling a data base.

11 A _____ _____ _____ is designed to supply organizational managers with information needed to plan, organize, staff, direct, and control the operations of the organization.

12 The first electronic spreadsheet was called _____.

13 _____ _____ are used to supervise the automatic loading of jobs into and out of the computer, schedule jobs for computer processing, initiate processing, and handle the termination of all jobs on the computer.

14 The multiple virtual storage operating system (MVS) is IBM's operating system for its _____ _____ (large mainframe, personal computer) systems.

15 Data transmission is the transfer of information according to a _____ _____.

16 In any data communications system, the data processing is done by the _____.

17 A _____ is an "electronic meeting" conducted among people at distant locations through the use of telecommunications.

18 An index to all the items in an organization's data base is called a _____ _____.

19 A person with the overall authority to design and manage a data base is called a _____ _____ _____.

20 A language used to extract data from a data base is called a _____ language.

21 DBMS means _____ _____ _____ _____.

22 An _____ _____ is used to control all on-line operations that take place within a computer system.

OUTLINE

OBJECTIVES

1 Understand the reasons for a
systems study.

2 Understand the steps involved
in the creation of an information processing system.

3 Understand the increasing security dangers faced by organizations using information processing systems.

4 Understand the importance of
hardware and software security.

5 Identify some of the ethical issues involved with using computers.

9 SYSTEMS DESIGN, SECURITY, AND ETHICS

Have you ever wondered how executives systematically determine improvements in how information is handled in their companies? One way is by conducting a systems study—an investigation to determine and develop needed informational improvements in specified areas. In some cases, these improvements will involve using a computer.

There are at least three reasons for making a systems study. First, substantial investment may be involved in using a computer, and a proper study reduces the risk of loss. Second, a systems study may help avoid common pitfalls resulting from inadequate planning. And, finally, the study may point the way to substantial benefits.

WHAT IS A SYSTEM?

A system is a composite of procedures, processes, methods, techniques, skills, and information capable of performing and/or supporting an operational role in attaining specified management objectives. A complete system includes equipment, material, services, personnel, related facilities, and information required for its operation so that it can be a self-sufficient unit in its operational and/or support environment.

A system does not have to be computer-based, although this would tend to provide a form of control to regulate the process. Computer-based systems are developed after much planning, expenditure of resources, and effort from all levels of management. Top management usually delegates the responsibility for developing computer-based systems to a computer-oriented system team.

If the specific function is to be accomplished, careful coordination is necessary. Coordination implies planning. The system begins with a user. The user has a need for technical support, but doesn't know how to use the computer to do the job. In another part of the organization, programmers, who know a great deal about the computer, often do not have an understanding of the user's needs. The solution is to call in a systems analyst, a professional whose basic responsibility is translating user needs into the technical specifications required by programmers. The systems analyst's job consists of: (a) determining company information needs; (b) gathering facts and analyzing the basic methods of current business systems; and (c) modifying, redesigning, and integrating existing procedures into new systems specifications that can provide the needed information. The systems analyst may also recommend justifiable equipment changes.

Systems analysts are aptly characterized as generalists. They must be familiar with the organization's objectives, personnel, products and services, industry, and special problems, and they should have a thorough grasp of programming. Systems analysts should also know the uses and limitations of computers and auxiliary information processing equipment, because they are interpreters between users and programmers. In addition to determining which jobs are candidates for computer processing, they must be able to organize a set of tasks into a series of inter-related programs, determine hardware resource requirements for programs, and estimate the time needed to design, write, and check out the programs.

To translate user needs into technical specifications under management control, the systems analyst uses a process known as systems analysis and design. Systems analysis and design is a step-by-step approach to system development, beginning with logical design and gradually moving to physical design.

SYSTEMS FUNCTIONS

No standards exist for systems analysis and design, however, as a system goes through the system life cycle, from concept to implementation, it must pass through each of the steps in Figure 9–1.

Problem Definition

The systems analyst's first responsibility is to prepare a written statement of the objectives and scope of the problem. Based on interviews with management and the user, the analyst writes a brief description of his or her understanding of the problem and reviews it with both groups, ideally in a joint management/user meeting. A clear statement of objectives is important because people respond to written statements. They ask for clarification; they correct obvious errors or misunderstandings. The analyst should provide a rough estimate of the cost of the project and an accurate assessment of the cost and schedule for the next phase—the feasibility study. These estimates will give management and the user a sense of the scope of the project.

Preliminary Study

The preliminary study, often called the feasibility study, is a high-level, capsule version of the entire process, and it is intended to answer a number of questions. What is the problem? Is there a feasible solution to the problem? Is the problem worth solving?

The feasibility study also recommends a direction to management. If the recommendation is accepted, then management must authorize the resources to perform the actual analysis.

Systems Analysis

Systems analysis is a logical process used to learn enough about the existing system to permit the design of a better one. Data are collected, organized, and evaluated; a conclusion is made whether to continue with the project. During this phase, the systems analyst will prepare cost studies for the existing system, make cost projections for system improvement, and supply a comparative analysis of the two.

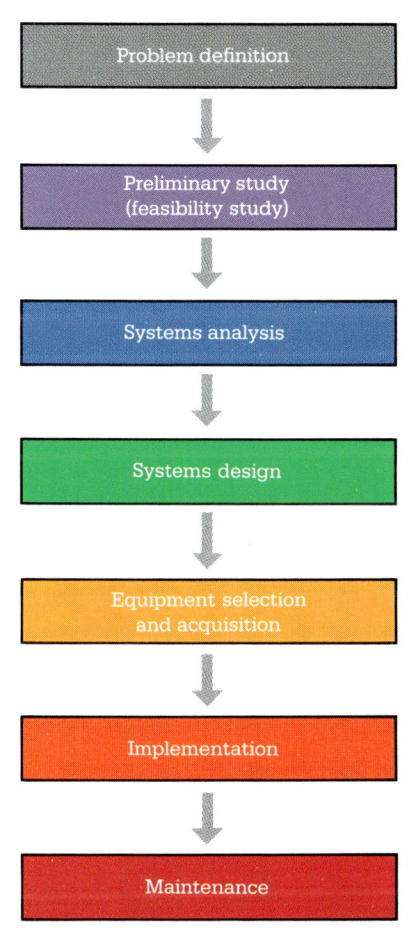

FIGURE 9–1
The steps in the system life cycle outlining the process of developing a computer-based information system

Systems Design

During the systems design phase, we begin to move from the logical system to the physical system. Several alternate solutions might be considered. For example, a given system might be implemented by a computer or manual means. If a computer is used, the system might be interactive or batch; a data base or traditional data files might be used.

Up to this point, the project has involved the time of a few systems analysts, and the cost has been limited. Detailed design may involve these analysts plus a few more, and the detailed design phase will take longer; thus, the costs begin to accelerate (Figure 9–2).

The systems design phase ends with management or the user deciding whether the new system's benefits are worth the cost, or whether programming will be able to support the system. If the decision is negative, the project ends. If the system is worth supporting, one of several alternatives will be selected. The systems analyst's description of the selected alternative will be used as a high level model for developing the physical system.

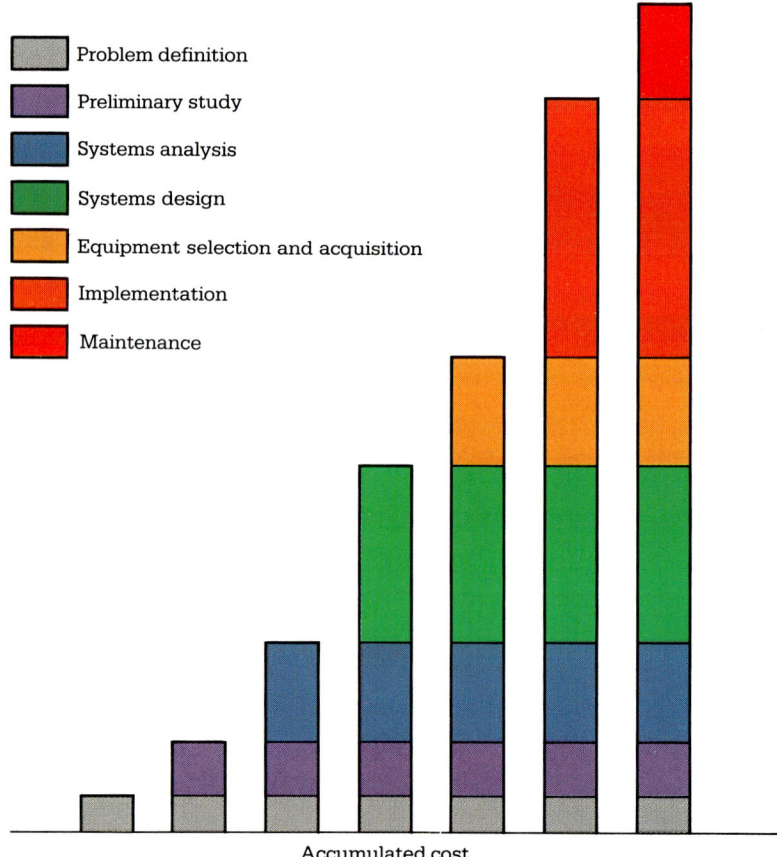

FIGURE 9–2
Cost of the system as it goes from phase to phase

Equipment Selection and Acquisition

During this phase, management acquires the computer that will do the job most effectively at the lowest possible cost. The systems analyst prepares a set of computer specifications, which are then placed out for proposal. The analyst reviews the vendors' bids, selects the vendor who most closely meets the specifications, and makes a recommendation to management. New hardware is selected, ordered, and installed. If current equipment has the required capacity, the systems analyst designs the system to use the available hardware.

Implementation

During the implementation phase, the system is physically created. Necessary programs are coded, debugged, tested, and documented. The replacement of the current system by the new system should be accomplished so that disruption of the operation is held to a minimum. The new system is tested with live data in the new system's operating environment, while the current system continues to operate in parallel with the new system until management is satisfied with the new system's operation and performance. In the interim, the user personnel must be trained and fully functional by the time the new system begins operation.

Maintenance

Following implementation, the system enters a maintenance phase. The objective is to keep the system functioning at an acceptable level. Maintenance is a programming function, but minor adjustments are sometimes necessary. Note that only adjustments to the system which support the original specifications are maintenance; adjustments that change functions or enhance output are not. Major changes to a system deserve the same study and care that went into the construction of the system in the first place, and a well-designed system must anticipate and allow for change.

COMPUTER CRIME AND SECURITY

Computer security involves technological and procedural safeguards for computer hardware, software, and data. When computer technology was young, computer security was a concern primarily for computer sites that stored national security data. At that time, the methods of protecting information were simpler; physical security was the main concern. In the past decade, the introduction of sophisticated software has increased the need for security measures other than physical protection. For example, in a multiprogramming environment, programs running simultaneously must be secured from one another. The introduction of microcomputers has also increased the complexity of security programs. In many instances, distributed information processing has increased access to information and has reduced the effectiveness of centralized organizational

Whether or not you are ready for it, the robot revolution has already begun. Tens of thousands of modern, sophisticated robot machines are at work today in factories throughout the world. Although robots have always been pictured as metallic human-like electronic devices, most aren't even remotely humanized. The majority are clumsy and can't see very well, but they are still very expensive. For these reasons, they have yet to fulfill their greatest promise and threat—the replacement of a great number of human workers.

No matter how long it takes them to reach their full potential, however, robots and the field of robotics are here to stay. Japan, the largest user of industrial robots, has tens of thousands of them manufacturing everything from automobiles to cameras. Today, the robotics industry grosses just below $100 million a year, but by 1990 this figure is expected to be $2 billion to $4 billion a year.

Robotic research is being conducted in the U.S., Japan, and other countries to increase the capabilities of and develop new uses for robots. Most advanced concepts about robots seem to come from university research laboratories. The robotic institutes at Carnegie-Mellon University, Stanford, and the Massachusetts Institute of Technology are a few of the educational institutions with research programs in artificial intelligence and robotics.

Let's take a look at how robotics could affect your life. Imagine going into a hypothetical shoe store/factory in the future. After your foot is measured by a computer-controlled measuring device, sample selections are shown to you on a computerized color display. After you select a shoe model and color and request alterations to suit your taste, an

In the automated shoe store/factory of the future, the customer will pick a shoe model and color and watch robots make the shoes on the spot.

order card is produced and read by computerized equipment in the production area, then the leather is cut to size. The shoe is assembled by robots and delivered to you in about ten minutes.

With a few qualifications, the technology to support an automated shoe store/factory is here. The computer-driven sizing and cutting being done in many areas of the garment industry could easily be applied to producing shoes, and the conversion of foot measurements into two-dimensional patterns is a straightforward task. At last, improved robots are becoming available that are dexterous enough to do such precise work as assembling shoes.

Robots are beginning to become part of the industrial workforce. They work without complaint, start on time, are never absent, and take no breaks or vacations. Here are a few examples of where they are at work today: machine tool loading, die casting, press transfer, materials handling, forging, tool handling, welding, and assembly.

control. The telecommunication links that connect distributed computer systems can further weaken security if adequate precautions are not observed.

In order to establish an effective security program, organizational and administrative controls must be developed and implemented. Planners must determine potential exposures, including the adverse effects each exposure might have on the information processing organization. This list can be used to develop a security plan. The need for security must be understood by the entire organization.

Physical security measures are intended to reduce or prevent disruption of service, loss of assets, and unauthorized access to equipment. Because of growing dependence on computers, disruption of service can be devastating to an organization. Unauthorized access to information can affect service by reducing confidence in the security of the information. Attempts to protect the system and data will be futile unless computer equipment is physically secure.

Developing countermeasures to security threats requires a thorough knowledge of the information processing installation and the entire organization. Threats can come from environmental hazards or from human action and can destroy or improperly modify the functioning of the system (Figure 9–3). If unanticipated, environmental hazards, such as fire, flooding, earthquake, severe storms, and power failures, often have an unpredictable and far-reaching impact. Human destruction of equipment or data is usually easier to contain. These damaging acts originate from many sources, ranging from sabotage to inadvertent errors in employee judgment.

Countermeasures that are used when designing a physical security program include: building design, placement of detection devices, fire/police notification systems, back-up air conditioning and power sources, secured doors and windows, personnel screening program, personnel education/awareness training, system access control, and control procedures. Some physical security countermeasures can also protect hardware. However, in many instances, these countermeasures are inadequate protection against unauthorized access because the perpetrator may have physical access to the system. Threats against hardware security are often more difficult to identify and quantify than are threats to physical security. Some possible countermeasures include: well-documented systems and procedures, storage protection, execution protection, input/output processing protection, cryptography (for data communications), predefined scheduling, and adherence to procedures. Many countermeasures require additional capabilities from the operating system and greater technical knowledge about the operation of the system and programs. Security problems associated with data transmission are complex, and countermeasures in this area are therefore harder to implement. For example, cryptographic technology ranges from simple algorithmic encryption of messages to complex hardware and software-oriented cryptography devices. Using these devices involves significant planning and requires changes in the daily operation of the computer installation.

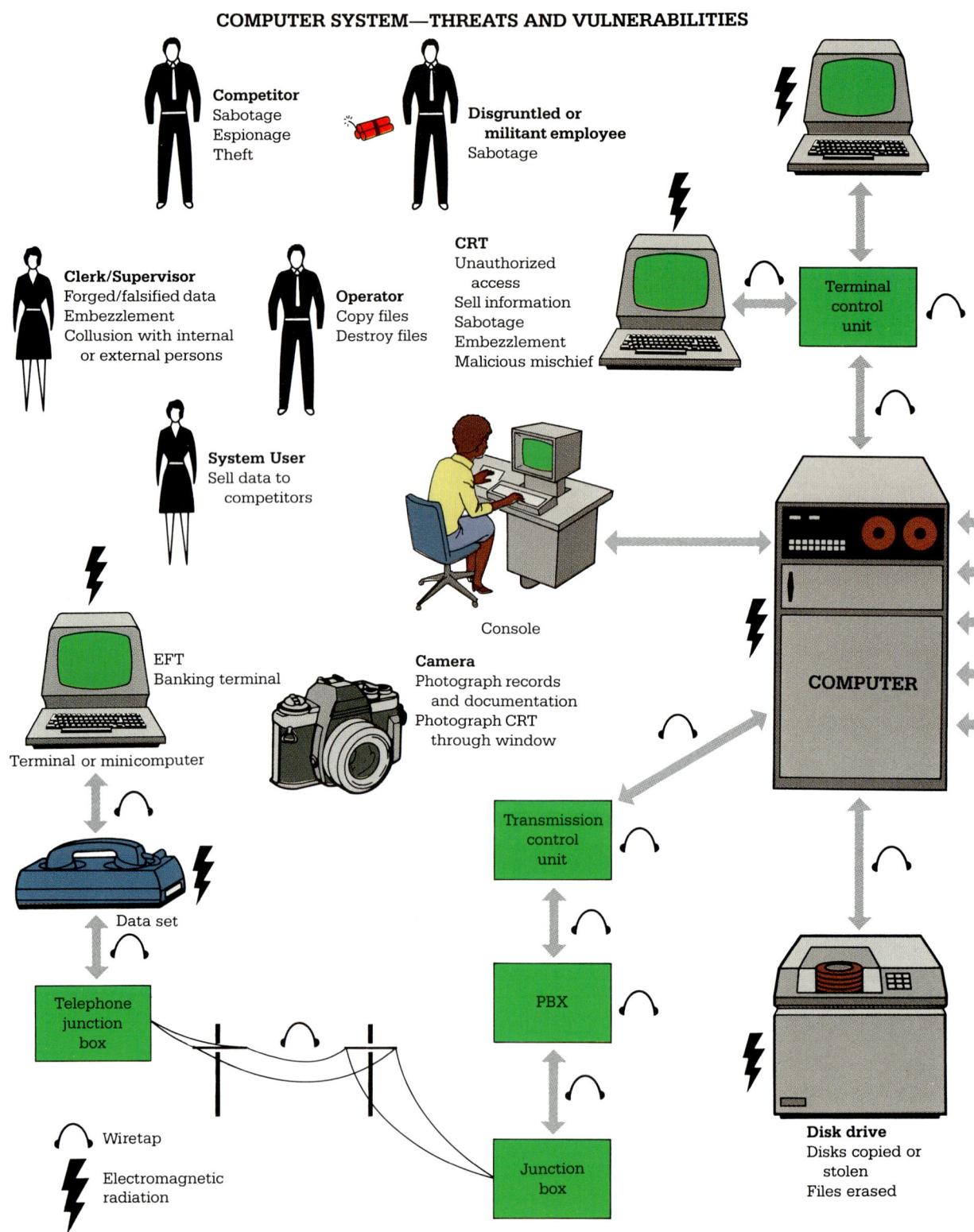

COMPUTER SYSTEM—THREATS AND VULNERABILITIES

Competitor
Sabotage
Espionage
Theft

Disgruntled or militant employee
Sabotage

Clerk/Supervisor
Forged/falsified data
Embezzlement
Collusion with internal
or external persons

Operator
Copy files
Destroy files

CRT
Unauthorized access
Sell information
Sabotage
Embezzlement
Malicious mischief

System User
Sell data to competitors

Terminal control unit

Console

EFT
Banking terminal

Terminal or minicomputer

Camera
Photograph records
and documentation
Photograph CRT
through window

COMPUTER

Data set

Transmission control unit

Telephone junction box

PBX

Junction box

Disk drive
Disks copied or stolen
Files erased

⌢ Wiretap

⚡ Electromagnetic radiation

FIGURE 9–3
A computer system's vulnerabilities (Reprinted with permission from Assets Protection Publishing; originally published in *Assets Protection Journal;* Volume 2, Number 3, 1977.)

202

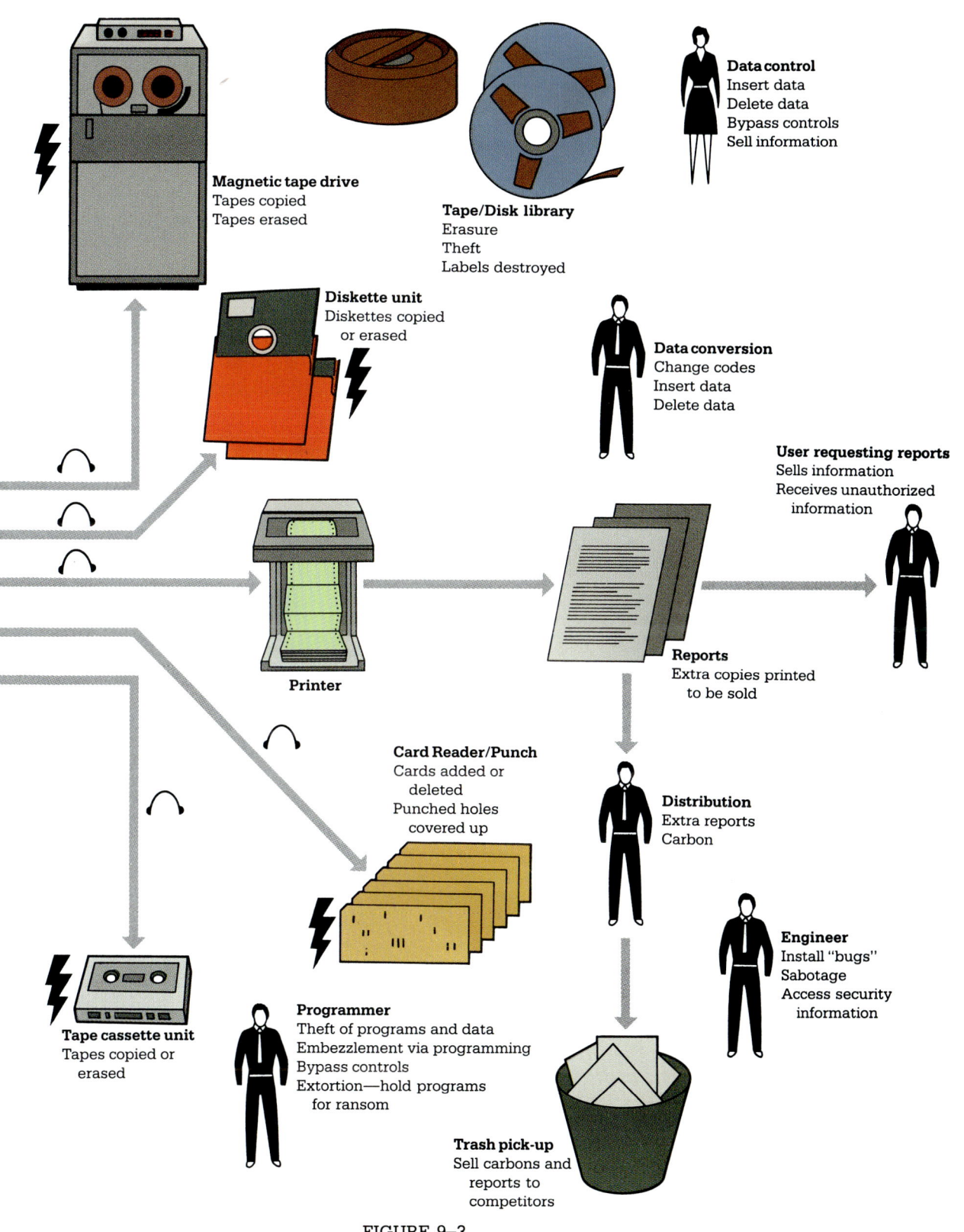

Magnetic tape drive
Tapes copied
Tapes erased

Tape/Disk library
Erasure
Theft
Labels destroyed

Data control
Insert data
Delete data
Bypass controls
Sell information

Diskette unit
Diskettes copied
or erased

Data conversion
Change codes
Insert data
Delete data

User requesting reports
Sells information
Receives unauthorized
information

Printer

Reports
Extra copies printed
to be sold

Card Reader/Punch
Cards added or
deleted
Punched holes
covered up

Distribution
Extra reports
Carbon

Engineer
Install "bugs"
Sabotage
Access security
information

Tape cassette unit
Tapes copied or
erased

Programmer
Theft of programs and data
Embezzlement via programming
Bypass controls
Extortion—hold programs
for ransom

Trash pick-up
Sell carbons and
reports to
competitors

FIGURE 9–3
(Continued)

Confidentiality and credibility of information is the heart of the computer security program. If the managers of a computer installation cannot guarantee the integrity and safety of information, users will be reluctant to use the services. Unauthorized use of a data base can be prevented by imposing controls at several points.

☐ Access to data should be controlled by physical security measures. Data file sources should be physically separate from access mechanisms.

☐ Especially sensitive data should be protected with multiple levels of password protection.

☐ System and data base documentation should list those employees authorized to access information.

☐ Application programs should be logged in properly, using electronically or manually recorded information.

The most critical elements in a security program are an awareness of the importance of security and a willingness on the part of information processing management to confront the task. Table 9–1 itemizes a physical security checklist.

ETHICAL ISSUES INVOLVING COMPUTERS

Computers are rapidly becoming the primary repositories of negotiable assets and information. The concentration of critical business and personal data in computer and data communications systems has created a power base in computer departments, placing power in the hands of technologists dealing with the processing, storage, and dissemination of data. Privacy and fair information practices are becoming major legislative issues.

Unlike the computer field, most professions have had considerable time to develop ethical concepts for dealing with new issues. Medical practitioners are attempting to resolve such issues as abortion, auditors ponder their responsibility to detect business fraud, and biologists debate issues in genetic research. In contrast, computer science has been in existence for only 35 years. Serious problems have developed because of the relative absence of ethical concepts and practices.

The ethical issues raised are a result of the various roles that computers play in society. Computers, for example, can serve as:

☐ Producers of new types of assets. Computer programs are a new kind of asset, possibly not subject to the same concepts of ownership as other assets.

☐ Repositories and processors of information. Unauthorized use of computer services or information stored in computers raises questions about the fair or appropriate uses of computer technology.

☐ Symbols of intimidation. The image of computers as infallible machines that replace fallible human beings should be carefully considered.

TABLE 9–1
Physical security checklist

Is computer visible from street?	Are dismissed employees of computer environment removed immediately and necessary guard personnel notified?
If computer area is visible to the general public, are windows of nonbreakable material?	
Is fire department aware that windows are of nonbreakable material?	Is your center alarmed to notify guard of intrusion?
Is installation located in a high crime rated area?	Do you have standby for power operated doors if power is off?
Would you consider your company vulnerable to vandalism because of the nature of business?	Are security personnel notified of employees permitted access during nonworking hours?
Have you evaluated your company as to whether it is a high, medium, or low risk center for attack?	Do company employees babysit service personnel during nonworking hours?
Do you have a 24-hour guard service? For entrances? For computer area only?	Are all visiting personnel identified by badge when visiting computer installation?
Do you use TV cameras in computer area?	Are operating personnel trained to challenge strangers without proper badge identification?
Do you use a man trap for access to the computer area?	
Are the number of doors leading into computer area kept to a minimum?	Are personnel educated as to security practices and encouraged to be alert at all times?
Do you monitor the status of emergency exits?	Do you agree that the greatest threat to security is from within?
Are doors to computer area locked at all times?	Are security personnel employees of company?
Is access to computer area by use of key, magnetic card, or cipher lock controlled?	If a breach of security was encountered at your installation, do you have professional assistance available?
Are access methods changed at regular intervals or after termination of an employee?	Are admission badges picked up from terminated employees?

Source: HSH National Management, Inc.

☐ Instruments of acts. Computer services and users of computers, data, and programs need to determine their degree of responsibility for the integrity and appropriateness of computer output.

To develop a code of ethics before component issues have been fully identified and before a general consensus on a definition of ethics has been reached appears to be unproductive. An empirical approach based on specific issues is necessary. One method of applying this approach is

More than 4 million children in the nation's public schools have physical, mental, or sensory disabilities. Three of the most exciting developments relating to special needs peripherals are speech synthesis, speech recognition, and modified keyboard technologies. These technologies enable computers to ''read'' for physically blind or dyslexic students, ''write'' for paralyzed or mobility-limited students, ''speak'' for those vocally handicapped, ''move'' for disabled individuals, and to some extent ''hear'' for deaf students— dramatically enhancing their ability to learn and to communicate.

to identify ethical issues by studying a series of cases to determine whether the acts described are ethical, unethical, or unrelated to ethical issues. Among acts to consider might be taking copies of programs from one employer to another when changing jobs, using idle computer time, or the unauthorized copying of a program stored on a floppy disk.

Obtaining agreement on one, simple ethical rule is often difficult. One might assume that the following rule would be accepted by a consensus of people in the computer field: ''Computer programs, data, and related documentation should always be treated as proprietary unless explicitly identified as being in the public domain.'' In other words, before programs or data are used, copied, sold, recreated, or given, the questions ''Do I have the authorization?'' and ''Is it fair to do this?'' should be asked. If not, permission of the rightful owner should be obtained.

One might compose another version of the rule. Consider the following: The information contained in computer programs, data, and related documentation should always be treated as being in the public domain unless explicitly identified as being proprietary. This rule certainly has merit. It encourages owners and custodians of programs and data to apply proprietary labels to them.

As computers are used for increasingly sophisticated applications, the issues of whether and how applications should be produced have become more important. Programmers, systems analysts, computer managers, and computer scientists must consider the effect of their work on the physical safety, mental well-being, rights, and economic conditions of people. Should programming or corporate managers have the authority to establish the need for adequate controls in a computer application? Are human rights violated by real time, covert, passive, identification verification by computer? Should a systems analyst become involved in management/union disputes over labor versus automation issues? General principles suggested by a consideration of these issues include the following:

- ☐ Engineers and scientists have a continuing obligation to ensure that their products are used in a socially responsible manner, however, they cannot be blamed for the manner in which others use their products.
- ☐ Human beings should not be treated as depersonalized objects.
- ☐ Human safety ethically requires more than meeting minimum legal requirements.
- ☐ All people involved in designing, assessing, and implementing computer systems should consider the human impact in terms of problems such as dehumanization of work, physical danger, or job loss.

Computers can be used for deceptive or intimidating actions. The public, computer customers, legislators, and workers can be victimized by unethical systems analysts, computer scientists, and company representatives. The questions in this category concern the dangers of computer applications and misperceptions of their meaning and impact. Do programmers have a responsibility to ensure the correct interpretation of program output? To what extent do computer scientists need to ensure the accurate reporting of their work in the media? Should a sales representative of a computer system manufacturer inform his customer about the possible impacts on employees? Attempts to answer these questions lead to the following principles:

☐ It is unethical to exploit popular computer applications and trust in computer accuracy in an attempt to lend validity to software or hardware proposals.

☐ It is unethical for a person to take no action when he knows that his work has been irresponsibly publicized.

☐ Any computer system proposal should assign responsibility for human factors.

A number of ethical issues concern computer-related products such as programs, program documentation, copies of programs, computer-related curricula, and computer equipment. Examples include copying programs, revealing the process used in programs, withholding program documentation, and failing to acknowledge the sources of intellectual efforts. Although these acts often result in criminal and civil legal actions, they may also be considered ethical issues because the initial decision to act and copy or take a program has ethical implications.

It has become necessary to establish some general principles concerning the proprietary value of program products. One way to avoid disputes is to assume that a program is proprietary unless it is explicitly identified as being in the public domain. Alternative suggestions include:

☐ In the absence of any agreement otherwise, programmers do not have a proprietary right to programs written for others.

☐ The ownership of programs developed at an educational institution must be negotiated between the institution and the instructor/student.

☐ An owner's dormant interest in his/her property does not justify appropriation of the property by another party.

Several ethical issues are related to the obligations between employees and employers, between universities, professors, and students, and between competitors concerning the appropriate use of computer services and programs, the responsibility for the results of computer use, and recognition for work. The issues emphasize the need for clear understanding about obligations. Should employees use computers for game-playing or personal gain? Is it fair to use a computer to take advantage of another person? Consideration of these and similar issues suggests the following general principles:

☐ System analysts and programmers should be responsible for ensuring that a program performs according to specifications.

□ Computer users should be responsible for supplying systems analysts and programmers adequate specifications.

□ Computer system weaknesses should not be exploited for personal satisfaction or unauthorized gain.

Many ethical concerns are shaping professional behavior in the information processing field. Addressing these questions provides a practical method for establishing a code of ethics for information processing.

SUMMARY

□ The steps involved in developing a system are: problem definition, preliminary study, systems analysis, system design, equipment selection and acquisition, implementation, and maintenance.

□ As reliance on computers has grown, techniques for safeguarding data have become increasingly sophisticated. Among the threats to computer security are environmental disasters, theft and fraud, mechanical failure, and deliberate or unintentional operator error.

□ Among the safeguards for computer data security are factors related to location, site construction, computer room access, software access security measures, encryption, duplicate files, production control, and business insurance.

□ Computer professionals as well as computer users are responsible for many ethical issues in the information processing field. Among them are unauthorized use of computer systems and illegal copying of programs.

REVIEW QUESTIONS

True or False

_____ 1 A systems study is the investigation made by a company to determine which computer to buy.

_____ 2 Systems analysis involves designing a system and programming the system on a computer system.

_____ 3 The objectives of the programming and implementation functions are to write, test, and check out computer programs.

_____ 4 During the equipment selection and acquisition phase, management acquires the computer and its associated equipment.

_____ 5 The purpose of the systems design phase is to improve a system so that it is superior to the existing one.

_____ 6 A system that uses a computer is always better than a manual system that does not use one.

_____ 7 One important area in the preliminary study is the definition of the problem.

_____ 8 A systems designer plans a new system as specified by the programmer and wiring technician.

_____ 9 The user need not be involved in the design of the system.

_____ 10 The introduction of microcomputers has increased the complexity of securing a computer system.

_____ 11 The most critical elements in a security program are an awareness of the importance of security and a willingness on the part of information processing management to confront the task.

_____ **12** Systems analysts and programmers should be responsible for ensuring that a program performs according to specifications.

_____ **13** The preliminary study is often called the feasibility study.

_____ **14** Dishonest programmers have been using computer systems for illegal purposes for years.

_____ **15** Basically, the issue of privacy deals with the use or misuse of computer-stored data.

Short Answer

1 A _____ is a composite of equipment, skills, techniques, and information capable of performing and/or supporting an operational role in attaining specified management objectives.

2 The steps in the system life cycle are _____, _____, _____, _____, _____, _____, and _____.

3 A system must be designed for the _____, not for the convenience of the computer.

4 During the _____ phase, necessary programs are coded, debugged, tested, and documented.

5 A _____ study is often used to determine the feasibility of a request for a change from one method to another in accomplishing certain processing functions.

6 The object of the _____ _____ phase is to determine what must be done to solve a problem.

7 Following implementation, the system enters a _____ phase.

8 _____ _____ involves the use of computers to intercept information, time, software, or valuable goods belonging to another.

9 Dishonest practices involving the use of computers are called _____ _____.

10 Actions taken to ensure that a computer system is used properly and ethically are called _____ _____.

11 It is _____ (ethical, unethical) to copy the contents of a floppy disk without the owner's permission.

12 An ethical issue concerning disclosure of information stored on computers is _____ _____.

13 The objective of the _____ phase is to keep the system functioning at an acceptable level.

14 The protection of data against destruction or accidental or intentional disclosure to unauthorized persons is called _____.

GLOSSARY

Access time The time required to move data from an auxiliary storage device to the computer's main memory or vice versa.

Acronym A word formed from the first letter (or letters) of the words in a phrase or name.

Algorithm A set of rules for solving a problem.

Alphanumeric A general term for alphabetic letters, numerical digits, and special characters (-,/,*,$,(,), + , etc.) that can be processed by machine.

Analysis The investigation of a problem by a consistent, systematic procedure.

APL A programming language. A terminal-oriented, symbolic programming language especially suitable for interactive problem solving.

Application The system or problem for which a computer is used.

Application program The computer program designed to solve a particular type of problem or perform a specific operation.

Applications software The programs written to perform specific user applications.

Arithmetic/logic unit (ALU) The area of the central processing unit where arithmetic and logical operations are performed.

Array (1) A series of related items. (2) An ordered arrangement or pattern of items or numbers, such as a determinant, matrix, vector, or a table of numbers.

Artificial intelligence A branch of computer science that uses computers to solve problems that appear to require imagination, intuition, or knowledge.

Assembler A computer program that takes nonmachine language instructions prepared by a computer operator and converts them into a form that the computer can use.

Assembly language A low-level symbolic programming language that allows a computer user to write a program using mnemonics instead of numeric instructions.

Automated teller machine A special purpose input/output device used by banks for data communications with the bank's computer system.

Auxiliary operation An operation performed on equipment not under the direct control of the central processing unit.

Auxiliary storage A memory device that supplements the main memory of a computer.

Bar graph A method of presenting business data as a clear comparison between two or more items.

BASIC Beginner's all-purpose symbolic instruction code. An easy-to-learn, easy-to-use algebraic programming language widely used in programming instruction, personal computing, business, and industry.

Batch processing A technique in which programs that are to be executed are coded and collected together into groups for processing purposes.

Binary A number system with a radix of two; the usual number system of computers and related equipment. It has two digits, 0 and 1.

Bit The smallest unit of information that the computer recognizes, a bit (binary digit) is represented by the presence or absence of an electronic pulse, 0 or 1.

Branch instruction An instruction used to transfer control from one sequence of a program to another.

Buffer An area of storage where data are held temporarily to facilitate transfer between devices operating at different speeds or on different time cycles.

Bug A mistake in a computer program or system, or a malfunction in a computer hardware component.

Byte A grouping of adjacent binary digits operated on by the computer as a unit.

Capacity The number of items of data (computer words, bytes, or characters) that a storage device is capable of containing.

Card   A storage medium in which data are represented by means of holes punched in vertical columns in a paper card.

Card reader   An input device that transfers information punched into cards to the computer's memory.

Cassette tape   A plastic cartridge that contains a length of magnetic tape on which to store programs and data.

Cathode ray tube (CRT)   An electronic tube with a screen for information display.

Central processing unit   The component of a computer system with the circuitry to control the interpretation and execution of instructions.

Character   A symbol, digit, letter, or punctuation mark stored or processed by computing equipment.

Chip   A thin silicon wafer on which electronic components are deposited in the form of integrated circuits.

COBOL   Common business oriented language. A high-level language developed for business data processing applications.

Code   (1) A set of rules outlining the way in which data may be represented. (2) Rules used to convert data from one representation to another. (3) To write a program or routine.

Coding   The writing of a list of instructions that will cause a computer to perform specified operations.

Compiler   A computer program that translates a source program written in a higher-level language into a series of machine language instructions.

Computer   A programmable electronic machine that can store, retrieve, and process data for purposes limited only by the creativity of the humans who use it.

Computer art   A picture produced by computing equipment.

Computer input microfilm (CIM)   A technology involving the use of an input device to read the contents of microfilm directly into the computer.

Computer output microfilm (COM)   A technology that involves recording computer output on microfilm.

Computer network   A complex consisting of two or more interconnected computer systems, terminals, and communication facilities.

Computer program   A series of instructions that guide the activities of a computer.

Computer science   The field of knowledge that includes all aspects of computer design and use.

Computer security   The protection of computer system equipment and data from unauthorized access.

Computer system   The combination of hardware and software used as a unit to process data.

Computing   The act of using electronic equipment for processing data.

Conditional transfer   An instruction that may cause a departure from the sequence of instructions being followed depending upon the result of an operation or the value of a variable.

Console   The part of a computer system that enables human operators to communicate with the computer.

Control program   A set of instructions for an operating system that is responsible for the overall management of the computer and its resources.

Cursor   A position indicator frequently employed in a display on a video terminal to indicate a character to be corrected or a position where data are to be entered.

Data   A representation of facts, concepts or instructions in a formalized manner suitable for communication, interpretation, or processing by humans or automatic means.

Data bank   Same as data base.

Data base   A collection of libraries of data.

Data base administrator (DBA)   The individual responsible for the orderly development and operation of a data base.

Data base management system (DBMS)   A collection of related programs for loading, accessing, and controlling a data base.

Data capture   The gathering or collecting of data for computer handling. Also called **data recording.**

Data communications system   A system consisting of computers, terminals, and communications links.

Data dictionary   Index of all items in an organization's data base.

Data preparation   The process of organizing information and storing it in a form that can be entered into the computer.

Data processing   One or more operations performed on data to achieve a desired objective.

Data transmission   Sending data between different parts of a system.

Debugging   Detection and elimination of all mistakes in a computer program and any malfunctions in the computing system itself.

Decision   The computer operation of determining if a certain relationship exists between words in storage or registers and altering a previously determined course of action if it does not exist.

Digit   One of the symbols of a number system that is used to designate a quantity.

Digital computer   A device that manipulates digital data and performs arithmetic and logic operations of these data.

Digital plotter   An output device that uses an automatically controlled pen to graph data.

Digitizing tablet   An input device generally consisting of a 28 cm × 28 cm (11 in × 11 in) surface underlaid by a fine grid of wires that converts graphic and pictorial data into binary inputs for use in a computer.

Direct access   The process of obtaining data from or placing data into storage where the time required is independent of the location of the data. Also called **random access.**

Disk access time　The time required to locate a specific track on a disk. Also called **seek time.**

Disk storage　A storage device that uses magnetic recording on flat rotating disks. It is a direct access storage device.

Display　A visual representation of data.

Distributed data base　Data base that is spread throughout the computer system of a network.

Distributed processing system　A set of interacting computer systems or data bases situated in different locations.

Documentation　The preparation of documents, during systems analysis and subsequent programming, that describe such things as the system, the programs prepared, and the changes made at later dates.

Downtime　A time period during which the computer system is malfunctioning.

EDP　Electronic data processing.

Electronic spreadsheet　A type of software program that can perform in minutes complex financial tasks that would take hours to complete manually.

Fifth generation computer development project　A plan, proposed by the Japanese, to develop, prior to 1990, a new generation of computers that will mimic human recognition systems, just as if they had eyes, ears, or noses, or could sense temperature.

File　A collection of related records treated as a unit.

Firmware　A program, contained on a silicon chip, that combines elements of hardware and software.

First generation　The first commercially available computers, produced from 1951–1959 and characterized by their use of vacuum tubes.

Floppy disk　A flexible disk (diskette) of oxide-coated mylar that is stored in paper or plastic envelopes. The entire envelope is inserted into the disk unit.

Flowchart　A form of algorithm that uses symbols and interconnecting lines to show the logic and sequence of specific program operations (program flowchart) or a system of processing to achieve objectives (system flowchart).

FORTRAN　Formula translator. A widely used, high-level programming language used to perform mathematical, scientific, and engineering computations.

Fourth generation computer　A modern digital computer that uses large-scale integration (LSI) and very large-scale integration (VLSI) circuitry.

Function key　Special keys on a keyboard associated with a particular graphic entity and used for executing certain procedures.

General purpose computer system　A computer system designed to solve a wide variety of problems.

Graphic digitizer　An input device that converts graphic and pictorial data into binary inputs for use in a computer.

Hand-held computer　A portable computer that can be programmed (in BASIC) to perform a wide variety of applications.

Hardware　The physical components of the computer system including mechanical, magnetic, electrical, and electronic devices.

HIPO chart　Chart used to provide an orderly approach to program development. Consists of two parts—the hierarchy chart and the input-process-output chart.

Impact printer　A printer that forms images on paper by striking the paper with an imprinting mechanism.

Information　The meaning that people assign to data.

Information processing　All the operations performed by a computer.

Information retrieval　The methods used to recover specific information from stored data.

Input　(1) The data that are entered into the computer. (2) The act of entering data.

Input/output device　A unit that is used to get data from the user into the central processing unit and to transfer data from the compiler's main storage to an auxiliary storage or output device.

Input/output symbol　A flowcharting symbol, represented by a parallelogram, used to indicate an input operation to the procedure or an output operation from the procedure.

Instructions　A group of characters, bytes, or bits that defines an operation to be performed by the computer.

Integrated circuit　A combination of interconnected circuit elements on a semiconductor chip.

Interblock gap　The distance on a magnetic tape, disk, or drum between the end of one block and the beginning of the next.

Interface　A common boundary between two pieces of hardware or between two computer systems.

Internal storage　Addressable memory directly controlled by the central processing unit.

Interpreter　A computer program that translates each source language statement into a sequence of machine instructions and then executes these machine instructions before translating the next source language statement.

Interrecord gap　The distance on a magnetic tape or magnetic disk between the end of one record and the beginning of the next.

Iterate　To repeat, automatically, under program control, the same series of processing steps until a predetermined stop or branch condition is reached.

Job　A specifically defined set of work to be done.

Joystick   A device for entering X-Y coordinates by moving a lever to change the position of a cursor on a graphical screen.

K   A computer shorthand term equaling the quantity 1024 and generally used as a measurement of computer memory capacity.

Kilobyte   A kilobyte equals 2^{10} or 1024 bytes and is commonly abbreviated as ''K'' and used as a suffix when describing memory size.

Language   A set of rules, representations, and conventions used to convey information.

Large-scale integration (LSI)   The process of placing a large number of integrated circuits on one silicon chip.

Library   A collection of programs, routines, and subroutines available to every user of the computer.

Library manager   The program that maintains the programs stored in an operating system.

Light pen   An electrical device resembling a pen that can be used to write or sketch on the screen of a cathode ray tube to provide input.

Line graph   A method of charting business data that clearly reveals trends via plot lines across a grid.

Line printer   An output peripheral device that prints data one line at a time.

Loop   A sequence of instructions in a program that can be executed repetitively until certain specified conditions are satisfied.

Machine language   The basic language of a computer. Programs written in machine language require no further interpretation by a computer.

Magnetic bubble storage   A memory that uses locally magnetized areas that can move about in a magnetic material, such as a plate of orthoferrite. It is possible to control the reading in and out of this area within the magnetic material and as a result, a very high capacity memory can be built.

Magnetic disk   A disk made of rigid material (hard disk) or heavy mylar (floppy disk) and used to hold magnetized information.

Magnetic ink character recognition (MICR)   The technique used in banking to encode account numbers and check values so they can be automatically debited from accounts.

Magnetic tape   A plastic strip having a magnetic surface for storing data in a code of magnetized spots.

Main storage   The fastest general purpose memory of a computer.

Management information system (MIS)   An information system designed to supply organizational managers with the necessary information needed to plan, organize, staff, direct, and control the operations of the organization.

Mass storage device   An auxiliary memory unit with a very large capacity.

Memory   The section of the computer where instructions and data are stored.

Microcomputer   A small, low-cost computer.

Microcomputer system   A system that includes microcomputer, peripherals, operating system, and applications programs.

Microprocessor   An integrated circuit that will perform a variety of operations in accordance with a set of instructions.

Microsecond   One-millionth of a second.

Millisecond   One-thousandth of a second.

Minicomputer   A computer that is distinguished from a microcomputer by higher performance, more powerful instruction sets, higher prices, and a wider selection of available programming languages and operating systems.

Modem   Modulator-demodulator. A device used at each end of a telephone line to convert binary digital data to audio tones suitable for transmission over the line and vice versa.

Monitor   A program to supervise the proper sequencing of programming tasks by the computer. It is an example of computer software and is often used synonymously with executive, supervisory routine, and operating system.

Mouse   A device that can control the movement of a cursor by being rolled along a flat surface by hand. Attached to computer by a long cable.

Multiplexer   A device that allows several communication lines to share one computer data channel.

Multiprocessing   The simultaneous execution of two or more sequences of instructions by several central processing units under common control.

Multiprogramming   Running two or more sets of instructions at the same time in the same computer.

Nanosecond   One-billionth of a second.

Natural language   A language that allows users to prepare programs in English or other natural language. Also called **problem-oriented language.**

Non-impact printer   A printer that produces a printed image without striking the paper.

Numerical analysis   The branch of mathematics concerned with the study and development of effective procedures for computing answers to problems.

OCR   Optical character recognition. Characters printed in a special type style that can be read by both machines and people.

Off-line   A term describing equipment, devices, or persons not in direct communication with the central processing unit of a computer.

On-line   A term describing equipment, devices, and persons that are in direct communication with the central processing unit of a computer.

Operating system   An organized collection of software, available to the computer at all times, that controls the overall operations of a computer.

Output device   A unit used for taking out data values from a computer and presenting them in the desired form to the user.

Paddle   A hand-held device connected to the computer that can move the display terminal cursor up/down or left/right.

Pascal   A high-level programming language that has become increasingly popular because it facilitates the use of good structured programming techniques.

Peripheral   A device, such as a visual display or printer, used for storing data and entering them into or retrieving them from the computer system.

Personal computer   A small, inexpensive microcomputer that can be used in the home for entertainment, education, business, control, and household tasks.

Picosecond   One-trillionth of a second.

Pie chart   A charting technique used to represent portions of a whole.

Pocket computer   A portable, battery-operated computer that can be programmed (in BASIC) to perform a wide number of applications.

Point-of-sale (POS) terminal   A device used in retail establishments to record sales information in a form that can be input directly into a computer.

Print   To transfer information, usually from the computer's internal storage, to a printing device.

Problem analysis   The process of understanding a problem. The goal is the formal and logical presentation of the problem for computer solution.

Problem definition   The formulation of the logic used to define a prob-

lem. A description of a task to be performed.

Processing   Generally, the arithmetic and logic operations performed on data in the course of executing a computer program.

Program   A set of coded instructions directing a computer to perform a particular function.

Program design   The process of describing the computer solution to a problem.

Program execution   The process of putting a program in the computer, along with any other information required, and instructing the machine to execute or run the program.

Program library   A collection of available computer programs and routines.

Program maintenance   The process of keeping the program functioning at an acceptable level including correcting previously undetected bugs and making appropriate changes to meet new requirements.

Program testing   Executing instructions with test data to ascertain that they can perform expected functions.

PROM   Programmable read only memory. A memory that is programmed by the end user, not the manufacturer.

Punch card   A cardboard card used in data processing operations in which tiny rectangular holes at hundreds of individual locations denote numerical values and alphanumeric codes.

Query language   A set of commands used to extract from a data base the data that meet specific criteria.

Random access memory (RAM)   A storage system in which each element of information has its own address (location) and from which any element can be easily and conveniently retrieved by using that address.

Read   To get information from any input or file storage media.

Read-only memory (ROM)   A solid-state storage chip that is programmed at the time of its manufacture and cannot be reprogrammed by the computer user.

Real time   A term referring to a system in which data are processed as soon as they are entered into the computer.

Record   A collection of related items of data treated as a unit.

Remote terminal   A device for communicating with computers from sites that are physically separated from the computer and often distant enough so that communication facilities such as telephone lines are used, rather than direct cables.

Response time   The time it takes the computer system to react to a given input. It is the interval between an event and the system's response to the event.

Rotational delay time   The time required for the disk to attain the desired position at the read/write head; also called **latency.**

Run   The single and continuous execution of a program by a computer on a given set of data.

Semiconductor   A material such as silicon with a conductivity between that of a metal and an insulator; it is used in the manufacture of solid-state devices, such as transistors and the complex integrated circuits that comprise computer logic hardware.

Semiconductor storage   A memory device whose storage elements are formed as solid-state electronic components on an integrated circuit chip.

Sequence   An arrangement of items according to a specified set of rules.

Sequencial access   A term used to describe files such as magnetic tape that must be searched serially from the beginning to find desired records.

Simulation   To represent the functioning of one system by another; that is, to represent a physical system by the execution of a computer program, or to represent a biological system by a mathematical model.

Software   A general term for computer programs, procedural rules, and the documentation involved in the operation of a computer system.

Sort   To arrange records according to a logical system.

Source document   An original paper from which basic data are extracted.

Special purpose computer system   A computer system capable of solving only a few selected types of numerical or logical problems.

Standalone graphics system   A graphics system that includes a microcomputer or minicomputer, storage, terminal, and other input/output devices.

Statement   In programming, an expression or generalized instruction in a source language.

Storage capacity   The number of items of data that a memory device is capable of containing.

Stored program computer   A computer that executes instructions that are stored within its main memory.

Subroutine   A subsidiary routine, within which initial execution never starts.

Supercomputer   Expensive computer systems characterized by their large size and fast processing speeds capable of executing many million instructions per second.

Symbol   (1) A letter, numeral, or mark that represents a numeral, operation, or relation. (2) An element of a computer language's character set.

System   The computer and all its related components, including peripheral devices, people, and programs.

Systems analyst   One who studies the activities, methods, procedures, and techniques of organizational systems in order to determine what actions need to be taken and how these actions can best be accomplished.

Systems programs   A set of computer programs that provide a particular service to the user.

Task   A basic unit of work to be accomplished by a computer.

Terminal   A peripheral device through which information is entered into or extracted from the computer.

Third generation   A series of computers that use integrated circuits and miniaturization as their main components.

Throughput   A measure of the amount of work that can be accomplished by the computer system during a given period of time.

Thumb wheels   Dials that provide input into a computer system.

Time sharing   A method of operation in which a computer facility is shared by several users for different purposes at (apparently) the same time. Although the computer actually services each user in sequence, the high speed of the computer makes it appear that the users are all handled simultaneously.

Top-down program design   The process of breaking a large, complicated problem into a series of smaller, easier-to-solve problems.

Touch-sensitive panel   An input device consisting of sets of horizontal and vertical wires, each mounted on a thin plastic sheet, then combined into a grid separated by a third plastic sheet, and mounted on a display screen.

Trackball   A device used to move the cursor on a computer display. Consists of a mounting (usually a box) that holds a ball that moves at the speed and in the direction of the ball's motion.

Turnaround time   The measure of time between the initiation of a job and its completion by the computer.

Universal Product Code (UPC)   A machine-readable code of parallel bars used for labeling products used in a point-of-sale automation system.

User-friendly   A term that implies the computer system or software is easy to use.

Very large-scale integration (VLSI)   The accumulation of hundreds of thousands of electronic circuit elements on a single semiconductor chip.

Videodisk   A disk that can store both pictures and text; also called **optical disk.**

Winchester disk   A fast auxiliary storage device consisting of a rigid magnetic disk in a sealed container.

Write   The process of transferring information from the computer to an output medium.

INDEX